Houghton Mifflin
Spelling and Vocabulary

Autumn leaves
with acorn and
pine needles,
South Carolina

Senior Authors
Edmund H. Henderson
Shane Templeton

Consulting Authors
Barbara Coulter
Joyce A. M. Thomas

Consultants
Jane Adrian
Judith Pierce Jefferson
Catherine Leeker
Jane Ann Malakosky
Elisabeth L. Rowlands

Houghton Mifflin Company   Boston

Atlanta   Dallas   Geneva, Illinois   Palo Alto   Princeton   Toronto

Acknowledgments

Select definitions in the Spelling Dictionary are adapted and reprinted by permission from the following Houghton Mifflin Company publications. Copyright © 1986 *The Houghton Mifflin Intermediate Dictionary*. Copyright © 1986 *The Houghton Mifflin Student Dictionary*. Copyright © 1985 *The American Heritage Dictionary, Second College Edition*.

PASSWORD is the registered trademark of the Super Password Company. Used by permission.

Literature excerpts:
from *Mister Stormalong* by Anne Malcolmson and Dell McCormick. Copyright © 1952 by Mabel McCormick and Anne Burnett Malcolmson. Copyright © renewed 1980 by Anne Burnett Malcolmson Van Storch and Joshua Tolford. Reprinted by permission of Houghton Mifflin Company.

from *Nature's Champions* by Alvin and Virginia Silverstein. Copyright © 1980 by Alvin and Virginia Silverstein. Reprinted by permission of Random House, Inc.

from *Philip Hall likes me. I reckon maybe.* by Bette Greene. Text copyright © 1974 by Bette Greene. Adapted and reprinted by permission of the publisher, Dial Books for Young Readers.

from "Winter Static Magic" by Doris Spaulding. Appeared in *Cricket* magazine, Volume 3, Number 4, December 1975. Copyright © 1975. Reprinted by permission of the author.

"A Zillion Stars" by Yoshiko Uchida. Copyright © 1983 by Yoshiko Uchida. Adapted and reprinted by permission of the author.

ISBN: 0-395-62669-2

56789-RT-97 96 95

How to Study a Word

1 **LOOK** at the word.

- What letters are in the word?
- What does the word mean? Does it have more than one meaning?

2 **SAY** the word.

- What are the consonant sounds?
- What are the vowel sounds?

3 **THINK** about the word.

- How is each sound spelled?
- Did you see any familiar spelling patterns?
- Did you note any prefixes, suffixes, or other word parts?

4 **WRITE** the word.

- Think about the sounds and the letters.
- Form the letters correctly.

5 **CHECK** the spelling.

- Did you spell the word the same way it is spelled in your word list?
- Do you need to write the word again in your Notebook for Writing?

Your Notebook for Writing

A Notebook for Writing is a good way to build your own personal word list. What words should you write in your notebook?

- new words from your reading and your school subjects
- words from your writing that you have trouble spelling
- spelling words that you need to study

When should you use your Notebook for Writing?

- when you are looking for exact or interesting words to use in your writing
- when you are proofreading your writing for misspelled words
- to help you study spelling

First, fold eight pieces of paper lengthwise. Also fold a cover sheet.

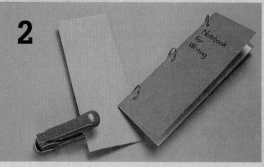

Staple the sheets, or punch holes and fasten with rings. Write **Notebook for Writing** and your name on the cover.

Beginning on the first page, write the numbers for the 36 units you will study. Write two numbers on each page.

As you begin a unit, use this part of your notebook to write the spelling words that you especially need to study.

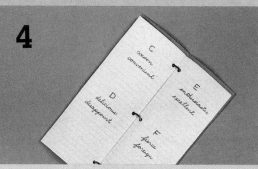

Write **My Own Words** on the first page of the second part. Write two alphabet letters on each page.

In this part of your notebook, keep your own personal word list.

Contents

Cycle Two

Cycle Four

Cycle Six

Student's Handbook

Theme: Summer Camp

1 Short Vowels

LOOK

at each word.

SAY

each word.

Basic Words   ■ Challenge

1. bunk	11. fond	21. trek
2. staff	12. crush	22. knapsack
3. dock	13. grasp	23. summit
4. slept	14. dwell	24. rustic
5. mist	15. fund	25. mascot
6. bunch	16. ditch	
7. swift	17. split	
8. stuck	18. swept	
9. breath	19. deaf	
10. tough	20. rough	

Camp
Mohawk

THINK

about the words.

A short vowel sound spelled by a single vowel and followed by a consonant sound is the **short vowel pattern.** Each word has a short vowel sound spelled with this pattern:

|ă| st**a**ff |ĕ| sl**e**pt |ĭ| m**i**st |ŏ| d**o**ck |ŭ| b**u**nk

• What letter usually spells each short vowel sound? How are the Elephant Words different?

WRITE

the words.

Practice   **Write the Basic Words to answer the questions.**

A. Which **two** words have the |ă| sound?

B. Which **five** words have the |ĕ| sound?

C. Which **four** words have the |ĭ| sound?

CHECK

your spelling.

D. Which **two** words have the |ŏ| sound?

E. Which **seven** words have the |ŭ| sound?

■ **Now write the five Challenge Words.** Underline the letters that spell the short vowel sounds.

Spelling-Meaning Hint   *Breathe* and *breath* have different vowel sounds, but they are related in spelling and meaning. **Think of this:** During the winter you can see your *breath* when you *breathe*.

Independent Practice

Spelling-Meaning   Look at the Spelling-Meaning Hint.

1-2. Write *breathe.* Then write the Basic Word that is related in spelling and meaning to *breathe.*

Word Analysis   Complete the exercises with Basic Words.

3-4. Write the two words that end with double consonants.

5-6. Write the two words that end with the |f| sound spelled *gh*.

7-9. Write the three words that have the |ch| or the |sh| sound.

Definitions   Write the Basic Word that fits each meaning.
10. a wharf
11. to hold on to firmly
12. a double-decker bed
13. unable to hear
14. moving very fast
15. a sum of money

short vowels

■ **Challenge Words**   Write the Challenge Word that fits each clue. Use your Spelling Dictionary.
16. a slow, hard journey
17. rural
18. holds camping supplies
19. peak
20. often seen at football games

Summing Up

A short vowel sound is usually spelled by a single vowel and followed by a consonant sound. This is the **short vowel pattern.** These single vowels usually spell these short vowel sounds:

|ă| **a** |ĕ| **e** |ĭ| **i** |ŏ| **o** |ŭ| **u**

Expanding Vocabulary

Context Clues Can you figure out the meaning of the word *adhered*, using the other words in this sentence?

The sticky wallpaper **adhered** firmly to the wall.

The words *sticky* and *firmly to the wall* tell you that *adhered* means "stuck."

Practice **Write the correct meaning of each underlined word. Use context clues.**

1. Six campers and one counselor <u>reside</u> in each cabin.
   a. write　　　　**b.** live　　　　　**c.** hike
2. The campers are <u>obligated</u> to keep their cabins clean.
   a. required　　**b.** allowed　　　**c.** chosen
3. Everyone loves the silence of the <u>tranquil</u> lake.
   a. noisy　　　　**b.** ugly　　　　　**c.** peaceful
4. The campers <u>vied</u> for the Best Camper Award.
   a. raced　　　　**b.** competed　　**c.** cooked

Proofreading

End Marks End every sentence with the correct mark.

DECLARATIVE: At camp we learned the names of birds.
INTERROGATIVE: Will we see a red-winged blackbird?
IMPERATIVE: Please hand me the binoculars.
EXCLAMATORY: How colorful the bluejay is!

Practice **Proofread these instructions. Find four misspelled words and two incorrect end marks. Write the instructions correctly.**

Did you ever row against a swift river current. It takes skil. Grasp the oars tightly, or they will be sweped away by the ruff water? Take a deep breth, and pull as hard as you can.

Review: Spelling Spree

Letter Swap   Write a Basic or Review Word by changing the underlined letter to a different letter or two different letters.

Example: spill *skill*

1. brush
2. flesh
3. old
4. bench
5. stiff
6. pitch
7. dead
8. death
9. touch
10. grass
11. fond
12. bank
13. swept
14. swell
15. duck
16. tough
17. must

Find a Rhyme   Write the Basic or Review Word that rhymes with the underlined word and makes sense in the sentence.

18. When I opened the car ____, out jumped a skunk.
19. Jeffrey ____ the floors and kept the place neat.
20. A man walked along the ____, carrying his sack.
21. Anna is ____ of swimming in the pond.
22. How did the truck get ____ in the sand?
23. The ____ current caused the boat to drift toward shore.
24. If you both want the apple, ____ it.
25. With grace and ____, Jane skied down the hill.

■ **Challenge Words**   Make up five book titles, using a Challenge Word in each title. Then, for each title, write a sentence that describes what the book is about. Remember to capitalize the first, last, and each important word in each title. Be sure to underline each title.

Example: The Lost Knapsack
This book is about a weekend camping trip.

📖 *Writing Application:* A Post Card   Your first day of summer camp has just ended. Write a post card to your best friend. Tell about the highlights of your day. What did you do? What are the other campers like? Where do you live? Try to use five words from the list on page 14.

1 Spelling Across the Curriculum

Recreation: *Summer Camp*

Theme Vocabulary

campfire
canoe
mosquitoes
prank
counselor
crafts
archery
poison ivy

Using Vocabulary Write the Vocabulary Words to complete the paragraph. Use your Spelling Dictionary.

This summer we went to Camp Huron. Pam, the camp __(1)__, was in charge of our cabin. She taught us how to paddle a __(2)__, hit the target in __(3)__, build a roaring __(4)__, and make different __(5)__. She also taught us how to avoid getting bitten by hungry __(6)__ and to recognize __(7)__ leaves, which can cause an itchy skin rash. At night we giggled a lot because Pam would often play a __(8)__ on us.

Understanding Vocabulary Write a Vocabulary Word to answer each riddle.

9. What does the job of both a stove and a furnace?
10. What is a sport you can play standing in one place?
11. What is green but can make you turn red?
12. What insects get slapped when they have dinner?

FACT FILE

Backpacking combines hiking and camping. Backpackers hike into the wilderness carrying food, clothing, shelter, bedding, and cooking equipment on their back.

Enrichment

👪 *Rhyme Time*

Players: 3 or more **You need**: paper, pencils, egg timer or watch with a second hand
How to play: One person is the moderator. That person chooses a spelling word and reads it aloud. The other players write the spelling word and as many words as they can that rhyme with it. After one minute, the moderator says "Stop." Each player gets a point for each correctly spelled word. The first player to score twenty-five points wins.

📖 *Writing*
Sports Roundup

You are a reporter for the Camp Sunacook newspaper. The camp has just held an important game or contest. Write an article covering the event. What was the sport, and who took part in it? Describe some of its surprising, thrilling, or funny moments. Try to use words from the lists in this unit. Be sure to proofread your article.

AD FOR THE PERFECT CAMP

What is your idea of the perfect summer camp? Where would it be, and what would the campers do? Draw an ad for this camp. Give the camp a name, and list its main features. Illustrate two or three features with drawings, and arrange your pictures and writing attractively. Try to use some of the spelling words in this unit.

(Theme: Elections)

2 Spelling |ā| and |ē|

LOOK
at each word.

SAY
each word.

Basic Words

1. speech
2. greet
3. claim
4. stray
5. brain
6. deal
7. male
8. raise
9. leaf
10. thief
11. lease
12. laid
13. waist
14. praise
15. beast
16. stain
17. seal
18. sway
19. fleet
20. niece

■ Challenge

21. candidate
22. succeed
23. campaign
24. nominate
25. cease

THINK
about the words.

Each word has the long *a* or the long *e* sound. The |ā| sound can be spelled *a*-consonant-*e* or with two letters. The |ē| sound is often spelled with two vowels. The patterns *ai* and *ea* are often followed by a consonant sound.

|ā| m**a**l**e**, br**ai**n, str**ay** |ē| l**ea**f, gr**ee**t

- What are three spelling patterns for the |ā| sound? What are two patterns for the |ē| sound? How is the |ē| sound spelled in the Elephant Words?

WRITE
the words.

CHECK
your spelling.

Practice   **Write the Basic Words to answer the questions.**

A. Which **ten** words have |ā|?

B. Which **eight** words have |ē| spelled *ea* or *ee*?

C. Which **two** words have |ē| spelled another way?

■ **Now write the five Challenge Words.** Underline the patterns that spell the |ā| and the |ē| sounds.

> *Spelling-Meaning Hint*   *Deal* and *dealt* are related in meaning and spelling even though they have different vowel sounds. **Think of this:** When it was Tom's turn to *deal*, he *dealt* the cards quickly.

Independent Practice

Spelling-Meaning   Look at the Spelling-Meaning Hint.
 1-2. Write *deal* and *dealt*. Underline two letters in each word that are the same but that spell different vowel sounds.

Word Analysis   Complete the exercises with Basic Words.

 3-4. Write the two words that rhyme with *chain*.

5-10. Write the word that begins with each consonant cluster.
  5. pr   **6.** sw   **7.** str   **8.** fl   **9.** gr   **10.** sp

Definitions   Write the Basic Word that fits each meaning.
11. a person who steals   **14.** to rent
12. a right to something   **15.** the daughter of one's
13. to lift   brother or sister

■ **Challenge Words**   Write the Challenge Words to complete this paragraph. Use your Spelling Dictionary.

   Is your class going to __(16)__ Paul for president of Student Council? Do you think he can __(17)__ in defeating Julie? So far Julie is the most likely __(18)__ for the office. Thank goodness the election is Tuesday. After the election all these __(19)__ activities will __(20)__ .

Summing Up

The |ā| sound can be spelled with the pattern *a*-consonant-*e*, *ai,* or *ay*.
The |ē| sound can be spelled with the pattern *ea* or *ee*.

Basic

1. speech
2. greet
3. claim
4. stray
5. brain
6. deal
7. male
8. raise
9. leaf
10. thief
11. lease
12. laid
13. waist
14. praise
15. beast
16. stain
17. seal
18. sway
19. fleet
20. niece

■ **Challenge**

21. candidate
22. succeed
23. campaign
24. nominate
25. cease

Review

1. free
2. gray
3. least
4. safe
5. gain

Expanding Vocabulary

Using a Thesaurus Where can you find an exact word to replace a general or overused word? Where can you find **synonyms**, words with the same or similar meanings? Use a **thesaurus**. Look at this thesaurus entry.

part of speech   definition   sample sentence

main entry word → **speech** *n.* a public talk. *The writer gave a* **speech** *at the high school.*

subentries → *address* a formal speech. *We listened to the President's* **address**.

lecture a speech providing information on a subject, given before a class. *The class heard a* **lecture** *about the planets.*

Practice **Read pages 254–255 to learn how to use your Thesaurus. Then use your Thesaurus to find the two subentries given for each of these words. Write the subentries.**

1. boast   **2.** protect   **3.** praise   **4.** eager

Dictionary

Guide Words In a dictionary each main word, or **entry word**, is listed in alphabetical order. Two **guide words** appear at the top of each dictionary page. They show the first and last entry words on that page.

guide words →

growl ǀ guard
growl ǀgroulǀ *n., pl.* **growls** A low, deep, angry sound.

Practice **1-8. Write the words that you would find on the page with the guide words *leader* ǀ *leather*.**

leash   leaf   leap   learn   leave

lease   league   lead   leak   least

Review: Spelling Spree

Word Clues   Write a Basic or Review Word to fit each clue.

1. walks on four legs
2. placed or put
3. to achieve
4. part of a plant
5. a homeless cat
6. boy or man
7. a color
8. to say hello
9. no cost
10. to swing back and forth
11. many ships
12. robber
13. sister's daughter
14. agreement with a landlord
15. discolored spot
16. opposite of *greatest*
17. between the ribs and the hips

Proofreading   18-25. Find eight misspelled Basic or Review Words in this talk. Write each misspelled word correctly.

> I am giving this speech today to gain your support. I clame to be the best person for class treasurer. First, I have a good bran for math. Second, I know how to deel with money and keep it saif. My chief concern is to get money for our after-school activities. I have lots of ideas about how we can raze money on our own. I hope I have earned your prais. Give me your seel of approval when you vote.

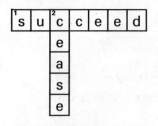

¹s	u	²c	c	e	e	d
		e			
		a			
		s			
		e			

■ **Challenge Words**   Make a crossword puzzle, using the Challenge Words. Write a clue for each word. Write the answers on the back. Trade puzzles with a classmate.

📖 *Writing Application:* A Campaign Speech You are running for mayor in the town of Pindersnap. Write a speech telling the voters what you will do for Pindersnap. Try to use five words from the list on page 20.

2 Spelling Across the Curriculum

Social Studies: *Elections*

Using Vocabulary Write the Vocabulary Words to complete the paragraph. Use your Spelling Dictionary.

To choose a candidate for President of the United States, each major political __(1)__ holds a meeting called a __(2)__. The __(3)__ decide who the Democratic candidate will be, and the __(4)__ choose their candidate. Each party also writes its __(5)__, a statement of the party's beliefs and goals. All citizens over eighteen should __(6)__ to vote. Each __(7)__ can cast one __(8)__ for one candidate.

Understanding Vocabulary Write *yes* if the underlined word is used correctly. Write *no* if it is not.

9. Mrs. Lewis marked her <u>ballot</u>.
10. On election day the people voted at a <u>convention</u>.
11. <u>Party</u> members worked to support their candidate.
12. The party's <u>platform</u> was fifty pages long.

FACT FILE

The right to vote is called suffrage. The United States has not always had suffrage for women. Susan B. Anthony worked to win this right, and suffrage for women became law in 1920.

Enrichment 2

👥 *Jotto*

Does it have a d?

deal

Players: 2   **You need:** paper, pencils
How to play: Each player writes the alphabet on a sheet of paper and then thinks of a spelling word. Player 1 asks Player 2 if a certain letter is in Player 2's word. Player 2 answers yes or no and, if the letter *is* in his or her word, tells Player 1 how many times the letter appears. Then Player 2 takes a turn. Players use their alphabets to keep track of correct letters. The first player to guess the other player's word scores a point.

A CARTOON STRIP

Make a cartoon strip that illustrates an election campaign. The campaign can be for president of a class, a club, or any other group. Show several candidates, each making a funny campaign promise. Write a title for your cartoon strip. Use words from the lists in this unit.

📖 Writing
Pen Pals

In some countries people do not vote for government leaders. Imagine that you have a pen pal in such a country. Write a letter about elections in the United States. Explain why the right to vote is important. Try to use words from the lists in this unit. Be sure to proofread your letter.

Theme: Baseball

3 Spelling |ī| and |ō|

LOOK
at each word.

SAY
each word.

Basic Words ■ Challenge

1. strike
2. thrown
3. stole
4. boast
5. sign
6. stroll
7. thigh
8. height
9. dough
10. owe

11. loaf
12. stroke
13. growth
14. stride
15. code
16. slope
17. hose
18. mild
19. flow
20. slight

21. opponent
22. sacrifice
23. site
24. plight
25. reproach

THINK
about the words.

Each word has the long *i* or the long *o* sound. Both sounds can be spelled vowel-consonant-*e* or with other patterns of one or more letters. The *oa* pattern is usually followed by a consonant sound.

|ī| str**i**ke, th**igh**, s**i**gn
|ō| h**o**se, b**oa**st, thr**ow**n, str**o**ll

• What are three spelling patterns for the |ī| sound? What are four patterns for the |ō| sound? How are the |ī| and the |ō| sounds spelled in the Elephant Words?

WRITE
the words.

CHECK
your spelling.

Practice   **Write the Basic Words to answer the questions.**

A. Which **seven** words have the |ī| sound?

B. Which **thirteen** words have the |ō| sound?

■ **Now write the five Challenge Words.** Underline the patterns that spell the |ī| and the |ō| sounds.

24

> ***Spelling-Meaning Hint***   How can you remember that *sign* has a silent *g*? Think of the related word *signal*, in which the *g* is pronounced.

sign
signal

Independent Practice

Spelling-Meaning   Look at the Spelling-Meaning Hint.

1-2. Write *sign* and *signal*. Then underline the letter that is silent in one word and pronounced in the other.

Word Analysis   Complete the exercises with Basic Words.

3-6. Write the four words that begin with the same cluster of three consonants.

7-9. Write the three words that end with the |ō| sound. Then circle the word in which the |ō| sound is the only sound.

Word Clues   Write the Basic Word that fits each clue.

10. the upper part of the leg
11. how tall a person is
12. can be used to wash a car or to water a garden
13. synonym for *brag*
14. small in amount
15. synonym for *gentle*

o-consonant-e
|ō|

■ **Challenge Words**   Write the Challenge Word that fits each meaning. Use your Spelling Dictionary.

16. to blame
17. a rival
18. location
19. to give up something valuable
20. a serious condition

Summing Up

The |ī| sound is often spelled with the pattern *i*-consonant-*e*, *igh*, or *i*.

The |ō| sound is often spelled with the pattern *o*-consonant-*e*, *oa*, *ow*, or *o*.

Basic

1. strike
2. thrown
3. stole
4. boast
5. sign
6. stroll
7. thigh
8. height
9. dough
10. owe
11. loaf
12. stroke
13. growth
14. stride
15. code
16. slope
17. hose
18. mild
19. flow
20. slight

■ Challenge

21. opponent
22. sacrifice
23. site
24. plight
25. reproach

Review

1. twice
2. goal
3. broke
4. shown
5. sigh

Expanding Vocabulary

Exact Words for *walk* Which sentence is clearer?

Tim **walks** to first base.   Tim **strides** to first base.

Walks tells you what Tim does, but *strides* is more exact. It tells you that Tim walks with energy, taking long steps. Use exact words when you speak and write.

Practice Write the best word to replace *walk* in each sentence. Use your Thesaurus.

stroll   march   tiptoe   wander   limp

1. The stray cats <u>walk</u> around the city, looking for food.
2. The injured players <u>walk</u> into the locker room.
3. The students in the band will <u>walk</u> in the parade.
4. On holidays the people <u>walk</u> past the colorful shops.
5. My parents <u>walk</u> to the crib to check on the baby.

Dictionary

Definitions A dictionary **entry** may include several numbered definitions. A **sample sentence** or **phrase** is often given to help you understand a specific meaning.

height |hīt| *n., pl.* **heights 1.** The distance from bottom to top: *The height of the flagpole is twenty feet.* **2.** The distance from foot to head: *My height increased two inches this year.* **3.** The highest point; peak: *the height of the storm.*

Practice Write 1, 2, or 3 to show which definition of *height* is used in each sentence.
1. The twins were exactly the same <u>height</u>.
2. The <u>height</u> of the building is ninety feet.
3. She won the Nobel Prize at the <u>height</u> of her career.
4. People were amazed by the <u>height</u> of the mountain.

Review: Spelling Spree

Letter Math   Add and subtract letters from the words below to make Basic or Review Words. Write the new words.

Example: sh + blown − bl =   *shown*

1. th + sigh − s =
2. fl + show − sh =
3. sl + hope − h =
4. tw + rice − r =
5. d + though − th =
6. m + wild − w =
7. s + fight − f − t =
8. grow + th =
9. str + bike − b =
10. c + rode − r =
11. str + joke − j =
12. load − d + f =
13. throw + n =
14. str + bride − br =
15. h + rose − r =

Proofreading   **16-25.** Find ten misspelled Basic or Review Words in this report. Write each word correctly.

Carlton Hays brok a world record in today's ball game. He stol more bases than any other baseball player. That has been his gole since he joined the team. Look at him strole across the field.

With a slite nod to the crowd, Carlton begins to speak. He does not bost about his talent. Carlton explains, "I ow my success to my teammates. They have shone what good teamwork can do." Some fans hold up a sine that says *Hooray for Hays!* Carlton is at the hight of his career.

■ **Challenge Words**   Write three Letter Math equations for each Challenge Word. Think of a word. Then add and subtract letters to make a Challenge Word. Write your answers on the back of your paper. Have a classmate solve your equations.

SHARKS COUGARS

📖 *Writing Application:* Creative Writing   Imagine that you play baseball or another sport. Write a paragraph describing the sights, sounds, and smells of an exciting game. Try to use five words from the list on page 26.

3 Spelling Across the Curriculum

Physical Education: *Baseball*

Theme Vocabulary

mound
inning
outfield
league
triple
shortstop
umpire
pitcher

Using Vocabulary Write the Vocabulary Words to complete the paragraph. Use your Spelling Dictionary.

Jason, the star __(1)__ in our baseball __(2)__ , throws a great fast ball. When Jason steps up to the __(3)__ , the crowd cheers. The __(4)__ has trouble calling balls and strikes. Jason plays through the ninth __(5)__ . He strikes out most players, and no one has hit a __(6)__ . His team-mates who play in the __(7)__ rarely see much action. The person who plays __(8)__ , the position between second and third base, is bored.

Understanding Vocabulary Write *yes* if the under-lined word is used correctly. Write *no* if it is not.

9. The <u>pitcher</u> threw a curve ball to the batter.
10. In yesterday's game, the <u>umpire</u> hit a home run.
11. The batter hit a fly ball into the left <u>inning</u>.
12. The Cardinals are in our baseball <u>league</u>.

FACT FILE

Jackie Robinson was the first black player on a major league baseball team. A great all-around player, he is honored in the National Baseball Hall of Fame.

Enrichment

3

👥 *Play Ball!*

Players: 2 teams of 3 or more, a pitcher
You need: a large drawing of a baseball diamond, 20 index cards with a Basic Word on each, game markers
How to play: The teams take turns being batters. The pitcher reads a word to a batter. If the batter spells the word correctly, he or she moves the marker one base, and a new batter is up. Each incorrect spelling is an out. After three outs the other team's players become batters. The first team to score three runs wins.

strike

second base

third base

first base

home plate

height

📖 *Writing*
A Tall Tale

In a tall tale one character has superhuman strength. This person is able to "save the day" or solve problems that ordinary people cannot resolve. Write a tall tale about a losing baseball team that has just hired an amazing new player. Try to use words from the lists in this unit. Be sure to proofread your story.

hank aaron

bob clemente

BASEBALL CARDS

Start a baseball card collection. Cut out pictures of baseball players from sports magazines. Glue each picture to an index card. Below each picture, write a short description of the player. Use list words. You may wish to trade cards with your friends.

4 Spelling |ōō| and |yōō|

LOOK
at each word.

SAY
each word.

Basic Words		■ Challenge
1. clue	11. duke	21. subdue
2. proof	12. mood	22. pursuit
3. cruise	13. scoop	23. presume
4. choose	14. mule	24. accuse
5. rule	15. youth	25. intrude
6. troop	16. bruise	
7. dew	17. loose	
8. route	18. rude	
9. view	19. loop	
10. lose	20. flute	

THINK
about the words.

Each word has the |ōō| or the |yōō| sound. These sounds can be spelled *u*-consonant-*e* or with two vowels. A consonant sound usually follows the patterns *oo*, *ui*, and *ou*.

|ōō| or |yōō| r**u**l**e**, cl**ue**, d**ew**, pr**oo**f, cr**ui**se, r**ou**te

• What are six patterns for the |ōō| or the |yōō| sound? How are these sounds spelled in the Elephant Words?

WRITE
the words.

Practice   Write the Basic Words to answer the questions.

A. Which **twelve** words have |ōō| or |yōō| spelled with the pattern *u*-consonant-*e* or *oo*?

B. Which **six** words have |ōō| or |yōō| spelled with the pattern *ue*, *ew*, *ui*, or *ou*?

CHECK
your spelling.

C. Which **two** words have other spellings for |ōō| or |yōō|?

■ **Now write the five Challenge Words.** Underline the patterns that spell the |ōō| and the |yōō| sounds.

> *Spelling-Meaning Hint* Can you see *view* in these words: *preview, review*? These words are all related in spelling and meaning. **Think of this:** The critic had a good *view* when she watched the movie *preview*.

view
pre*view*
re*view*

Independent Practice

Spelling-Meaning   Look at the Spelling-Meaning Hint.

1-2. Write *preview*. Then write the Basic Word that you see in *preview*.

Word Analysis   Complete the exercises with Basic Words.

3-6. Write the four words that have the final |z| sound.

7-9. Write three words by adding letters to the consonant clusters.

   7. cl____   **8.** tr____   **9.** pr____

Classifying   Write the Basic Word that belongs in each group.

10. spoon, shovel, ____   **13.** violin, tuba, ____
11. queen, prince, ____   **14.** road, highway, ____
12. fog, mist, ____   **15.** donkey, horse, ____

clue
|oo|

■ **Challenge Words**   Write the Challenge Word that completes each sentence. Use your Spelling Dictionary.

16. The police officer tried to ____ the noisy crowd.
17. The police are in ____ of the bank robber.
18. Will the witness ____ the suspect of stealing?
19. We have laws so that others do not ____ on our privacy.
20. Do not ____ that a person who looks suspicious is guilty.

Summing Up

The |oo| and the |yoo| sounds are often spelled with the pattern *u*-consonant-*e, ue, ew, oo, ui,* or *ou*.

Expanding Vocabulary

Easily Confused Words   Could a hat be *loose* or *lose*? Could you *loose* or *lose* a pencil? *Loose* is usually an adjective that can mean "not fitting tightly" or "not tied up." *Lose* is a verb that can mean "to fail to find" or "to fail to win."

My **loose** hat fell off.
I often **lose** my pencil.

Practice   Write *loose* or *lose* to complete each sentence.

1. The chickens are ____ in the yard.
2. The rope was tied in a ____ knot.
3. We will ____ the game if we do not practice beforehand.
4. Brian has a ____ front tooth.
5. Did Melissa ____ her wallet during recess?

Proofreading

Commas in Compound Sentences   In a compound sentence, two sentences are joined by the conjunction *and, but,* or *or.* Use a comma before the conjunction.

You must stop at a red light, or you will get a ticket.

Practice   Proofread the beginning of this detective story. Find four misspelled words and two missing commas. Write the story correctly.

> *The Case of*
> ## The Missing Instrument
>
> Who took the floot? Officer Mackey talked to the groupe in the music store. They said the rude yuth was innocent and Mackey knew the story was true. Mackey needed a clew but she did not know where to look.

Review: Spelling Spree

Puzzle Play   Write a Basic or Review Word to fit each clue. Circle the letter that would appear in the box. Write these letters in order to spell three mystery words that name a job.

Example: not polite _ _ □ _   *ru(d)e*

1. pick □ _ _ _ _ _
2. young person _ _ _ _ □
3. good dessert _ _ _ □ _
4. stubborn animal _ _ _ □
5. evidence _ _ _ _ □
6. a feeling _ □ _ _
7. an instrument □ _ _ _ _

8. bunch _ _ _ _ □
9. misplace _ □ _ _
10. to govern _ _ □ _
11. hurt spot _ _ _ □ _ _
12. to dish out _ □ _ _ _
13. path _ _ _ _ □

Crack the Code   Some Basic and Review Words have been written in the code below. Use the code to figure out each word. Then write the words correctly.

CODE	L	V	Q	P	Z	S	B	W	E	H	A	R	J	O	T	X
LETTER	c	i	l	v	b	e	r	t	u	k	s	w	p	h	o	d

Example: ZBEVAS   *bruise*

14. QTTAS
15. XSR
16. LBEVAS

17. ZQSR
18. AOTTW
19. BEXS

20. XEHS
21. LQES
22. WBTTJ

23. WBES
24. QTTJ
25. PVSR

■ **Challenge Words**   Create your own Puzzle Play, using the Challenge Words as the answers to the clues. Think of a mystery word that can be made by combining one letter from each Challenge Word. Write your answers on the back of your paper. Have a classmate complete your puzzle.

Writing Application: A Police Report   Imagine that you have witnessed a car accident. No one was hurt, but a fender was dented. Write a report for the police. Try to use five words from the list on page 32.

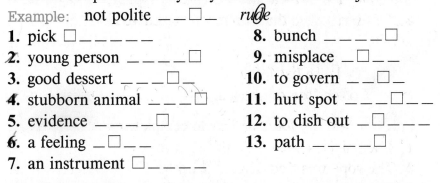

4 Spelling Across the Curriculum

Careers: *Police Work*

Theme Vocabulary

deputy
squad
badge
officer
warrant
criminal
headquarters
rookie

Using Vocabulary Write the Vocabulary Words to complete the paragraph. Use your Spelling Dictionary.

A thief had escaped from Briar County Jail. Rosalind Davis was the assistant sheriff, or __(1)__ , in charge while Sheriff Kane was away. Captain Davis was no __(2)__ . She had been a police __(3)__ in a big city for several years. Davis quickly organized a __(4)__ to help her track down the wanted __(5)__ . Then wearing her __(6)__ and carrying a __(7)__ for arrest, she hurried down the steps of the police __(8)__ .

Understanding Vocabulary Write *T* if the sentence is true. Write *F* if it is not.

9. A squad works like a team.
10. A deputy is in charge of a sheriff.
11. A rookie has a lot of experience.
12. A warrant allows an officer to make an arrest.

FACT FILE

The most famous police department may be Scotland Yard in London, England. It has led the world in solving crimes. It was the first to use fingerprinting.

Enrichment

👪 *The Detective Game*

Players: 3-4 **You need:** game board with 20 spaces, pencils, index cards, game markers
How to play: Each person writes ten "clues"—questions that can be answered with unit words. Each question is on a separate card with the answer on the back. Place the clues in a pile with the questions facing up. Players take turns picking a card, reading the clue aloud, and trying to spell the answer correctly. If the answer is correct, the player can move one space. If it is also spelled correctly, the player can move two more spaces. The first player to cross *Finish* wins.

What is the moisture on grass called?

WHO DID IT?

A detective often follows a trail of clues. One clue leads to the next. Make a map showing a trail of at least ten footprints. Write a word on each footprint. The last letter of one word must be the first letter of the next word. Try to use words from this unit and earlier units.

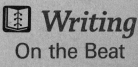

📖 *Writing*
On the Beat

105

You are the writer for a new TV series called *Police!* Write a summary of the first episode. Who are the characters? Describe the plot. What is the problem, and how is it solved? Try to use words from the lists in this unit. Be sure to proofread your summary.

5 Spelling |ou|, |ô|, and |oi|

LOOK

at each word.

SAY

each word.

Basic Words		■ Challenge
1. hawk	11. launch	21. grouse
2. claw	12. royal	22. poise
3. bald	13. scowl	23. loiter
4. tower	14. haunt	24. somersault
5. stalk	15. joint	25. awkward
6. prowl	16. coward	
7. loyal	17. fawn	
8. pause	18. thousand	
9. moist	19. drown	
10. ounce	20. fault	

THINK

about the words.

Each word has the |ou|, the |ô|, or the |oi| sound. These sounds are usually spelled with two letters. The patterns *ou*, *au*, and *oi* are usually followed by a consonant sound.

|ou|	**ou**nce, tow**er**	|oi|	m**oi**st, l**oy**al
|ô|	cl**aw**, p**au**se, b**al**d		

- What are two patterns for the |ou| sound? What are three patterns for the |ô| sound? What consonant follows the *a* spelling of |ô|? What are two patterns for the |oi| sound?

WRITE

the words.

CHECK

your spelling.

Practice Write the Basic Words to answer the questions.

A. Which **seven** words have the |ou| sound?

B. Which **nine** words have the |ô| sound?

C. Which **four** words have the |oi| sound?

■ **Now write the five Challenge Words.** Underline the patterns that spell the |ou|, the |ô|, and the |oi| sounds.

**moist
moisten**

> **Spelling-Meaning Hint** How can you remember that *moisten* has a silent *t*? Think of the related word *moist*, in which the *t* is pronounced.

Independent Practice

Spelling-Meaning Look at the Spelling-Meaning Hint.

1-2. Write *moist* and *moisten*. Underline the letter that is pronounced in one word and silent in the other.

Word Analysis Complete the exercises with Basic Words.

3-7. Write the five words that begin with a consonant cluster. (*Th* is not a consonant cluster. It spells one sound.)

8-9. Write the two rhyming words that have the |oi| sound.

Analogies An **analogy** compares word pairs that are related in the same way. Write a Basic Word to complete each analogy.
Example: **Hot** is to **cold** as **lost** is to **found**.

10. *Heart* is to *muscle* as *elbow* is to _____.
11. *Foot* is to *inch* as *pound* is to _____.
12. *Bear* is to *cub* as *deer* is to _____.
13. *Mammal* is to *rabbit* as *bird* is to _____.
14. *Airplane* is to *takeoff* as *ship* is to _____.
15. *One* is to *ten* as a *hundred* is to a _____.

■ **Challenge Words** Write the Challenge Word that fits each clue. Use your Spelling Dictionary.

16. to linger	**18.** to balance	**20.** to roll the body in
17. a game bird	**19.** clumsy	a complete circle

Summing Up

The |ou|, the |ô|, and the |oi| sounds are usually spelled with these patterns: |ou| *ou, ow* |ô| *aw, au, a* before *l* |oi| *oi, oy.*

Basic

1. hawk
2. claw
3. bald
4. tower
5. stalk
6. prowl
7. loyal
8. pause
9. moist
10. ounce
11. launch
12. royal
13. scowl
14. haunt
15. joint
16. coward
17. fawn
18. thousand
19. drown
20. fault

■ Challenge

21. grouse
22. poise
23. loiter
24. somersault
25. awkward

Review

1. south
2. dawn
3. false
4. cause
5. howl

Expanding Vocabulary

Metric Measurements *Ounce* and *gram* belong to different systems of measurement. *Gram* belongs to the metric system, which is based on the number 10. The prefixes below are commonly used with basic metric units.

PREFIX			PREFIX + BASE WORD		
kilo-	=	1000	**kilogram**	=	1000 grams
centi-	=	1/100	**centigram**	=	1/100 gram
milli-	=	1/1000	**milligram**	=	1/1000 gram

Practice Add *kilo-*, *centi-*, or *milli-* to *gram*, *meter*, or *liter* to write a word that fits each definition.

1. 1/1000 liter
2. 1000 grams
3. 1/1000 meter
4. 1000 meters
5. 1/100 meter
6. 1000 liters
7. 1/1000 gram
8. 1/100 liter

Dictionary

Spelling Table How can you find a word in a dictionary when you do not know how to spell it? Use the **spelling table**. It lists different spellings for the vowel and consonant sounds. If you wanted to find |houl|, you would check each spelling for the |ou| sound until you found *howl*.

SOUND	SPELLINGS	SAMPLE WORDS
|ou|	**ou, ough, ow**	**lou**d, **bough**, **now**

Practice For each pronunciation below, write the spellings given in the spelling table on page 275 for the vowel sound. Then find the word in your Spelling Dictionary. Write it correctly.

1. |drout|
2. |yēld|
3. |klĕnz|
4. |vōlt|

Review: Spelling Spree

The Third Word   Write the Basic or Review Word that belongs in each group.

1. connection, hinge, _____
2. stop, wait, _____
3. scratch, dig, _____
4. mistake, blame, _____
5. morning, sunrise, _____
6. fake, untrue, _____
7. ship, voyage, _____
8. frown, pout, _____
9. wail, hoot, _____
10. wet, damp, _____
11. faithful, true, _____
12. hundred, million, _____
13. spook, ghost, _____
14. ton, pound, _____
15. east, north, _____
16. calf, foal, _____

Proofreading   17-25. Find nine misspelled Basic or Review Words in this description. Write each word correctly.

At dawn the forest is awake. Like a king in his royle tawer, the bawld eagle watches the sunrise. The hauk is no caward. It searches the forest floor, ready to stauk mice. A river and a thousand birdsongs almost droun out a wolf's howl. A mother deer and her fawn run down to the shining stream. Though the wolf is on the proul, it is too distant to couse them much fear.

■ **Challenge Words**   Create your own Third Word activity. For each Challenge Word think of two other words that belong in the same category. Write the answers on the back of your paper. Then have a classmate complete your activity.

📖 *Writing Application:*   Comparison and Contrast
Look at the pictures of a turkey and a peacock. Write two paragraphs comparing and contrasting them. Think about their shape, size, features, and colors. Try to use five words from the list on page 38.

5 Spelling Across the Curriculum

Science: *Birds*

Theme Vocabulary

falcon
ostrich
penguin
cardinal
flamingo
mallard
condor
quail

Using Vocabulary   Write the Vocabulary Words to complete the paragraph. Use your Spelling Dictionary.

At the zoo I saw birds from near and far. A huge vulture, a (1) , came from South America. Two long-necked birds, a pink (2) and a fluffy (3) , came from Africa. A funny black-and-white (4) came from the South Pole. From North America there was a red (5) with a crested head, a green-headed (6) swimming in a pond, and a plump (7) with a short tail. The hawklike (8) had the look of a hunter.

Understanding Vocabulary   Write a Vocabulary Word to answer each question.

9. Which bird can swim but cannot fly?
10. Which bird is a kind of duck?
11. Which bird can run but cannot fly?
12. Which bird likes to wade?

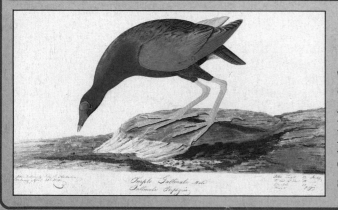

FACT FILE

John James Audubon was an artist who loved birds. Audubon observed many kinds of wild birds and painted lifelike pictures of them in their natural setting.

Enrichment

5

👪 All-About-Birds Chart

With your classmates gather information about several birds named in this unit or other birds that interest you. Make a chart to display what you learn. Include columns labeled *Name, Appearance, Size, Environment, Feeding Habits,* and *Special Facts.* Under *Appearance,* draw a picture of each bird. Under *Environment,* describe the kind of place where each bird lives. Under *Special Facts,* tell something unusual about each bird.

📖 Writing
Poems Taking Shape

Write a four-line poem about a bird. Use the following form:

adjective, noun—
adjective, adjective, adjective—
verb
adverb, adverb, adverb

Finally, draw the shape of the bird around the poem.

Powerful falcon—
Rare, keen-eyed, courageous—
Diving
    Fast, fast, fast.

BIRD MOBILE

Make a bird mobile. On construction paper draw five different bird shapes. Cut out the shapes, and make a small hole at the top of each one. Draw details, such as eyes and feathers, on both sides of each shape. On one side write a sentence describing the bird. Try to use list words. Use string to tie your bird shapes together.

6 Review: Units 1–5

Unit 1   Short Vowels   pp. 12-17

staff	bunch	slept	breath	tough
ditch	fond	grasp	rough	deaf

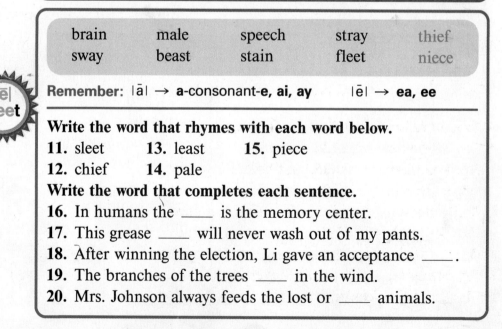

short vowels

Remember: A short vowel sound is usually spelled by a single vowel and is followed by a consonant sound.

|ă| → **a** |ĕ| → **e** |ĭ| → **i** |ŏ| → **o** |ŭ| → **u**

Write the word that fits each clue. Circle the words that have the |ĕ| sound.

1. a group
2. unable to hear
3. strong
4. loving
5. a walking stick
6. rhymes with *death*

Write the word that belongs in each group.

7. hold, grab, ____
8. hole, pit, ____
9. napped, dozed, ____
10. bumpy, uneven, ____

Unit 2   Spelling |ā| and |ē| pp. 18-23

brain	male	speech	stray	thief
sway	beast	stain	fleet	niece

seal   fleet

Remember: |ā| → **a**-consonant-**e, ai, ay** |ē| → **ea, ee**

Write the word that rhymes with each word below.

11. sleet
13. least
15. piece
12. chief
14. pale

Write the word that completes each sentence.

16. In humans the ____ is the memory center.
17. This grease ____ will never wash out of my pants.
18. After winning the election, Li gave an acceptance ____.
19. The branches of the trees ____ in the wind.
20. Mrs. Johnson always feeds the lost or ____ animals.

Half of the words from each unit are reviewed on these pages.
The rest are reviewed on pages 229–231.

Review **6**

Unit 3 Spelling |ī| and |ō| pp. 24-29

thigh	stroll	height	dough	owe
growth	stride	mild	loaf	stroke

o-consonant-e

ose

|ō|

Remember: |ī| → **i-consonant-e, igh, i**

|ō| → **o-consonant-e, oa, ow, o**

Write the word that completes each sentence.

21. Will you join us for a _____ around the neighborhood?
22. The black horse won the race without breaking _____.
23. Bread, pastry, and other baked goods are made from _____.
24. The bells rang at the _____ of midnight.
25. The part of the leg above the knee is the _____.

Write the word that means the opposite of each word below.

26. work   27. decline   28. pay   29. stormy   30. depth

Unit 4 Spelling |o͞o| and |yo͞o| pp. 30-35

dew	clue	cruise	view	lose
mule	mood	duke	youth	loose

clue

|o͞o|

Remember: |o͞o| and |yo͞o| → **u-consonant-e, ue, ew, oo, ui, ou**

Write the word that fits each meaning.

31. to look at   34. early life
32. a nobleman   35. not bound together
33. a sea trip   36. state of mind

Write the word that completes each sentence.

37. The grass sparkled with morning _____.
38. A missing book was a _____ to the mystery.
39. Many trees _____ their leaves in the fall.
40. I tied the gear onto the gray _____.

6 Review

Unit 5 Spelling |ou|, |ô|, and |oi| pp. 36-41

pause	moist	ounce	loyal	stalk
fawn	scowl	joint	launch	thousand

Remember: |ou| → **ou, ow** |ô| → **aw, au, a** before **l**
         |oi| → **oi, oy**

Write the word that completes each analogy.
41. *Hot* is to *warm* as *wet* is to ____.
42. *Smile* is to *grin* as *frown* is to ____.
43. *Bad* is to *good* as *unfaithful* is to ____.
44. *Tree* is to *trunk* as *plant* is to ____.

Write the word that fits each clue.
45. knee
46. less than a pound
47. brief stop
48. a number
49. motorboat
50. young deer

■ Challenge Words Units 1-5 pp. 12-41

opponent	somersault	summit	accuse	succeed
candidate	sacrifice	subdue	loiter	knapsack

Write the word that means the opposite of each word.
51. provoke
52. teammate
53. base
54. hurry

Write the word that completes each analogy.
55. *Sharp* is to *dull* as *defend* is to ____.
56. *Swimmer* is to *dive* as *gymnast* is to ____.
57. *Sweet* is to *sour* as *fail* is to ____.
58. *Cycling* is to *saddlebag* as *hiking* is to ____.
59. *Gift* is to *present* as *offering* is to ____.
60. *Job* is to *applicant* as *public office* is to ____.

Spelling-Meaning Strategy

Consonant Changes: Silent to Sounded

You know that words, like people, can be related to each other. Read this paragraph.

> When you are riding your bicycle, you should always stop at a stop **sign.** Use a hand **signal** when you want to make a turn.

sign
signal

Think

- How are *sign* and *signal* related in meaning?
- Which letter is silent in one word and pronounced in the other?

Here are more related words in which a consonant is silent in one word and pronounced in the other.

colum**n**	heir	muscle
columnist	inherit	muscular

Apply and Extend

Complete these activities on a separate piece of paper.

1. Look up the meaning of each word in the word box above. Then write a short paragraph, using one pair of words from the box. Can you make the meaning of each word clear?
2. With a partner list as many words as you can that are related to *sign, column, heir,* and *muscle.* Then look on page 269 of your Spelling-Meaning Index. Add any other words that you find in these families to your list.

Summing Up Sometimes you can remember how to spell a word with a silent consonant by thinking of a word that is related in meaning in which the letter is pronounced.

LITERATURE AND WRITING

Personal Narrative

Usually Beth likes to talk to Philip, but today she has something else on her mind. Why is Beth eager to get home?

As I took a flying leap across the frozen drainage ditch that separated the road from the field, I heard Philip calling me.

"Hey, Beth!" He was still standing on the blacktop just where the bus left him. "You shouldn't be going through the field. You might step into an ice puddle."

Of all days to have to stop and start explaining things to Philip Hall. But at any other time I'd be thinking that he wouldn't be fretting about my feet if he didn't really like me. Now would he? "Frosty feet are nothing," I told him, "when you have a spanking new puppy waiting to meet you."

"What if Mr. Grant wouldn't swap a collie dog for one of your pa's turkeys?" asked Philip, grinning as though he hoped it was so.

"That's all you know! When I left the house this morning, my pa was picking out six of our fattest turkeys for swapping." I turned and began running across the field.

from Philip Hall likes me. I reckon maybe. *by Bette Greene*

Think and Discuss

1. What information does the author present through the **dialogue** to explain why Beth wants to get home?
2. Where does this part of the story take place? What **details** help you picture the scene?
3. From whose **point of view** is this story told? How do you know?

The Writing Process

The excerpt on page 46 lets you share Beth's experience from her **point of view.** You too can write a personal narrative to share an experience. Write a **beginning** that will catch your readers' attention. Add **details** to make your story interesting and to let your readers "see" what happens. Use **dialogue** to help develop the plot and characters.

Assignment: Write a Personal Narrative

Step One: Prewriting

1. List interesting experiences that you have had. Discuss them with a classmate, and choose a topic.
2. Write three beginnings. Choose the one you like best.

Step Two: Write a First Draft

1. Think about your purpose and your audience.
2. Do not worry about mistakes—just write!

Step Three: Revise

1. Where could you add details and dialogue to help your reader see, hear, and feel your experience?
2. Use your Thesaurus to find exact words.
3. Read your story to a classmate. Make other changes.

Step Four: Proofread

1. Did you use end marks correctly?
2. Did you spell all words correctly? Copy any words that you misspelled into your Notebook for Writing.

Step Five: Publish

1. Copy your story neatly. Add an interesting title.
2. Tape-record your story, and share it with friends.

Composition Words

tough
boast
lose
loyal
stroll
bruise
scowl
slept

Proofreading Marks

¶ Indent
∧ Add something
ℓ Take out something
≡ Capitalize
/ Make a small letter

Theme: Tales

7 Spelling \ôr\, \âr\, and \är\

LOOK
at each word.

SAY
each word.

Basic Words		■ Challenge
1. hare	11. tore	21. folklore
2. scar	12. lair	22. unicorn
3. torch	13. snare	23. ordeal
4. soar	14. carve	24. marvelous
5. harsh	15. bore	25. hoard
6. sore	16. fare	
7. lord	17. cork	
8. flair	18. barge	
🐘 9. warn	19. flare	FINISH
🐘 10. floor	20. rare	

THINK
about the words.

Each word has a vowel sound + *r*. The \ôr\ sounds are close to the \ō\ sound. The \âr\ sounds are close to the \ā\ sound. The \är\ sounds are close to the \ä\ sound.

\ôr\ **torch, sore, soar**   \âr\ **hare, flair**   \är\ **scar**

- What are three spelling patterns for \ôr\? How are the \ôr\ sounds spelled in the Elephant Words? What are two patterns for \âr\? What is one pattern for \är\?

WRITE
the words.

Practice   Write the Basic Words to answer the questions.

A. Which **seven** words have \ôr\ spelled *or*, *ore*, or *oar*?
B. Which **two** words have \ôr\ spelled other ways?
C. Which **seven** words have \âr\ spelled *are* or *air*?
D. Which **four** words have \är\ spelled *ar*?

CHECK
your spelling.

■ **Now write the five Challenge Words.** Underline the patterns that spell the \ôr\ and the \âr\ sounds.

> ***Spelling-Meaning Hint***   When you form the past tense of *scar*, double the *r* before adding *-ed*. Otherwise, you will have the word *scared*, which is the past tense of *scare*.

scar
scar**red**

Independent Practice

Spelling-Meaning   Look at the Spelling-Meaning Hint.
  1-2. Write *scar*. Then write the past tense of *scar*, and under-
      line the double consonant.

Word Analysis   Complete the exercises with Basic Words.

  3-6. Write the word that sounds the same as each word.
      3. boar   **4.** fair   **5.** worn   **6.** hair

  7-10. Write the two pairs of words that sound alike but are
      spelled differently.

Definitions   Write the Basic Word that fits each meaning.
  11. a wild animal's den
  12. unpleasant or severe
  13. bottom surface of a room
  14. a bottle stopper
  15. to make by cutting

|âr|

flare   flair

■ **Challenge Words**   Write the Challenge Word that fits each
  meaning. Use your Spelling Dictionary.
  16. a difficult experience   **19.** legends, fables, myths
  17. a secret supply   **20.** an imaginary animal
  18. causing wonder   similar to a horse

Summing Up

The |ôr| sounds are often spelled with the pattern *or, ore,* or *oar.*
The |âr| sounds are often spelled with the pattern *are* or *air.*
The |är| sounds are usually spelled with the pattern *ar.*

Expanding Vocabulary

Idioms   Read the sentence below. Is Ben now bald?

Ben **tore his hair out** over the tough decision.

The phrase *tore his hair out* is an idiom. It means that Ben suffered greatly. An **idiom** has a meaning that is different from the meanings of its separate words.

Practice   **Write the meaning of each underlined idiom.**

a. to rise to give a formal speech
b. to be part of something from the beginning
c. nervous
d. to be obvious

1. The spelling mistake sticks out like a sore thumb.
2. All eyes were on Tom when he took the floor.
3. Mary was on pins and needles while waiting for her test.
4. Abby got in on the ground floor of the new project.

Dictionary

Pronunciation Key   How can you find out how to pronounce *warn*? The dictionary entry gives its pronunciation. The **pronunciation key** helps you understand the symbols used in the pronunciation by giving one or more sample words for each symbol. Part of a pronunciation key is shown below.

PRONUNCIATION   PRONUNCIATION KEY
warn |wôrn| ŏ pot   ō go   ô paw, for

Practice   **Write the correct spelling for each dictionary pronunciation. Use the pronunciation key on page 277.**

1. |lōop| lope, loop
2. |skăr| scar, scare
3. |prâr′ ē| prayer, prairie
4. |flôr| floor, flour
5. |sôr′ ē| sore, sorry
6. |fâr| fare, far

Review: Spelling Spree

Crack the Code   Use the following code to find a Basic or Review Word in each item below. Write each word correctly.

CODE	1	2	3	4	5	6	7	8	9	10	11	12	13	14	15	16	17	18
LETTER	a	b	c	d	e	f	g	h	i	k	l	o	q	r	s	t	u	v

Example: 8-1-14-15-8 *harsh*

1. 3-1-14-18-5
2. 16-12-14-5
3. 2-12-14-5
4. 2-1-14-7-5
5. 11-1-9-14
6. 6-11-1-14-5

7. 15-12-1-14
8. 11-12-14-4
9. 2-12-1-14-4
10. 15-3-1-14
11. 8-1-14-5
12. 16-12-14-3-8

13. 15-12-14-5
14. 15-13-17-1-14-5
15. 6-1-14-5
16. 3-12-14-10
17. 15-16-1-9-14-15

Proofreading   18-25. Find eight misspelled Basic or Review Words in this tale. Write each word correctly.

Once upon a time the hare had tiny ears. A bird with a hars voice and shap claws saw a snair on the forest flor. This rar bird tried to worn the hare about the trap, but the hare did not listen. A hors with a flar for saving animals pulled the sore hare out by its ears. That is how the hare got its big ears.

■ **Challenge Words**   Create a Crack the Code activity. Write a message with a numbered code, using each Challenge Word. Then write the message correctly on the back of the paper. Trade papers with a classmate. Decode each other's messages.

Writing Application: Creative Writing   Imagine that at one time zebras did not have black and white stripes. Write a tale that explains how zebras got their stripes. Try to use five words from the list on page 50.

7 Spelling Across the Curriculum

Language Arts: *Tales*

Theme Vocabulary

superhuman
stubborn
astound
exhausted
rugged
beware
feat
cunning

Using Vocabulary Write the Vocabulary Words to complete the paragraph. Use your Spelling Dictionary.

Pecos Bill will __(1)__ you with his extraordinary, or __(2)__, strength. Once he dug a ditch through __(3)__ Texas country to the Gulf of Mexico and was not even __(4)__ by this incredible __(5)__! Although his girlfriend Slue-Foot Sue was a good rider, Bill told her to __(6)__ of Widow Maker, his wild horse. Sue, being a __(7)__ person, refused to listen. She used her __(8)__ to find a way to ride the horse and was never seen again.

Understanding Vocabulary Write *yes* if the underlined word is used correctly. Write *no* if it is not.

9. The <u>rugged</u> mountains were difficult to climb.
10. Did Pecos Bill have big <u>feat</u>?
11. She was <u>stubborn</u> and easy to get along with.
12. This amazing adventure will <u>astound</u> you.

FACT FILE

The tale of John Henry may be based on a true event. To prove that no machine could replace him, Henry raced his hammer against a steam-powered drill and won.

Enrichment 7

 Writing
A Limerick

A limerick is a humorous five-line poem. The first, second, and last lines rhyme, and the third and fourth lines rhyme. Here is an example:

> There once was a boy named Pete,
> Who performed an amazing feat.
> He soared through the air,
> With incredible flair,
> Then landed with grace on both feet.

Write a limerick about another amazing character. Try to use words from the lists in this unit. Be sure to proofread your paper.

SHAPE WORDS

Can you draw the letters of a word to show the word's meaning? Can you write the word *square* so that it looks like a square? Can you write *hare* so that it looks like a hare? Draw words from the lists in this unit in ways that illustrate their meanings.

Creature Lore

A unicorn is an imaginary animal similar to a horse but with a horn in the middle of its forehead. With a partner make a list of other imaginary creatures, or make up some creatures of your own. Draw them on a poster. Write a caption for each picture, using list words.

Theme: Using a Microscope

8 Spelling |ûr| and |îr|

LOOK

at each word.

SAY

each word.

Basic Words

1. smear
2. germ
3. blur
4. peer
5. stir
6. squirm
7. nerve
8. early
9. worth
10. pier

11. thirst
12. burnt
13. rear
14. term
15. steer
16. pearl
17. squirt
18. stern
19. hurl
20. worse

■ Challenge

21. interpret
22. yearn
23. emerge
24. dreary
25. career

THINK

about the words.

Here are more words with a vowel sound + *r*. The |ûr| sounds have a weak vowel sound. The |îr| sounds are close to the |ē| sound.

|ûr| g**er**m, st**ir**, bl**ur**, **ear**ly, w**or**th |îr| p**eer**, sm**ear**

• What are five spelling patterns for the |ûr| sounds? What are two patterns for the |îr| sounds? How are the |îr| sounds spelled in the Elephant Word?

WRITE

the words.

CHECK

your spelling.

Practice **Write the Basic Words to answer the questions.**

A. Which **eleven** words have |ûr| spelled *ir, ur,* or *er*?
B. Which **four** words have |ûr| spelled *ear* or *or*?
C. Which **four** words have |îr| spelled *eer* or *ear*?
D. Which **one** word has |îr| spelled another way?

■ **Now write the five Challenge Words.** Underline the patterns that spell the |ûr| and the |îr| sounds.

Spelling-Meaning Hint   Can you see *worth* in these words: *worthy, worthless, worthwhile*? These words are all related in spelling and meaning. **Think of this:** A *worthy* friend is *worth* your time.

worth
worthy
worthless
worthwhile

Independent Practice

Spelling-Meaning   Look at the Spelling-Meaning Hint.
  1-2. Write *worthy*. Then write the Basic Word that you see in *worthy*.

Word Analysis   Complete the exercises with Basic Words.

  3-6. Write the four words that begin or end with *st*.

  7-8. Write the two words that have the |kw| sounds.

  9-10. Write the two words that sound alike.

Analogies   Write the Basic Word that completes each analogy.
11. *Good* is to *better* as *bad* is to _____.
12. *Jump* is to *leap* as *throw* is to _____.
13. *Frozen* is to *thawed* as *raw* is to _____.
14. *Sunrise* is to *sunset* as *late* is to _____.
15. *Flower* is to *daisy* as *gem* is to _____.

|ûr|

squirt

■ **Challenge Words**   Write the Challenge Word that fits each clue. Use your Spelling Dictionary.
  16. opposite of *cheerful*
  17. opposite of *disappear*
  18. to have a deep longing
  19. a chosen profession
  20. to explain the meaning or importance of

Summing Up

The |ûr| sounds are often spelled with the patterns *er, ir, ur, ear,* and *or.*
The |îr| sounds are often spelled with the patterns *eer* and *ear.*

Basic

1. smear
2. germ
3. blur
4. peer
5. stir
6. squirm
7. nerve
8. early
9. worth
10. pier
11. thirst
12. burnt
13. rear
14. term
15. steer
16. pearl
17. squirt
18. stern
19. hurl
20. worse

■ Challenge

21. interpret
22. yearn
23. emerge
24. dreary
25. career

Review

1. learn
2. curve
3. world
4. firm
5. year

Expanding Vocabulary

Blended Words   When one word can do a better job than two, a new word may be created. When the two words are combined, some letters may be dropped. The new word is a **blended word**.

sports + broad**cast** = **sportscast**

Practice   Write blended words by combining the underlined parts in each pair of words.

1. twist + whirl
2. sky + hijack
3. motor + cavalcade
4. helicopter + airport
5. television + marathon
6. squirm + wriggle

Proofreading

Singular and Plural Possessive Nouns   A **possessive noun** shows ownership. To form a possessive noun, add *'s* to a singular noun or a plural noun that does not end with *s*. When a plural noun ends with *s*, add only an apostrophe.

Penny's notebook   mice's tails   students' jars

Practice   Proofread this diary entry. Find four misspelled words and two incorrect possessive nouns. Write the paragraph correctly.

September 27

This yer we are using a microscope. It brings a new world into view. Everything is a blir when I per through the lens, so I adjust the knob. I have seen a sponges skeleton, a jurm, and several insects wings!

Review: Spelling Spree

Puzzle Play   Write a Basic or Review Word to fit each clue. Circle the letter that would appear in the box. Write these letters in order to spell two words that name science subjects.

Example: to look hard □ _ _ _   ⓟeer

1. a bending line □ _ _ _ _ _
2. throw with force □ _ _ _
3. find out _ □ _ _ _
4. a blotch _ □ _ _ _
5. solid _ □ _ _
6. wiggle □ _ _ _ _ _
7. value _ _ _ □ _
8. to guide _ _ _ _ □

9. twelve months □ _ _ _
10. scorched □ _ _ _ _
11. place for ships _ □ _ _
12. less well _ □ _ _ _
13. white gem _ _ _ _ _ □
14. Earth _ □ _ _ _
15. causes disease □ _ _ _
16. not late _ _ _ _ □

Find a Rhyme   For each sentence write a Basic Word that rhymes with the underlined word and that makes sense in the sentence.

17. Is there a scientific ____ for <u>germ</u>?
18. Put that <u>fern</u> in the ____ of the boat.
19. This photo of Rover is not clear. It is just a ____ of <u>fur</u>!
20. We stopped to ____ at the <u>deer</u> in the forest.
21. What should you do <u>first</u> to satisfy your ____?
22. <u>Sir</u>, the chef must ____ the sauce.
23. The tennis player lost his ____ and missed the <u>serve</u>.
24. Do not ____ that water on my clean <u>shirt</u>!
25. Why do you <u>fear</u> sitting in the ____ of the bus?

■ **Challenge Words**   Think of a synonym for each Challenge Word. Then write ten sentences. Use a Challenge Word or a synonym in each sentence. Use your Spelling Dictionary.

📖 *Writing Application:* A Description   Look at the picture. It shows a close-up view of a drop of pond water. Write a paragraph describing the details that you see. Try to use five words from the list on page 56.

8 Spelling Across the Curriculum

Science: *Using a Microscope*

Theme Vocabulary

microscope
slide
magnify
bacteria
focus
cell
experiment
laboratory

Using Vocabulary Write the Vocabulary Words to complete the paragraph. Use your Spelling Dictionary.

You can perform an interesting __(1)__ in the science __(2)__. First, scrape the inside of your cheek with a tongue depressor. Smear some of the scraping onto a glass __(3)__. Examine it under a __(4)__. The instrument will __(5)__ the sample about a hundred times. If the image is blurry, turn the knob to bring it into __(6)__. A skin __(7)__ from your cheek is almost transparent and has a round, flat shape. Do you see any germs or __(8)__ ?

Understanding Vocabulary For each sentence write *T* if the statement is true. Write *F* if it is not.

9. You can look at the stars with a microscope.
10. Some bacteria cause disease.
11. If you magnify things, you make them look smaller.
12. When the image is not clear, adjust the focus.

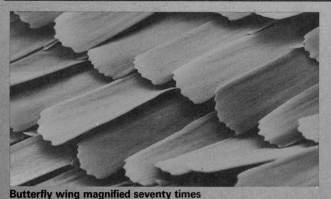

Butterfly wing magnified seventy times

FACT FILE

Most microscopes use light to magnify, but an electron microscope uses a beam of electrons. An electron microscope can make an object appear 500,000 times bigger than its actual size.

Enrichment

8

👪 A Tiny, Tiny Universe

Under a microscope or a magnifying glass, the most ordinary things can take on an unusual appearance. With a partner gather leaves, small rocks, dirt, pond water, and other familiar objects. Examine each object with a magnifying glass or a microscope. Draw each magnified object on construction paper. Write a caption for each drawing. Try to use list words from this unit. Staple the illustrations together to make a booklet.

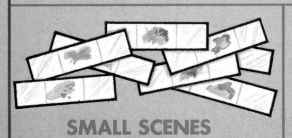

SMALL SCENES

Create a comic strip about "The Amazing Adventures of Professor Lens." Think of a humorous situation that involves this comical scientist and his microscope. Draw three or four frames on construction paper. Draw cartoon characters in each frame, and write dialogue in speech balloons. Try to use words from the lists in this unit.

📖 Writing
Extra! Extra!

Imagine that you are a reporter covering the story of Dr. Marjory Kim. With the aid of her microscope, Dr. Kim has just discovered a cure for the common cold. Write a newspaper article that explains the who, what, where, when, why, and how of her discovery. Try to use words from the lists in this unit. Be sure to proofread your paper.

Theme: Wheelchair Basketball

9 Compound Words

LOOK
at each word.

SAY
each word.

Basic Words		■ Challenge
1. basketball	11. highway	21. extraordinary
2. wheelchair	12. daytime	22. self-assured
✗ 3. cheerleader	13. whoever	23. quick-witted
4. newscast	14. test tube	24. limelight
5. weekend	✗15. turnpike	25. junior high
✗6. everybody	16. shipyard	school
7. up-to-date	17. homemade	
✗8. grandparent	18. household	
9. first aid	19. salesperson	
10. wildlife	20. brother-in-law	

THINK
about the words.

Each word is a compound word. A **compound word** is made up of two or more smaller words.

wheel + **chair**   = wheelchair   **first** + **aid** = first aid
up + **to** + **date**   =   up-to-date

• What three ways can compound words be written? What words make up each compound word in the list?

WRITE
the words.

Practice   **Write the Basic Words to answer the questions.**

A. Which **sixteen** compound words are written as one word?

B. Which **two** compound words are written with hyphens?

CHECK
your spelling.

C. Which **two** compound words are written as separate words?

■ **Now write the five Challenge Words.** Draw a line between the words that make up each compound word.

> *Spelling-Meaning Hint*   Can you see *wild* in the words *wildlife* and *wilderness*? These words are related in meaning and spelling. **Think of this:** Many kinds of *wildlife* live in the *wilderness*.

wild
wildlife
wilderness

Independent Practice

Spelling-Meaning   Look at the Spelling-Meaning Hint.

1-2. Write *wild*. Then write the Basic Word that is related to *wild* in spelling and meaning.

Word Analysis   Write the Basic Words that include the underlined parts of these words.

3. ar<u>mch</u>air
4. <u>turntable</u>
5. <u>house</u>boat

6. <u>test</u> pilot
7. <u>homesick</u>
8. <u>everything</u>

9. <u>mother-in-law</u>
10. <u>daydream</u>

daytime

Making Inferences   Write the word that fits each clue.

11. If you play this game, it is good to be tall.
12. What you build here will be used in the water.
13. A person in an accident might need this right away.
14. This person is always older than your mother or father.
15. You can listen to this on the radio many times a day.

■ **Challenge Words**   Write the Challenge Word that fits each definition. Use your Spelling Dictionary.

16. confident
17. mentally alert
18. very unusual

19. the center of public attention
20. the seventh, the eighth, and sometimes the ninth grades

Summing Up

A **compound word** is made up of two or more smaller words. A compound word may be written as one word, as a hyphenated word, or as separate words.

Basic

1. basketball
2. wheelchair
3. cheerleader
4. newscast
5. weekend
6. everybody
7. up-to-date
8. grandparent
9. first aid
10. wildlife
11. highway
12. daytime
13. whoever
14. test tube
15. turnpike
16. shipyard
17. homemade
18. household
19. salesperson
20. brother-in-law

■ Challenge

21. extraordinary
22. self-assured
23. quick-witted
24. limelight
25. junior high
    school

Review

1. afternoon
2. ninety-nine
3. everywhere
4. all right
5. breakfast

Expanding Vocabulary

Compound Words In 1891 a sport was invented in which a soccer ball was thrown into a peach basket. Eventually *basket* was added to *ball* to form a new name for this game—*basketball*. The meaning of a compound word combines the meanings of the two words from which it is formed.

Practice Write compound words by adding *basket* or *ball* to each word below. Use your Spelling Dictionary.

1. bearing
2. waste
3. snow
4. room
5. weave
6. foot
7. game
8. eye

Dictionary

Stress A **syllable** is a word part that has one vowel sound. In a word with more than one syllable, one syllable is said more strongly, or with more **stress.** The dictionary pronunciation for a word shows which syllable is stressed. The stressed syllable is followed by an **accent mark** (′).

who·ev·er |hoo ĕv′ ər| *pron.* Anyone that.

Practice Look at each word and its pronunciation. Write each word in syllables. Then underline the stressed syllable.

1. tulip |too′ lĭp|
2. sorrow |sŏr′ ō|
3. neglect |nĭ glĕkt′|
4. furnish |fûr′ nĭsh|
5. dolphin |dŏl′ fĭn|
6. explain |ĭk splān′|
7. diet |dī′ ĭt|
8. destroy |dĭ stroi′|

Review: Spelling Spree

Combining Words   Write Basic or Review Words by combining the words in the box with the words in the numbered list.

yard	life	where	way	ever	right
cast	aid	in-law	person	made	tube
fast	pike	parent	hold		

1. test
2. who
3. ship
4. all

5. sales
6. news
7. turn
8. grand

9. wild
10. high
11. every
12. house

13. first
14. home
15. brother
16. break

Proofreading   17-25. Find nine misspelled Basic or Review Words in this sportscast. Write each word correctly.

Marshall Arena is the setting for the exciting weelchair baskitball championship. It seems that everbody wants to attend. The score in the game this afternon was one hundred to ninty-nine. Guard Rob Dean seemed to be everywhere at once. One chearleader yelled so much that her voice was hoarse. The games continue all weekend. This concludes our daytim newscast. Join us this evening for another up to date report.

■ **Challenge Words**   Write five headlines about a basketball game. Use one Challenge Word in each headline. Capitalize the first, last, and each important word in each headline.

Writing Application: A Persuasive Letter   Write a letter to your principal, asking to use some school sports equipment. Include two good reasons to support your argument. Try to use five words from the list on page 62.

9 Spelling Across the Curriculum

Recreation: *Wheelchair Basketball*

Theme Vocabulary

referee
court
foul
dribble
forward
gymnasium
penalty
trophy

Using Vocabulary Write the Vocabulary Words to complete the paragraph. Use your Spelling Dictionary.

Wheelchair basketball is usually played on a regulation-size __(1)__ , often in a school __(2)__ . Any player—a center, a guard, or a __(3)__ —is allowed to push the wheels twice. Then the player must __(4)__ , or bounce, the ball at least once. If a rule is broken, the __(5)__ will call a __(6)__ , or violation. The __(7)__ can be the loss of the ball. In a tournament the winning team gets a __(8)__ .

Understanding Vocabulary Write *yes* if the underlined word is used correctly. Write *no* if it is not.

9. The player caused a <u>foul</u> and scored two points.
10. Each player got a <u>penalty</u> for winning the game.
11. The <u>referee</u> called a time-out.
12. One player made a basket from center <u>court</u>.

FACT FILE

The National Wheelchair Basketball Association sponsors tournaments for youths between the ages of eight and nineteen and for adults. Competitions have been held since 1949.

Enrichment

9

👪 *What Word Am I?*

Players: 10 players, 1 referee **You need**: 20 large cards, each shaped like a basketball, with a Basic Word on each

How to play: Form two teams of five players. The referee pins a card on each player's back. Each player takes a turn and has one minute to try to guess his or her word by asking other team members questions about the word. The player must guess and spell the word correctly. For each correct word, the team gets a point. If a word is spelled incorrectly, the other team gets a turn. The first team to get five points wins.

📖 *Writing*
A Sports Interview

Imagine that you will interview a famous wheelchair basketball player. Make a list of *who, what, where, when, why,* and *how* questions to ask. Then write an interview between you and the player, using your questions. Try to use words from the lists in this unit. Be sure to proofread your paper.

COMPOUND THE FUN!

Make at least five rebus puzzles that represent compound words from the lists in this unit. On an index card write or draw words, letters, numbers, or pictures that illustrate the parts of a compound word. Write the compound word correctly on the back of the card. Can your classmates solve your puzzles?

10 Homophones

LOOK
at each word.

SAY
each word.

Basic Words

1. poll
2. pole
3. main
4. mane
5. sole
6. soul
7. hall
8. haul
9. peace
10. piece
11. loan
12. lone
13. heal
14. heel
15. flea
16. flee
17. pore
18. pour
19. berry
20. bury

■ Challenge

21. canvass
22. canvas
23. stationary
24. stationery

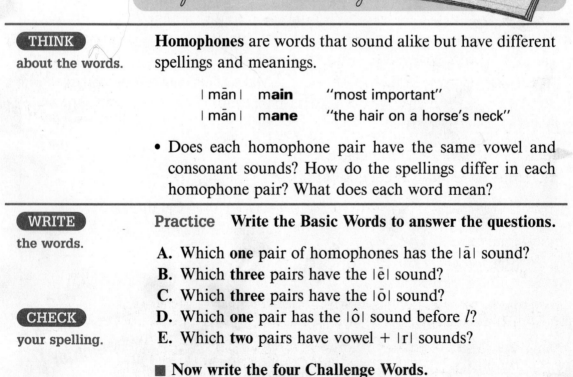

An Election Poll
☐ Yes
☐ No
☐ Undecided

THINK
about the words.

Homophones are words that sound alike but have different spellings and meanings.

| mān | **m**ain   "most important"
| mān | **m**ane   "the hair on a horse's neck"

- Does each homophone pair have the same vowel and consonant sounds? How do the spellings differ in each homophone pair? What does each word mean?

WRITE
the words.

Practice   Write the Basic Words to answer the questions.

A. Which **one** pair of homophones has the |ā| sound?
B. Which **three** pairs have the |ē| sound?
C. Which **three** pairs have the |ō| sound?
D. Which **one** pair has the |ô| sound before *l*?
E. Which **two** pairs have vowel + |r| sounds?

CHECK
your spelling.

■ Now write the four Challenge Words.

> **Spelling-Meaning Hint**   The words *sole* and *solitary* have different vowel sounds but are related in spelling and meaning. **Think of this:** The *sole* resident of the valley led a *solitary* life.

so|le
so|litary

Independent Practice

Spelling-Meaning   Look at the Spelling-Meaning Hint.

1-2. Write *solitary*. Then write the Basic Word that is related in spelling and meaning to *solitary*.

Context Sentences   Write the Basic Word in parentheses that completes each sentence correctly.

3. The ____ showed that many people have pets. (poll, pole)
4. The squirrel ran up the telephone ____. (poll, pole)
5. That horse has a beautiful black ____. (main, mane)
6. What is the ____ idea of the paragraph? (main, mane)
7. If you give the dog a bone, he may ____ it. (berry, bury)
8. A ____ is a small, juicy fruit. (berry, bury)
9. A tiny opening in the skin is a ____. (pore, pour)
10. Please ____ the milk into a glass. (pore, pour)

berry   bury

Definitions   Write the Basic Word that fits each meaning.

11. a corridor	**13.** to pull	**15.** to run away
12. freedom from war	**14.** an insect	**16.** a portion

■ **Challenge Words**   Write the Challenge Word that fits each definition below. Use your Spelling Dictionary.

17. to poll or survey	**19.** a heavy cloth
18. not changing	**20.** writing paper

Summing Up

Homophones are words that sound alike but have different spellings and meanings.

Basic

1. poll
2. pole
3. main
4. mane
5. sole
6. soul
7. hall
8. haul
9. peace
10. piece
11. loan
12. lone
13. heal
14. heel
15. flea
16. flee
17. pore
18. pour
19. berry
20. bury

■ Challenge

21. canvass
22. canvas
23. stationary
24. stationery

Review

1. wait
2. weight
3. meet
4. meat

Expanding Vocabulary

Homophones   Why do homophones sound alike but have different spellings and meanings? Look at the histories of *miner* and *minor*. You will see that they have different origins.

> **Miner** may come from the Common Celtic *meini-*, meaning "ore." **Minor** comes from the Latin word *minor*, meaning "less."

Practice   Write *miner* or *minor* to complete each sentence correctly. Use your Spelling Dictionary.

1. The coal ____ worked underground all day.
2. Roberto had a ____ part in the play.
3. Kristen received only ____ injuries in the car accident.
4. An old ____ once discovered gold in that shaft.

Dictionary

Homophones   Because homophones sound alike, people sometimes confuse them. A dictionary entry will tell you if a word has a homophone.

> **lone** |lōn| *adj.* **1.** Without others: *A lone sailor stood watch.*
>   **2.** By itself: *A lone tree stood in the meadow.*
>   ♦ *These sound alike* **lone, loan.**

Practice   Look up the words below in your Spelling Dictionary. Write the homophone given for each word.

1. seen   2. hoard

Write the correct spelling for each pronunciation.

3. Have you |sēn| the results of the poll?
4. The hikers kept a |hôrd| of food in their camper.
5. Ten police officers quickly rushed to the |sēn|.
6. A |hôrd| of people gathered at the burning house.

Review: Spelling Spree

Homophone Riddles   Write a pair of Basic or Review Words to complete each statement. Write the words in the correct order. Capitalize the first word of a quotation.

1-2. A foot doctor might say to your foot, "____, ____."

3-4. A race between a ham and a steak is a ____ ____.

5-6. A dog might say to an insect, "____, ____."

7-8. A single spirit is a ____ ____.

9-10. A part of a treaty is called a ____ of a ____.

11-12. A horse's most important hair is its ____ ____.

13-14. A survey of long sticks is a ____ ____.

15-16. An animal storing its food might ____ a ____.

Proofreading   **17-24.** Find eight misspelled Basic or Review Words in this notice. Write each word correctly.

- Do you pore a lot of milk onto your cereal?
- How do you hall heavy books to school?
- Do you por over the comics in the newspaper?
- Should parents lone their children money?
- Should people exercise to lose wieght?
- Should you wate for a friend who is always late?

  The fifth graders are taking a poll in the main holl.

  Give us a piece of your mind. Don't be a lon ranger!

■ **Challenge Words**   Look at the Homophone Riddles activity. Write a homophone riddle for each pair of Challenge Words. Write your answers on the back of your paper. Trade riddles with a classmate, and answer each other's riddles.

📖 *Writing Application:* Instructions   Imagine that you own a polling service. Write a paragraph of instructions for your Employee's Handbook. Explain how to conduct interviews. Try to use five words from the list on page 68.

10 Spelling Across the Curriculum

Math: *Surveys*

Theme Vocabulary

survey
sample
data
random
predict
questionnaire
percentage
graph

Using Vocabulary Write the Vocabulary Words to complete the paragraph. Use your Spelling Dictionary.

How can you __(1)__ whether students want to have a sports day? To find out you must conduct a __(2)__. You can do this by handing out a printed __(3)__ or by interviewing. Because you cannot question everyone, choose a test group, or __(4)__. Select a specific group, or choose people at __(5)__. The information, or __(6)__, you gather will tell you what __(7)__ of students want a sports day. Show the results on a bar or line __(8)__.

Understanding Vocabulary Write *yes* if the underlined word is used correctly. Write *no* if it is not.

9. A large <u>percentage</u> of the children swim daily.
10. The survey provided new <u>data</u> on the city's growth.
11. Rebecca is an excellent <u>questionnaire</u>.
12. Take a <u>survey</u> to find out if people like the product.

FACT FILE

In the 1930s George Gallup developed scientific ways to take national surveys. Gallup polls provide information to businesses and other groups.

Enrichment 10

OOPS!

Using the wrong homophone can sometimes make us laugh. Can you imagine an opinion pole or a swim meat? Create homophone cartoons, using a homophone pair from the lists in this unit. Think of a title that is serious or silly, depending on which homophone is used. For example, you might use the serious title "An Opinion Poll" and the silly title "An Opinion Pole." Draw a cartoon for each title.

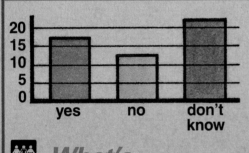

What's Your Opinion?

How much allowance should a fifth grade student receive? Should schools have a dress code? With a classmate write a list of questions about topics that interest you. Try to use words from the lists in this unit. Survey your classmates. Record the results on a bar graph.

📖 Writing
Speaking of Spokes

Ms. Random Data is conducting a survey to find out what people look for when they buy a bicycle. Write the conversation that takes place between Ms. Data and Noah Knowit All, a person who has some definite but unusual opinions. Try to use words from the lists in this unit. Be sure to proofread your paper.

(Theme: Theater)

11 Final |ər|

LOOK
at each word.

SAY
each word.

Basic Words   ■ **Challenge**

1. theater   11. flavor   21. character
2. actor   12. finger   22. clamor
3. mirror   13. mayor   23. tremor
4. powder   14. polar   24. scholar
5. humor   15. clover   25. chamber
6. anger   16. burglar
7. banner   17. tractor
8. pillar   18. matter
9. major   19. lunar
10. thunder   20. quarter

THINK
about the words.

Each word ends with the schwa sound + *r*. The **schwa sound**
is a weak vowel sound that is often found in an unstressed
syllable. It is shown as |ə|. Because the |ə| sound can be
spelled with any vowel, pay careful attention to its spelling.

|ər| ang**er**, act**or**, pill**ar**

• What are three spelling patterns for the final |ər| sounds?

WRITE
the words.

**Practice   Write the Basic Words to answer these questions
about the final |ər| sounds.**

CHECK
your spelling.

A. Which **nine** words have these sounds spelled *er*?
B. Which **seven** words have these sounds spelled *or*?
C. Which **four** words have these sounds spelled *ar*?

■ **Now write the five Challenge Words.** Underline the
patterns that spell the final |ər| sounds.

> *Spelling-Meaning Hint*   How can you remember how to spell the final |ər| sounds in *major*? Think of the |ôr| sounds in the related word *majority*.

major
major ity

Independent Practice

Spelling-Meaning   Look at the Spelling-Meaning Hint.

1-2. Write *major* and *majority*. Then underline the two letters in *majority* that help you remember how to spell the final |ər| sounds in *major*.

Word Analysis   Complete the exercises with Basic Words.

3-6. Write the four words that have double consonants.

7-9. Write the word that rhymes with each word below.

    7. linger   **8.** molar   **9.** chowder

Definitions   Write the Basic Word that fits each meaning.
10. having to do with the moon
11. the quality of being funny
12. a building where plays or movies are presented
13. a plant with leaves divided into three leaflets
14. the chief government officer of a city or a town
15. a rumbling noise that comes after a flash of lightning

■ **Challenge Words**   Write the Challenge Word that fits each clue. Use your Spelling Dictionary.

16. a knowledgeable person
17. a room in a house
18. opposite of *silence*
19. a shaking movement
20. a person in a book, a movie, or a play

Summing Up

In words of more than one syllable, the final |ər| sounds are often spelled with the patterns *er, or,* and *ar.*

Expanding Vocabulary

Meanings for *quarter* Did you know that *quarter* has several meanings? Look at this dictionary entry for *quarter*.

quar·ter |kwôr′ tər| *n., pl.* **quarters 1.** Any of four equal parts into which something can be divided: *I cut the apple into quarters.* **2.** A coin used in the United States or Canada that is worth 25 cents. **3.** One of four time periods that make up a game. **4.** A district or section of a city.

Practice Write 1, 2, 3, or 4 to show which meaning of *quarter* is used in each sentence.

1. The score was tied after the first quarter.
2. Two dimes and a quarter are on the table.
3. There are lots of parks in this quarter of town.
4. Only a quarter of the chicken pie is left.

Proofreading

Comparing with *good* and *bad* The adjectives *good* and *bad* have special forms for making comparisons.

	good	bad
COMPARING TWO:	better	worse
COMPARING MORE THAN TWO:	best	worst

Practice Proofread this setting for a new play. Find four misspelled words and two incorrect forms of *good* or *bad*. Write the title and paragraph correctly.

> ## *The Flavor of Autumn*
>
> SETTING: A farm. The worse of summer is over, and best weather has arrived. The moon is about to entar its last quarter. An old tracter rests in a patch of clovar. Far away, thunder roars.

Review: Spelling Spree

Letter Math   Add and subtract letters from the words below to make Basic or Review Words. Write the new words.

1. c + doll − d + ar =
2. rang − r + er =
3. l + tuna − t + r =
4. cl + drove − dr + r =
5. humid − id + or =
6. pole − e + ar =
7. bent − b + er =
8. b + many − m − y + ner =
9. m + bath − b − h + ter =
10. fl + save − s − e + or =
11. d + rocket − r − ket + tor =
12. th + blunt − bl − t + der =
13. p + crowd − cr + er =
14. admire − ad − e + ror =

Question Clues   Write a Basic or Review Word to answer each question.

15. What *er* word is one-fourth of a dollar?
16. What *or* word is most important?
17. What *er* word responds to a question?
18. What *ar* word might hold up a bridge?
19. What *ar* word might break into a building?
20. What *er* word is part of a hand?
21. What *or* word pulls a plow?
22. What *er* word has a stage?
23. What *or* word performs on a stage?
24. What *or* word governs a city?
25. What *or* word deserves respect?

■ **Challenge Words**   Create your own Question Clues activity. Write five questions. Each question should give a clue to a Challenge Word and should include the letters that spell the final |ər| sounds. Write the answers on the back of your paper. Trade papers with a partner. Answer each other's questions.

Writing Application: A Plot   Imagine that you are a famous writer planning a new play. Write a summary of the plot. Who are the main characters? What are the major scenes? Try to use five words from the list on page 74.

11   Spelling Across the Curriculum

Performing Arts: *Theater*

Theme Vocabulary

audition
script
playwright
role
dialogue
cue
applause
sets

Using Vocabulary   Write the Vocabulary Words to complete the paragraph. Use your Spelling Dictionary.

How do you get a part in a Broadway show? With dozens of other performers, you __(1)__ for a __(2)__, or part. You learn your lines from the __(3)__. At the tryouts the director, the producer, and the __(4)__ are your audience. The stage is bare. There are no props and no __(5)__. On a __(6)__ from the director, you might begin a __(7)__ with another actor. Then you listen. If you hear loud __(8)__, you may have earned the part!

Understanding Vocabulary   Write a Vocabulary Word to answer each riddle.

9. What does an actor do to apply for a job?
10. What has many pages and is divided into scenes?
11. What makes up the scenery for a stage play?
12. What do you hear at the end of a good play?

Scene from *Twelfth Night* by William Shakespeare

FACT FILE

William Shakespeare, English playwright and poet of the 1500s, had a great understanding of people. He is considered the greatest playwright in the English language.

Enrichment 11

The Play's the Thing!

There's a lot of confusion at City Hall. The keys to the city have disappeared! Who is responsible? Will the mayor head a search party? Will the burglar be caught? A broken mirror and a dog collar are the only clues. With a group of classmates, write a one-act play about the crime. Describe the time and setting of the play and list the characters. Include dialogue, using words from the lists in this unit. Then perform the play for your classmates.

THEATER COLLAGE

Make a collage of a theater scene. Draw a theater stage on a piece of construction paper. Then find or draw pictures of people and things you want to show in your stage play. Arrange the pictures to show a moment in a play, and paste them onto the stage. Label the pictures, using words from the lists in this unit.

Writing
Character Sketches

Imagine that you are taking notes for a play you are going to write. Write sketches of three or four characters you will have in your play. What do they look like? How old are they? What kinds of clothes do they wear? What does each character like or dislike? Tell something interesting about their lives. Try to use words from the lists in this unit. Be sure to proofread your paper.

12 Review: Units 7–11

Unit 7 Spelling |ôr|, |âr|, and |är| pp. 48-53

|âr|

flare flair

flair	harsh	soar	warn	~~floor~~
cork	carve	snare	bore	lair

Remember: |ôr| → **or, ore, oar** |âr| → **are, air** |är| → **ar**

Write the word that completes each sentence.
1. Please put the ____ back in the bottle.
2. The baby spilled a glass of milk all over the clean ____.
3. Kim has a ____ for designing clothes.
4. A lioness and her cubs live in a ____.
5. Long, dull stories about animals ____ me.

Write the word that is a synonym for each word below.
6. fly   8. cruel   10. cut
7. alert   9. trap

Unit 8 Spelling |ûr| and |îr| pp. 54-59

|ûr|

squirt

germ	peer	stir	smear	pier
pearl	burnt	rear	worse	squirt

Remember: |ûr| → **er, ir, ur, ear, or** |îr| → **eer, ear**

Write the word that belongs in each group.
11. ruby, jade, ____
12. front, middle, ____
13. spread, wipe, ____
14. splash, spray, ____

Write the word that fits each meaning.
15. to look closely   18. an organism that causes disease
16. damaged by heat   19. to mix
17. a dock or wharf   20. less well

Half of the words from each unit are reviewed on these pages.
The rest are reviewed on pages 232–234.

Review **12**

Unit 9   Compound Words   pp. 60-65

up-to-date	first aid	wildlife	wheelchair
newscast	homemade	whoever	brother-in-law
salesperson	test tube		

Remember: A compound word may be written as one word, as two or more words joined by hyphens, or as separate words.

daytime

Write the compound word that has each part below.

21. person   **23.** home   **25.** in   **27.** who
22. first   **24.** chair   **26.** test

Write the compound words that complete this paragraph.

   Try to watch the six o'clock __(28)__ tonight. The town dump is polluting our water and harming the __(29)__ in the nearby woodlands. Tune in to hear the results of an __(30)__ government study.

Unit 10   Homophones   pp. 66-71

hall	peace	sole	berry	flea
haul	piece	soul	bury	flee

berry   bury

Remember: Homophones are words that sound alike but have different spellings and meanings.

Write the words that complete these sentences.

   Help me __(31)__ this dresser down the __(32)__. We can have no __(33)__ until the last __(34)__ of furniture is in place.

Write the word that fits each clue.

35. the bottom of a shoe
36. can make a dog scratch
37. something you might
   pick from a bush

38. spirit
39. to put in the ground
40. to run away

Unit 11   Final |ər| pp. 72-77

mirror	thunder	major	pillar	theater
quarter	mayor	finger	lunar	polar

Remember: The final |ər| sounds are often spelled **er, or,** or **ar** in words of more than one syllable.

Write six words by adding the missing letters.

41. thund _ _   **43.** fing _ _   **45.** maj _ _

42. theat _ _   **44.** mirr _ _   **46.** quart _ _

Write the word that completes each analogy.

47. *State* is to *governor* as *city* is to ____ .

48. *Sun* is to *solar* as *moon* is to ____ .

49. *Heat* is to *tropical* as *cold* is to ____ .

50. *Tent* is to *pole* as *building* is to ____ .

■ Challenge Words   Units 7-11   pp. 48-77

junior high school	marvelous	dreary	stationary
extraordinary	folklore	tremor	stationery
character	interpret		

Write the word that fits each clue.

51. opposite of *unremarkable*

52. after elementary school

53. opposite of *terrible*

54. to explain

55. beliefs handed down through generations

Write the word that belongs in each group. Circle the words that are homophones.

56. pen, envelope, ____

57. gloomy, dismal, ____

58. actor, dialogue, ____

59. vibration, shake, ____

60. unchanging, fixed, ____

theater
actor
lunar

Spelling-Meaning Strategy

Vowel Changes: Long to Short Vowel Sound

Words from the same word family are often related in both spelling and meaning. Knowing how to spell one word in the family may help you spell the other words. Read this sentence.

Although Uncle Jonathan was in very good **health** for a man of eighty, his broken leg took several months to **heal**.

Think

- How are *heal* and *health* related in meaning?
- What vowel sound do you hear in each word?
- How is each vowel sound spelled?

Here are more related words in which a long vowel sound in one word is spelled the same as a short vowel sound in the other.

dream	cave	wise
dreamt	cavity	wisdom

Apply and Extend

Complete these activities on a separate piece of paper.

1. Look up the words in the word box above in your Spelling Dictionary. Write six sentences, using these words.

2. With a partner list as many words as you can that are related to *heal, dream, cave,* and *wise.* Then look on page 271 of your Spelling-Meaning Index. Add any other words that you find in these word families to your list.

Summing Up Knowing that words are related can often help you remember how to spell them, even though one word has a long vowel sound and the other has a short vowel sound.

Instructions

If you shuffle your feet on a carpet in winter and then touch a piece of metal, you will feel a light shock. This is caused by static electricity. The following instructions are for experiments that will help you learn about static electricity. What materials are used?

It's fun to experiment with static electricity. First, place a dinner knife on a table with the blade hanging over the edge. Next, cut two pieces of thread one foot long. Make two small, rounded paper wads of dry tissue. Then tie each of these paper balls to the end of each piece of thread. Fasten both pieces of thread to the end of the knife so they hang down freely, about two inches apart. Slowly move a comb towards the paper balls. Because there is no static electricity, nothing happens.

Then rub the comb briskly with wool. Move the comb towards the paper balls. The electrically "charged" comb attracts the paper balls.

Finally, hold the comb between the paper balls for a few seconds. When the balls touch the comb, they receive the same charge. After the paper balls become charged, the comb pushes them away.

based on "Winter Static Magic" by Doris Spaulding

Think and Discuss

1. What materials would you need to perform these experiments?
2. What is the **topic sentence** for these instructions?
3. What six **steps** are given in the first paragraph?
4. What **order words,** such as *first* or *finally,* are used?

The Writing Process

The paragraphs on page 82 give instructions for some science experiments. When you write instructions, begin with a **topic sentence** that states what your instructions are for. Then give each **step** of the instructions in order. Use **order words** to help make the sequence clear.

Assignment: Write Instructions

Step One: Prewriting

1. Make a list of things you know how to do. Discuss them with a classmate, and choose one to write about.
2. List all the steps, and number them in order.

Step Two: Write

1. Think about your purpose and your audience.
2. Do not worry about mistakes—just write!

Step Three: Revise

1. Does your topic sentence tell what your instructions are about?
2. Are the steps explained clearly? Are they in order?
3. Use your Thesaurus to help you find exact words.
4. Read your instructions to a classmate or your teacher. Make any other changes you want.

Step Four: Proofread

1. Did you use commas correctly in compound sentences?
2. Did you spell all words correctly? Copy any words that you misspelled into your Notebook for Writing.

Step Five: Publish

1. Copy your instructions neatly, and add a title.
2. Share your instructions. Make an instruction booklet.

Composition Words

stir
carve
piece
household
flavor
homemade
smear
pour

Proofreading Marks

⁋ Indent
∧ Add something
ℓ Take out something
≡ Capitalize
/ Make a small letter

(Theme: Holidays)

13 More Compound Words

LOOK
at each word.

SAY
each word.

Basic Words   ■ **Challenge**

1. firecracker   11. warehouse   21. starry-eyed
2. sweetheart   12. chalkboard   22. high-spirited
3. touchdown   13. worthwhile   23. awestruck
4. post office   14. watermelon   24. outspoken
5. classmate   15. throughout   25. halfhearted
6. baby-sit   16. furthermore
7. flashlight   17. whereabouts
8. grapefruit   18. masterpiece
 9. holiday   19. great-grandchild
10. welfare   20. part of speech

Be Mine

THINK
about the words.

You have learned that a compound word is made up of two or more smaller words. Each of these words is a compound word:

firecracker   baby-sit   post office

- What words make up each compound word on the list? How are the Elephant Words different?

WRITE
the words.

Practice   Write the Basic Words to answer the questions.

A. Which **sixteen** compound words are written as one word?

B. Which **two** compound words are written with hyphens?

CHECK
your spelling.

C. Which **two** compound words are written as separate words?

■ **Now write the five Challenge Words.** Draw a line between the smaller words in each compound word.

> *Spelling-Meaning Hint* Did you know that *office* is related in spelling and meaning to *official*? **Think of this:** My parents talked to an *official* from the *post office*.

office
official

Independent Practice

Spelling-Meaning Look at the Spelling-Meaning Hint.
1-2. Write *official*. Then write the Basic Word that has one part that is related in spelling and meaning to *official*.

Word Analysis The underlined word in each compound word is part of a Basic Word. Write the Basic Word.

3. mean<u>while</u>   7. <u>sweet</u> potato
4. <u>out</u>side   8. <u>flash</u> bulb
5. <u>class</u>room   9. car<u>fare</u>
6. <u>water</u> lily   10. every<u>where</u>

sweet heart

Making Inferences Write a Basic Word that fits each clue.
11. This makes a loud popping noise.
12. Labor Day is one.
13. A composer or an artist might create one.
14. This can be found on a wall in most classrooms.
15. This is a place where furniture can be kept.

■ **Challenge Words** Write the Challenge Word that fits each meaning. Use your Spelling Dictionary.
16. frank and honest   19. having little interest
17. lively   20. full of youthful hope and
18. full of wonder   confidence

Summing Up

A compound word is made up of two or more smaller words. A compound word may be written as one word, as a hyphenated word, or as separate words.

13 Part C Spelling and Language Study

Basic

1. firecracker
2. sweetheart
3. touchdown
4. post office
5. classmate
6. baby-sit
7. flashlight
8. grapefruit
9. holiday
10. welfare
11. warehouse
12. chalkboard
13. worthwhile
14. watermelon
15. throughout
16. furthermore
17. whereabouts
18. masterpiece
19. great-grandchild
20. part of speech

■ Challenge

21. starry-eyed
22. high-spirited
23. awestruck
24. outspoken
25. halfhearted

Review

1. airport
2. homesick
3. seat belt
4. make-believe
5. however

Expanding Vocabulary

Compound Words   Compound words name many places and buildings. Often the second part of the word names the general place or building. The first part is more specific.

post office   cornfield   outer space   warehouse

Practice   **Write a compound word to fit each meaning by matching a word on the left with a word on the right. Use your Spelling Dictionary to check the correct spellings.**

camp   super   light   market   rise   hall
city   high   house   site

1. a store that sells food and other household goods
2. a tall building with many stories
3. a tower with a powerful light that is used to guide ships
4. an area used for camping
5. the building that houses local government offices

Proofreading

Proper Nouns and Adjectives   A **proper noun** names a specific person, place, or thing. A **proper adjective** is formed from a proper noun. Remember to capitalize these words.

PROPER NOUN: Japan   PROPER ADJECTIVE: Japanese

Practice   **Proofread this journal entry. Find four misspelled words and four words that should be capitalized. Write the journal entry correctly.**

tuesday, april 16 I'm in china! A classmate met me at the arport. Today is a holaday, the chinese New Year, and I just heard a firecraker. So far, I'm not at all home sick.

86

Review: Spelling Spree

Picture Clues   Write a Basic or Review Word for each clue.

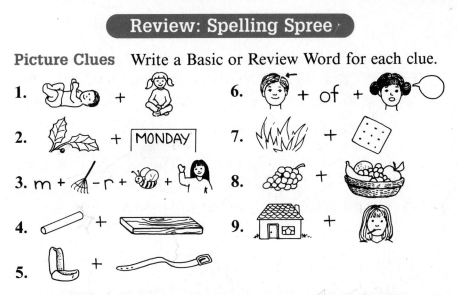

Compound Mix-Ups   Write a Basic or Review Word by matching part of the first word with part of the second word.

Example: fireworks, crackerjack   *firecracker*

10. hardware, firehouse
11. lamppost, officeholder
12. flash flood, lightweight
13. airtight, porthole
14. anywhere, hereabouts
15. first class, roommate
16. anyhow, everlasting
17. worthless, meanwhile

18. great-grandparent, childlike
19. rainwater, muskmelon
20. sweetbread, heartbreak
21. mastermind, mouthpiece
22. through street, outbreak
23. welcome, thoroughfare
24. touch-and-go, downhill
25. furthermost, moreover

■ **Challenge Words**   For each Challenge Word, draw a cartoon character whose face or actions express the meaning of the word. Write the Challenge Word on the back of the cartoon. Then have a classmate look at each cartoon and guess the word.

📖 *Writing Application:* An Announcement   You are planning a holiday event for your town. Write a newspaper announcement, providing details about the event. What holiday is being celebrated? Why will this event be special? Try to use five words from the list on page 86.

13 Spelling Across the Curriculum

Social Studies: *Holidays*

Theme Vocabulary

Martin Luther King Day
Thanksgiving Day
Valentine's Day
Memorial Day
Veterans Day
New Year's Day
Labor Day
Arbor Day

Using Vocabulary Write the Vocabulary Word that fits each definition. Use your Spelling Dictionary.

1. This day is the first day of the year.
2. This is a day when sweethearts exchange cards.
3. This day honors the birthday of a civil rights leader.
4. This day honors workers.
5. This day honors soldiers who have died in wars.
6. This day is for giving thanks.
7. This day is observed in many areas by planting trees.
8. This day honors those who served in the military.

Understanding Vocabulary Write the Vocabulary Word that best fits each activity.

9. Start a new calendar.
10. Send cards with hearts.
11. Listen to a speech honoring workers.
12. Help plant trees in your community.

FACT FILE

The Fourth of July, or Independence Day, celebrates the signing of the Declaration of Independence. On July 4, 1776, the American colonies broke ties with Britain.

Enrichment 13

👪 *April Fool!*

Players: 5-6 **You need:** one April Fool card; 48 word cards, one for each separate word that makes up each Basic and Review Word (Do not include Elephant Words.)

How to play: One player deals all of the cards face down. Players lay down any words that form compound words from the unit lists. The players then take turns drawing cards from each other's hands to try to form compound words. Play continues until all the cards are laid down and one player is left with the April Fool card. That player is out, and the player with the most compound words wins.

📖 *Writing*

Let's Celebrate!

Every country has its own holidays. Choose a country. Write a short research report about one of its holidays. What person or event does the holiday honor? What festivities take place? Are any special foods prepared? Try to use words from the lists in this unit. Be sure to proofread your paper.

HOLIDAY CALENDAR

Make a holiday picture calendar for next year. Show all twelve months with the dates and the names of the important holidays in each month. Include the holidays listed in this unit and any others that you want.

14 Final |l| or |əl|

LOOK
at each word.

SAY
each word.

Basic Words

1. jewel
2. sparkle
3. angle
4. shovel
5. single
6. normal
7. angel
8. legal
9. whistle
10. fossil
11. puzzle
12. bushel
13. local
14. gentle
15. level
16. label
17. pedal
18. ankle
19. needle
20. devil

■ Challenge

21. mineral
22. artificial
23. vital
24. neutral
25. kernel

THINK
about the words.

Each word is a two-syllable word with the final |l| or |əl| sounds. (Some dictionaries show only the final consonant sound because the schwa sound is so weak.)

|l| or |əl| spark**le**, jew**el**, leg**al**

• What are three patterns for the final |l| or |əl| sounds? How are the |əl| sounds spelled in the Elephant Words?

WRITE
the words.

Practice   Write the Basic Words to answer these questions about the final |l| or |əl| sounds.

CHECK
your spelling.

A. Which **eight** words have these sounds spelled *le*?
B. Which **six** words have these sounds spelled *el*?
C. Which **four** words have these sounds spelled *al*?
D. Which **two** words have these sounds spelled other ways?

■ **Now write the five Challenge Words.** Underline the patterns that spell the final |l| and |əl| sounds.

angel
angelic

> **Spelling-Meaning Hint**   How can you remember how to spell the schwa sound in *angel*? Think of the |ĕ| sound in the related word *angelic*.

Independent Practice

Spelling-Meaning   Look at the Spelling-Meaning Hint.

1-2. Write *angel* and *angelic*. Then underline the letter in *angelic* that helps you remember how to spell the schwa sound in *angel*.

Word Analysis   Complete the exercises with Basic Words.

3. Write the word that has the |k| sound spelled *c*.

4-7. Write the four words that have the |ĕ| sound in the first syllable.

8-9. Write the two words that have double consonants.

Classifying   Write the Basic Word that belongs in each group.

10. thread, thimble, ____

11. knee, elbow, ____

12. siren, horn, ____

13. pint, quart, ____

14. triple, double, ____

15. hoe, rake, ____

■ **Challenge Words**   Write the Challenge Word that completes each sentence. Use your Spelling Dictionary.

16. Robin painted her room beige, a ____ color.

17. A natural substance such as quartz is a ____.

18. The heart and lungs are ____ organs.

19. Each yellow ____ on this ear of corn is tender and juicy.

20. These ____ pearls are made of plastic.

Summing Up

The final |l| or |əl| sounds in a two-syllable word are often spelled with the pattern *le, el,* or *al*.

Basic

1. jewel
2. sparkle
3. angle
4. shovel
5. single
6. normal
7. angel
8. legal
9. whistle
10. fossil
11. puzzle
12. bushel
13. local
14. gentle
15. level
16. label
17. pedal
18. ankle
19. needle
20. devil

■ Challenge

21. mineral
22. artificial
23. vital
24. neutral
25. kernel

Review

1. simple
2. special
3. metal
4. nickel
5. double

Expanding Vocabulary

The Latin Roots _ped_ and _loc_ A **word root** is a word part that has meaning but cannot stand alone. It is added to other word parts to form whole words. The words _pedal_ and _local_ each contain a root from Latin, an ancient language.

ROOT	MEANING	WORD	WORD MEANING
ped	foot	pedal	a lever worked by the foot
loc	place	local	of a limited area or place

Practice Write the word that fits each meaning. Underline the Latin word root. Use your Spelling Dictionary.

dislocate   centipede   locomotion   location   pedestal

1. an insect with many legs
2. a certain place
3. to put out of place
4. a base or support
5. the act of moving from one place to another

Dictionary

Parts of Speech A dictionary gives the part of speech of each entry word. The part of speech is often abbreviated.

_n._	noun	_adj._	adjective	_prep._	preposition
_v._	verb	_adv._	adverb	_pron._	pronoun

Some words can be used as more than one part of speech. For example, _shovel_ can be used as either a noun or a verb.

> **shov·el** |shŭv′ əl| _n., pl._ **shovels** A tool with a long handle and a flattened scoop: _I dug out the ditch with a shovel._ _v._ **shoveled, shoveling** To pick up or move with a shovel: _Shovel the snow._

Practice Write the two parts of speech given in your Spelling Dictionary for each word. Do not abbreviate.

1-2. sparkle   **3-4.** special   **5-6.** early   **7-8.** throughout

Review: Spelling Spree

Phrase Fillers Write the Basic or Review Word that best completes each phrase.

1. a ____ of wheat
2. ____ and thread
3. a shrill ____
4. to tilt at an ____
5. a ____ -decker bus
6. a costly ____ necklace
7. a very ____ occasion
8. the ____ driving age

9. below sea ____
10. to ____ a bicycle
11. a dinosaur ____
12. five pennies for a ____
13. a sprained ____
14. a mischievous little ____
15. ____ body temperature of 98.6 degrees Fahrenheit

Proofreading 16-25. Find ten misspelled Basic or Review Words in this mystery. Write each word correctly.

The Special Secret

I had solved the puzzel! Finding the jewel would be simpel. The locol sheriff told me where to find the statue of an anjel. I got a shovle and headed for the abandoned town. There stood the statue. I took a singel step and began to dig. I soon struck metel. With a gentel tug I pulled out a box. The lable was ripped. Through a crack I could see something sparkel.

■ **Challenge Words** Make a mini-dictionary. Get five sheets of paper, and write a Challenge Word at the top of each one. Write two definitions for each word. Then write a sample sentence for each definition. Put the pages in alphabetical order, and staple them together.

📖 *Writing Application:* Creative Writing Write a plot summary for a fairy tale about a farmer who plants a field of corn. Instead of corn, jewels grow on the stalks. Try to use five words from the list on page 92.

14 Spelling Across the Curriculum

Science: *Gems*

Theme Vocabulary

topaz
sapphire
emerald
diamond
onyx
ruby
opal
jade

Using Vocabulary Write a Vocabulary Word to complete each sentence. Use your Spelling Dictionary.

1. Pale green ____ is carved into statues.
2. The blue ____ may reflect starlike rays of light.
3. A red ____ is found in the gravel of riverbeds.
4. The rare yellow ____ is mined in Brazil.
5. The six-sided green ____ is often found in granite.
6. The ____, often dyed, is used in carving cameos.
7. The multicolored ____ is found in rock cavities.
8. The usually colorless ____ is the hardest gem.

Understanding Vocabulary Write a Vocabulary Word to answer each question.

9. Which gem looks like it has a rainbow inside of it?
10. Which gem is the color of a clear sky during the day?
11. Which gem is the color of a cherry?
12. Which gem is the color of a bright sun?

FACT FILE

A rough diamond has not been cut and polished to bring out its brilliance. "Diamond in the rough" describes someone whose good qualities are still undeveloped.

Enrichment 14

 **Bingo!**

Players: 3, a reader **You need:** game cards divided into 16 boxes with a spelling for the |əl| ending in each box

How to play: The reader reads a Basic or Review Word from the lists. Players write the word in a box that has the same spelling for the |əl| sounds. The first person to write four correctly spelled words in a row wins.

A CROWNING ACHIEVEMENT

Design a decorative object fit for royalty. It might be a crown, a sword handle, a throne, a ring, or anything that has jewels on it. Include at least three different gems in your design. Draw the object and write a short description of it. Try to use words from the lists in this unit.

 **Writing**
A Fallen Star

Write a science fiction story about a scientist who travels to another planet and returns with a strange new jewel. The jewel has amazing powers that are very useful but that are also very dangerous. What powers does the jewel have? What happens as a result? Try to use words from the lists in this unit. Be sure to proofread your story.

Theme: Traffic Safety

15 VCCV Pattern

LOOK
at each word.

SAY
each word.

Basic Words

1. traffic
2. permit
3. witness
4. collect
5. tunnel
6. perhaps
7. pattern
8. object
9. million
10. arrive
11. barrel
12. furnish
13. shoulder
14. velvet
15. effort
16. sorrow
17. essay
18. empire
19. publish
20. subject

■ **Challenge**

21. collide
22. exceed
23. trespass
24. option
25. sincere

THINK
about the words.

A **syllable** is a word part that has one vowel sound. Each word has two syllables and the vowel-consonant-consonant-vowel (VCCV) pattern. Divide between the consonants to find the syllables. Look for familiar spelling patterns.

VC | CV   VC | CV
ar | r i v e   per | m i t

• Where is each word in the list divided into syllables?

WRITE
the words.

Practice   Write the Basic Words to answer the questions.

A. Which **ten** words are divided into syllables between double consonants?

CHECK
your spelling.

B. Which **ten** words are divided into syllables between two different consonants?

■ **Now write the five Challenge Words.** Draw a line between the syllables in each word.

> *Spelling-Meaning Hint*   How can you remember how to spell the |sh| sound in *objection*? Think of the related word *object*. The *t* is kept in *objection*, even though the sound changes.

**objection
object**

Independent Practice

Spelling-Meaning   Look at the Spelling-Meaning Hint.
1-2. Write *objection*. Then write the Basic Word that helps you remember how to spell the |sh| sound in *objection*.

Word Analysis   Complete the exercises with Basic Words.

3. Write the word that has the final |ər| sounds.

4-5. Write the two words that end with the |əl| sounds.

6-7. Write the two words that end with the |ō| or the |ā| sound.

Synonyms   Write the Basic Word that is a synonym for each word below.

8. maybe
9. equip
10. allow
11. observer

12. gather
13. design
14. kingdom
15. topic

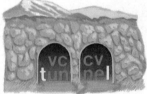

■ **Challenge Words**   Write the Challenge Word that fits each meaning. Use your Spelling Dictionary.

16. honest
17. a choice
18. to go beyond

19. to strike together with force
20. to go onto someone's property without permission

Summing Up

To find the syllables of a VCCV word, divide the word between the consonants. Look for patterns you have learned, and spell the word by syllables.

Basic

1. traffic
2. permit
3. witness
4. collect
5. tunnel
6. perhaps
7. pattern
8. object
9. million
10. arrive
11. barrel
12. furnish
13. shoulder
14. velvet
15. effort
16. sorrow
17. essay
18. empire
19. publish
20. subject

■ Challenge

21. collide
22. exceed
23. trespass
24. option
25. sincere

Review

1. arrow
2. corner
3. person
4. mistake
5. bottom

Expanding Vocabulary

The Latin Roots *mit* and *ject*   *Permit* and *object* have Latin word roots that appear in other English words.

ROOT	MEANING	WORD	WORD MEANING
mit	send	permit	to send through or allow
ject	throw	object	to throw or go against

Practice   **Write the word that completes each sentence. Then circle the Latin root. Use your Spelling Dictionary.**

transmit   submit   admit   project   reject

1. Telephone wires ＿＿ messages from coast to coast.
2. When selecting apples, ＿＿ any that are bruised.
3. An usher will ＿＿ you to the theater.
4. I will ＿＿ these slides onto that blank wall.
5. William would not ＿＿ to his brother's wishes.

Dictionary

Different Pronunciations   In some words, such as *subject*, the stressed syllable changes, depending on how the word is used in a sentence. Which syllable of *subject* is stressed when it is used as a noun? as a verb?

sub·ject |sŭb′ jĭkt| *n., pl.* **subjects** Something thought about or discussed; topic. |səb jĕkt′| *v.* **subjected, subjecting** To cause to undergo: *My doctor subjected me to some tests.*

Practice   **Write the underlined word in each sentence. Circle the stressed syllable. Use your Spelling Dictionary.**

1. Please do not <u>subject</u> us to more talk of sports.
2. I can talk about any <u>subject</u> with my best friend.
3. This zoo does not <u>permit</u> visitors to feed the animals.
4. If you must leave early, get a <u>permit</u> from the office.

Review: Spelling Spree

Word Addition   Each word below has the VCCV pattern. Combine the first syllable of the first word with the second syllable of the second word to write a Basic or Review Word.

Example: effect + comfort   *effort*

1. subway + inject
2. escape + hearsay
3. misfit + intake
4. patty + lantern
5. millet + trillion
6. perfect + admit
7. furnace + tarnish
8. sorry + borrow
9. barber + squirrel
10. arrange + burrow
11. witty + harness
12. ember + expire
13. perfect + lesson
14. perfume + mishaps
15. correct + manner
16. observe + inject

Proofreading   17-25. Find nine misspelled Basic or Review Words in this safety message. Write each word correctly.

Make an effert to learn the trafic laws. Always wear a safety belt across your sholder. Slow down at a corner or when entering a tunel. Stop and look when you arive at a stop sign. Your state may puplish a book that will help you to get a learner's permit. If you master the rules from top to botton, your driving will be as smooth as velvit, and you will not colect tickets.

■ **Challenge Words**   Make a crossword puzzle. Use all of the Challenge Words as well as other words from this unit. Write the answers to the puzzle on the back of your paper. Trade puzzles with a classmate, and complete each other's puzzles.

Writing Application: A Traffic Report   Imagine that you are a helicopter pilot observing a traffic jam. Write a report, describing the jam and explaining what caused it. Try to use five words from the list on page 98.

15 Spelling Across the Curriculum

Social Studies: *Traffic Safety*

Theme Vocabulary

vehicle
yield
intersection
crosswalk
speedometer
caution
right of way
pedestrian

Using Vocabulary Write a Vocabulary Word to complete each safety rule. Use your Spelling Dictionary.

1. I was going ten miles an hour according to my ____ .
2. A bicycle, like any ____ , must be well maintained.
3. Bikers must use ____ when riding on busy streets.
4. Look both ways at the ____ of two streets.
5. When entering a road, ____ to oncoming traffic.
6. Stop for people crossing the street in a ____ .
7. A green light gives you the ____ .
8. When possible, a ____ should use the sidewalk.

Understanding Vocabulary Write *yes* if the underlined word is used correctly. Write *no* if it is not.

9. The <u>speedometer</u> showed that I was lost.
10. Turn left at the <u>intersection</u> of First and L streets.
11. A green light at an intersection means <u>yield</u>.
12. Before riding your <u>vehicle</u>, check the tires.

TAKE SAFETY TO HEART
MASSACHUSETTS
SUGGESTS USE
OF SEAT BELTS

FACT FILE

Familiar sayings often give wise warnings. The saying "Better safe than sorry" is especially true in driving. It means that extra caution can prevent accidents.

Enrichment 15

 ## Wall-to-Wall Road Signs

Have you ever seen a sign that says *Caution: Deer Crossing* or *No Left Turn*? With your classmates make a list of ten road signs that give information to drivers. The signs may have words or just symbols. Check an encyclopedia or your library for a complete list of signs. Then design and create a mural that shows a long road with each kind of road sign. At every sign have a cartoon character explaining what the sign means. Try to use some words from the lists in this unit.

Writing
Safety Slogans

You are helping with a safe-driving campaign. Your main job is to make up catchy slogans for bumper stickers. Write several attention-getting slogans. They can refer to particular traffic rules or remind people to use good sense on the road. Try to use words from the lists in this unit. Be sure to proofread your slogans.

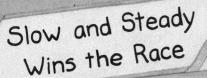

Slow and Steady Wins the Race

DO AND DON'T POSTER

Make a *Do and Don't* bicycle safety poster. Draw a line down the middle of the poster. Write *DO* at the top left and *DON'T* at the top right. In the appropriate column write one thing that good bicyclists should or should not do. Try to use words from the lists in this unit. Then draw a picture to illustrate each rule.

Theme: Congressional Representatives

16 VCCCV Pattern

LOOK
at each word.

SAY
each word.

Basic Words   ■ **Challenge**

1. district   11. mischief   21. Congress
2. address   12. complex   22. abstain
3. complain   13. partner   23. conscience
4. explain   14. orphan   24. function
5. improve   15. constant   25. extreme
6. farther   16. dolphin
7. simply   17. employ
8. hundred   18. sandwich
9. although   19. monster
10. laughter   20. orchard

THINK
about the words.

Each two-syllable word has the VCCCV pattern. In each word two different consonants spell one sound, as in *laughter*, or form a cluster, as in *complain*. Divide VCCCV words into syllables before or after those two consonants. Look for familiar patterns, and spell the word by syllables.

VCC | CV: **laugh | ter**   VC | CCV: **com | plain**

• Where is each word in the list divided into syllables?

WRITE
the words.

Practice   Write the Basic Words to answer the questions.

A. Which **seven** words are divided before or after two consonants that spell one sound?

CHECK
your spelling.

B. Which **thirteen** words are divided before or after two consonants that form a cluster?

■ **Now write the five Challenge Words.** Draw a line between the syllables in each word.

> *Spelling-Meaning Hint* Did you know that *simply* is related in spelling and meaning to *simple, simplify,* and *simplicity*? **Think of this:** These *simple* directions will get you to my house as *simply* as possible.

simple
simply
simplify
simplicity

Independent Practice

Spelling-Meaning   Look at the Spelling-Meaning Hint.

1-2. Write *simple*. Then write the Basic Word that is related in spelling and meaning to *simple*.

Word Analysis   Complete the exercises with Basic Words.

3. Write the word that has a final |ō| sound.

4. Write the word that has a final |oi| sound.

5-9. Write the five words that have the |f| sound.

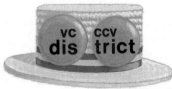

Word Clues   Write the Basic Word that fits each clue.

10. an area or region
11. synonym for *difficult*
12. someone to dance with
13. a lunch meal
14. where apples are grown
15. to express unhappiness

■ **Challenge Words**   Write the Challenge Word that fits each meaning. Use your Spelling Dictionary.

16. purpose or use
17. very great
18. to hold back by choice
19. sense of right and wrong
20. U.S. Senate and House of Representatives

Summing Up

When two different consonants in a VCCCV word spell one sound or form a cluster, divide the word into syllables before or after those two consonants. Look for familiar patterns that you have learned, and spell the word by syllables.

Basic

-1. district
2. address
3. complain
4. explain
5. improve
6. farther
7. simply
8. hundred
9. although
10. laughter
11. mischief
12. complex
13. partner
14. orphan
15. constant
16. dolphin
17. employ
18. sandwich
19. monster
20. orchard

■ Challenge

21. Congress
22. abstain
23. conscience
24. function
25. extreme

Review

1. empty
2. hungry
3. handsome
4. distrust
5. illness

Expanding Vocabulary

Words from Names   Some words come from names. For example, the sandwich is named after the Earl of Sandwich, who liked to eat meat between two slices of bread.

Practice   **Write the words that match these definitions.**

| madras | saxophone | polar bear |
| Dalmatian | lima bean | |

1. a bean first grown in Lima, Peru
2. a musical instrument invented by Adolphe Sax
3. a bear found mainly near the North Pole
4. a spotted dog first bred in Dalmatia, Yugoslavia
5. a fine cotton cloth first made in Madras, India

Proofreading

Commas in a Series   A **series** is a list of three or more items in a sentence. Use a comma after each item except the last.

Billy, Jessie, and Luis wrote letters to Senator Barnes.

Practice   **Proofread this part of Rebecca's letter. Find four misspelled words and two missing commas. Write the letter correctly.**

Dear Senator Barnes:

   I am writing to complane about the state park in our district. I found a hundred emty bottles cans and food wrappers there today. My class is willing to help inprove the condition of the park. Can you please adress the problem?

Review: Spelling Spree

Syllable Match Match the syllables at the top with the numbered syllables to write Basic Words.

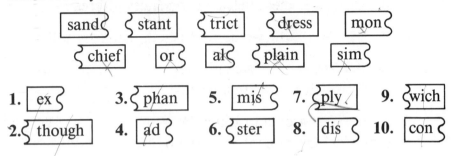

sand   stant   trict   dress   mon
chief   or   al   plain   sim

1. ex
2. though
3. phan
4. ad
5. mis
6. ster
7. ply
8. dis
9. wich
10. con

Contrast Clues   The second part of each clue contrasts with the first part. Write a Basic or Review Word for each clue.

11. not simple, but ____
12. not nearer, but ____
13. not full, but ____
14. not tears, but ____
15. not trust, but ____
16. not health, but ____
17. not ugly, but ____
18. not worsen, but ____
19. not well-fed, but ____
20. not a whale, but a ____
21. not a garden, but an ____
22. not praise, but ____
23. not alone, but with a ____
24. not a thousand, but a ____
25. not fire from a job, but ____

```
r d a o s e f
e x t r e m e
a m q e g p y
z i p e l l m
d s u t r o x
a k r e y y l
```

■ **Challenge Words** Make a Word Square puzzle. Write each Challenge Word across, down, or diagonally. Fill in other unit words or letters to complete the puzzle. Trade puzzles with a partner. Examples are shown.

Writing Application: A Persuasive Letter   Should Monday be part of the weekend? Should the legal driving age be raised or lowered? Write a letter to a senator. Tell about a law that you would like to see passed, changed, or abolished. Give at least two reasons to support your opinion. Try to use five words from the list on page 104.

16   Spelling Across the Curriculum

Social Studies: *Congressional Representatives*

Theme Vocabulary

committee
Constitution
represent
Capitol
compromise
Senate
adjourn
session

Using Vocabulary   Write the Vocabulary Words to complete the paragraph. Use your Spelling Dictionary.

The United States __(1)__ meets in the __(2)__ building. During a regular __(3)__ , which lasts several months, senators discuss national issues. A new amendment might be added to the __(4)__ . Some senators may work together on a small __(5)__ . Because the senators __(6)__ different groups, they may disagree on an issue. They listen to each other's points of view. Often a __(7)__ might be reached before it is time to __(8)__ .

Understanding Vocabulary   Write the Vocabulary Word that answers each question.

9. What is one way to resolve an argument?
10. What document states our nation's basic laws?
11. What might people at a meeting do at lunchtime?
12. What is one group that represents the states?

FACT FILE

Each state is represented in the Senate and in the House of Representatives. Each state has one representative in the House for every 500,000 people living in the state.

Enrichment 16

👪 *Password*

Players: 2 teams of 2, a scorekeeper **You need:** 25 word cards with a Basic or Review Word on each card, a watch with a second hand
How to play: A player on the first team draws a word card and gives his or her partner a one-word clue for the word. The partner tries to guess the word and spell it correctly. The first player can give as many one-word clues as possible in one minute. The team scores a point for a correct answer. The teams take turns until one team gets five points.

CALENDAR OF EVENTS

Pretend that you are a senator. Make a day-by-day calendar. Get seven pieces of paper, and write a day of the week on each one. List your activities for each day. For example, on Monday you might meet with a committee working to save the dolphins. Try to use the words from the lists in this unit. Decorate the pages, and staple them together.

📖 Writing
Are You Qualified?

The Constitution requires a person to have certain qualifications in order to run for the Senate or the House of Representatives. Write a short research report. Include the qualifications for a senator and a representative. Try to use words from the lists in this unit. Be sure to proofread your report.

Theme: Poetry

17 VV Pattern

LOOK
at each word.

SAY
each word.

Basic Words

1. poem
2. idea
3. create
4. diary
5. area
6. giant
7. usual
8. radio
9. cruel
10. quiet

11. diet
12. liar
13. fuel
14. riot
15. dial
16. lion
17. ruin
18. trial
19. rodeo
20. science

■ Challenge

21. appreciate
22. variety
23. enthusiastic
24. mosaic
25. eventually

Poems

THINK
about the words.

Each word has two vowel letters that appear together but spell two different vowel sounds. To find the syllables in a word that has the VV pattern, divide between the vowels. Look for familiar patterns. Spell the word by syllables.

V | V   V | V
po | em   **cre | ate**

• Does the first vowel letter in the VV pattern have a long or a short vowel sound? What is different about the Elephant Word?

WRITE
the words.

Practice Write the twenty Basic Words. Draw a line between the two vowels in each VV pattern.

CHECK
your spelling.

■ **Now write the five Challenge Words.** Draw a line between the two vowels in each VV pattern.

> *Spelling-Meaning Hint*   How can you remember how to spell the schwa sound in *poem*? Think of the lĕl sound in the related word *poetic*.

po**e**m
po**e**tic

Independent Practice

Spelling-Meaning   Look at the Spelling-Meaning Hint.

1-2. Write *poem* and *poetic*. Then underline the letter in *poetic* that helps you remember how to spell the schwa sound in *poem*.

Word Analysis   Complete the exercises with Basic Words.

3. Write the word that begins with the lkwl sounds.

4. Write the word that begins with the ljl sound.

5-8. Write the four words with the lo͞ol or the ly͞ool sound.

Definitions   Write the Basic Word that fits each meaning.

9. a wild cat of Africa

10. to invent

11. a thought or a plan

12. a region, as of land

13. a journal

14. the face of a clock

15. a disturbance by a large crowd of people

■ **Challenge Words**   Write the Challenge Word that fits each clue. Use your Spelling Dictionary.

16. opposite of *sameness*

17. to enjoy and understand

18. synonym for *eager*

19. sooner or later

20. a design made by gluing together pieces of tile

Summing Up

When the two vowels in a VV pattern spell two vowel sounds, divide the word into syllables between the vowels. Look for familiar patterns that you have learned, and spell the word by syllables.

Basic

1. poem
2. idea
3. create
4. diary
5. area
6. giant
7. usual
8. radio
9. cruel
10. quiet
11. diet
12. liar
13. fuel
14. riot
15. dial
16. lion
17. ruin
18. trial
19. rodeo
20. science

■ Challenge

21. appreciate
22. variety
23. enthusiastic
24. mosaic
25. eventually

Review

1. title
2. listen
3. wrote
4. finish
5. music

Expanding Vocabulary

Easily Confused Words Is the library *quite* or *quiet*? Is a needle *quite* small or *quiet* small? *Quiet* is usually an adjective that means "silent or nearly silent" or "calm." *Quite* is an adverb that means "completely" or "rather."

> I live on a **quiet** street.
> The baby is **quite** tired.

Practice **Write *quite* or *quiet* to complete each sentence.**
1. Mom was ____ surprised by my haircut.
2. The baby fell asleep while listening to the ____ music.
3. It was so ____ that we could hear a pin drop.
4. Dinner is not ____ ready yet.
5. After the raging storm the sea was ____ .
6. I am ____ content to watch television tonight.

Proofreading

Commas After Introductory Words **Introductory words** are words such as *yes, no, oh, well, first, next,* and *last* when they begin a sentence. Use a comma after these words.

> First, pick a theme for your poem.
> Oh, I already did.

Practice **Proofread Matt's instructions. Find four misspelled words and three missing commas. Write the instructions correctly.**

Do you find it hard to write a pome? Well here are some hints. First lisen to your favorite kind of music. This will put you in the mood to create and help you get an idear. Next, find a quite place. Last start to write.

Review: Spelling Spree

Hint and Hunt   Write the Basic or Review Word that answers each question.

1. What should you do when someone is speaking?
2. Where might you write your private thoughts?
3. What can tell you but never show you the news?
4. What does a car need to run?
5. What has a tune and a beat?
6. What takes place in a courtroom?
7. What gives a hint about the subject of a book?
8. What kind of book teaches facts about our planet?
9. What kind of writing is most like a song?

Word Maze   **10-25.** Begin at the arrow and follow the Word Maze to find sixteen Basic or Review Words. Write the words in order.

■ **Challenge Words**   Create your own Word Maze for the Challenge Words and any other words from this unit. Begin the maze at the left side of your paper. Put extra letters between the words. Write the answers on the back. Trade papers with a classmate, and complete each other's mazes.

📖 *Writing Application:* A Poem   Write a poem. It could be about a special person or place, your dreams, or your feelings about something. It could even be pure nonsense! Try to use five words from the list on page 110.

17 Spelling Across the Curriculum

Language Arts: *Poetry*

Theme Vocabulary

poet
rhythm
haiku
stanza
limerick
rhyme
image
ballad

Using Vocabulary Write the Vocabulary Words to complete the paragraph. Use your Spelling Dictionary.

There are many different kinds of poems. For example, a __(1)__ might write a Japanese __(2)__, a short poem with seventeen syllables. It creates a single picture, or __(3)__, in your mind. A story poem is called a __(4)__. Each __(5)__ tells part of the story. A funny poem of five lines is a __(6)__. It has a bouncing beat, or __(7)__. The first, second, and fifth lines have the same last sounds. The third and fourth lines also __(8)__.

Understanding Vocabulary Write a Vocabulary Word to answer each riddle.

9. *Home* and *roam* are examples of this.
10. This is like the beat of a drum.
11. This poem has a plot and characters.
12. This poem is meant to make you chuckle.

FACT FILE

Emily Dickinson was a great American poet of the 1800s. Her poems were short and untitled. She wrote over 1700 poems, but few were published during her lifetime.

Enrichment 17

👪 *A Poetry Reading*

In a small group plan a poetry lesson to present to your class. Look through poetry books to find samples of different kinds of poems. For each poem list the features that you will talk about during the lesson. For example, does the poem use rhyme or rhythm? Is it a special kind of poem, such as a limerick, a ballad, or a haiku? How do the titles of the poems reflect their content? Tell why you chose these particular poems. Make your lesson lively.

📖 *Writing*
A Haiku

A haiku is usually about nature. It has five syllables in the first line, seven in the second, and five in the third. Here is an example:

Deer, white tails blazing
Birds soaring across the sky—
Summer is coming.

Write a haiku. Try to use words from the lists in this unit. Be sure to proofread your poem.

BIRTHDAY GREETINGS

Make a birthday card for a friend or a relative. On the outside draw a funny, colorful illustration. On the inside write a short poem sending your birthday greetings. The poem should have something to do with the drawing. Try to use words from the lists in this unit.

18 Review: Units 13–17

Unit 13 More Compound Words pp. 84-89

post office	grapefruit	holiday	welfare
firecracker	furthermore	chalkboard	throughout
warehouse	great-grandchild		

Remember: A compound word may be written as one word, as two or more words joined by hyphens, or as separate words.

Write the compound word that has each part below.

1. out 2. more 3. fare 4. ware 5. grand 6. fire

Write the word that answers each question.

7. What is sometimes eaten for breakfast?
8. What do teachers write on when they teach a lesson?
9. What do you call a day of celebration?
10. Where can a person mail packages?

Unit 14 Final |l| or |əl| pp. 90-95

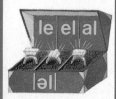

normal	jewel	shovel	whistle	fossil
needle	local	bushel	pedal	devil

Remember: The final |l| or |əl| sounds in a two-syllable word are often spelled **le, el,** or **al.**

Write the word that fits each meaning.

11. usual   14. a wicked person
12. a digging tool   15. a lever that is worked by foot
13. a sewing tool   16. a gem

Write the words to complete the paragraph.

While gathering a __(17)__ of clams at our __(18)__ beach, I picked up a pretty rock. Then I gave a __(19)__ of surprise. In the rock was a perfect __(20)__ of a fish.

Half of the words from each unit are reviewed on these pages. The rest are reviewed on pages 235–237.

Review **18**

Unit 15   VCCV Pattern   pp. 96-101

permit	witness	million	perhaps	object
barrel	velvet	effort	subject	shoulder

Remember: To find the syllables of a VCCV word, divide the word between the two consonants.

Write the word that fits each meaning.

21. disapprove of
22. an earnest attempt
23. possibly

24. a license
25. tells what a sentence is about

Write the word that belongs in each group.

26. hundred, thousand, ____
27. satin, silk, ____
28. trial, courtroom, ____

29. vat, keg, ____
30. wrist, elbow, ____

Unit 16   VCCCV Pattern   pp. 102-107

hundred	complain	laughter	farther	although
dolphin	orchard	employ	sandwich	constant

Remember: When two different consonants in a VCCCV word spell one sound or form a cluster, divide the word into syllables before or after those consonants.

Each word below is missing a syllable. Write the word.

31. or l ____
32. ____ l though

33. em l ____
34. ____ l plain

Write the word that fits each clue.

35. 10 × 10
36. a sea animal
37. may be made with cheese

38. not changing
39. opposite of *nearer*
40. sound of happiness

18 Review

Unit 17   VV Pattern   pp. 108-113

poem	diary	create	radio	quiet
fuel	dial	science	ruin	rodeo

Remember: When the two vowels in a VV pattern spell two vowel sounds, divide the word into syllables between the vowels.

Write the word that completes each analogy.

41. *Television* is to *channel selector* as *radio* is to ___.
42. *Acrobat* is to *circus* as *cowhand* is to ___.
43. *Fable* is to *story* as *haiku* is to ___.
44. *Algebra* is to *math* as *biology* is to ___.
45. *Movie* is to *television* as *song* is to ___.

Write the word that is a synonym for each word below.

46. invent   **47.** oil   **48.** journal   **49.** silent   **50.** wreck

■ **Challenge Words**   Units 13-17   pp. 84-113

enthusiastic	halfhearted	conscience	function	kernel
high-spirited	eventually	artificial	trespass	sincere

Write the word that fits each clue.

51. purpose   **54.** opposite of *dishonest*
52. intrude   **55.** a seed
53. opposite of *eager*

Write the word that completes each sentence.

56. The wild horse was too ___ to be easily tamed.
57. Abby's ___ would not allow her to lie.
58. These silk flowers look real even though they are ___.
59. Mario loves skating and is an ___ ice hockey player.
60. If you follow this path, you will ___ come to a pond.

Spelling-Meaning Strategy

Vowel Changes: Schwa to Short Vowel Sound

Thinking of related words may help you remember how to spell an unclear vowel sound. Read this paragraph.

> The man insisted that what he had done was **legal**. The committee questioned the **legality** of his actions and hired a lawyer.

leg**a**l
leg**a**lity

Think
- How are *legal* and *legality* related in meaning?
- What vowel sound does the letter *a* spell in each word?

Here are more related words in which the same letter spells the schwa sound in one word and the short vowel sound in another.

local	normal	mortal
locality	normality	mortality

Apply and Extend

Complete these activities on a separate piece of paper.

1. Look up the words in the word box above in your Spelling Dictionary, and write their meanings. Then write a short paragraph, using one pair of words.
2. With a partner list as many words as you can that are related to *legal, local, normal,* and *mortal*. Then look on page 272 of your Spelling-Meaning Index. Add any other words that you find in these families to your list.

Summing Up When you do not know the spelling of the schwa sound in a word, the short vowel sound in a related word may help you figure out which vowel to use.

Story

In this part of a tall tale, Stormy wants to be a cabin boy on a ship. What is unusual about Stormy?

"Excuse me, sir," said the schoolboy. "I hear you need a cabin boy."

The captain clung to the wheel to keep from slipping into the arms of the youngster who had jumped aboard. The youngster was large for his age. He stood about thirty feet tall and looked as if he weighed several tons. No wonder the *Silver Maid* was listing!

"If you don't shift your weight more to the port side, I'll need a salvage crew more than a cabin boy!" roared Captain Snard.

Stormy, the little fellow who was causing the trouble, blushed with embarrassment. "I'm sorry, sir," he stammered, and carefully placed one foot beside the port rail. The ship creaked and righted itself.

"Well!" said the captain, wiping his brow and looking up at the lad. "What makes you think you can be a cabin boy?"

Tears came to the young boy's eyes. "The sea is in my blood, sir," he said. "All my life I've wanted to join the China trade."

from Mr. Stormalong
by Anne Malcolmson and Dell J. McCormick

Think and Discuss
1. What is different about the main **character** Stormy? What kind of person is Stormy?
2. What is the **setting** of this part of the story?
3. What might be the **plot** of the rest of this story?

The Writing Process

The excerpt on page 118 is the beginning of a story. A good story has a **setting** that tells where and when the story takes place. A good story makes the **characters**—whether they are people, animals, or creatures—come to life. A good story has a **plot** that tells what happens. The beginning presents a problem. The middle tells what complications develop. The end tells how the problem is solved.

Assignment: Write a Story

Step One: Prewriting

1. Make a list of story ideas. Discuss your ideas with a classmate. Choose one idea to write about.
2. Outline your plot. Does the ending work?

Step Two: Write a First Draft

1. Think about your purpose and your audience.
2. Do not worry about mistakes—just write!

Step Three: Revise

1. Does your plot have a beginning, a middle, and an end?
2. Where can you add details to describe the characters?
3. Use your Thesaurus to find exact words.
4. Read your story to a classmate. Make other changes.

Step Four: Proofreading

1. Did you use commas in a series correctly?
2. Did you spell all words correctly? Copy any words that you misspelled into your Notebook for Writing.

Step Five: Publish

1. Copy your story neatly, and add a title.
2. Share your story by acting it out with some classmates.

Composition Words

flashlight
puzzle
jewel
giant
dolphin
tunnel
laughter
monster

Proofreading Marks

¶ Indent
∧ Add something
ℓ Take out something
≡ Capitalize
/ Make a small letter

Theme: Robots

19 VCV Pattern

LOOK
at each word.

SAY
each word.

Basic Words

1. robot
2. behave
3. repeat
4. rapid
5. detail
6. equal
7. value
8. nation
9. evil
10. closet

11. camel
12. adore
13. tulip
14. credit
15. aware
16. vanish
17. shadow
18. prefer
19. record
20. novel

■ Challenge

21. logic
22. laser
23. device
24. module
25. nuisance

THINK
about the words.

Each word has the VCV pattern. Divide a VCV word into syllables before or after the consonant. Look for familiar patterns. Note the spelling of the unstressed syllable.

VC | V		V | CV		
val | ue	**clos | et**	**ro | bot**	**a | ware**	**re | peat**

• Look at the first syllables in the examples. Which ones have the short vowel pattern? end with a vowel sound?

WRITE
the words.

Practice   **Write the Basic Words to answer the questions.**

A. Which **nine** words, including *record*, have first syllables with the short vowel pattern?

CHECK
your spelling.

B. Which **eleven** words have first syllables that end with a vowel sound?

■ **Now write the five Challenge Words.** Underline the words with a short vowel pattern in the first syllable.

> *Spelling-Meaning Hint* Can you see the word *nation*
> in the words *national, nationality,* and *international*? These
> words are related in spelling and meaning.

nation
national
nationality
international

Independent Practice

Spelling-Meaning   Look at the Spelling-Meaning Hint.
1-2. Write *national.* Then write the Basic Word that you see in
national.

Word Analysis   Complete the exercises with Basic Words.

3-4. Write the two words that have only the |ə| sound in the first
syllable.

5-9. Write the five words that have a long vowel sound in the
second syllable.

Classifying   Write the Basic Word that belongs in each group.
10. greater, less, _____   13. disc, tape, _____
11. elephant, horse, _____   14. rose, daisy, _____
12. story, poem, _____   15. clothes, hanger, _____

■ **Challenge Words**   Write the Challenge Word that fits each
clue. Use your Spelling Dictionary.
16. sound reasoning   19. a broom or a can opener
17. astronaut's work place   20. a machine that sends a
18. synonym for *pest*   powerful beam of light

Summing Up

To find the syllables of a VCV word, divide the word before or after
the consonant. Look for spelling patterns you have learned. Note
carefully the spelling of the unstressed syllable, and spell the word
by syllables.

Basic

1. robot
2. behave
3. repeat
4. rapid
5. detail
6. equal
7. value
8. nation
9. evil
10. closet
11. camel
12. adore
13. tulip
14. credit
15. aware
16. vanish
17. shadow
18. prefer
19. record
20. novel

■ **Challenge**

21. logic
22. laser
23. device
24. module
25. nuisance

Review

1. human
2. model
3. basic
4. amaze
5. total

Expanding Vocabulary

Word History   Flowers may be named for how they look.

> **Tulip** comes from the Turkish word *tulibend*, meaning "turban." The people of Turkey thought the flower looked like a turban, a hat worn in their country.

Practice   **Write the word that matches each history.**

rhododendron   daisy   snapdragon   dandelion   gladiolus

1. from Middle English *dayeseye*, "day's eye"
2. named for its blossoms shaped like a dragon's jaw
3. from Latin *gladius*, "sword," for its sword-shaped leaves
4. from Latin *dens leonis*, "lion's tooth," for its jagged leaves
5. from the Greek *rhodon dendron*, "rose tree"

Dictionary

Homographs   The sentence *She had a novel idea for a novel* includes two homographs. **Homographs** are words that are spelled the same but have different meanings and histories. They are numbered and listed separately in the dictionary.

> **nov·el**[1] | nŏv′ əl | *adj.* Very new, unusual, or different.
> **nov·el**[2] | nŏv′ əl | *n., pl.* **novels** A made-up story that is long enough to fill a book.

Practice   **Write *novel¹*, *novel²*, *stalk¹*, or *stalk²* to complete each sentence. Use your Spelling Dictionary.**

1. The flower ＿＿ was covered with blossoms.
2. Emma is reading a great mystery ＿＿＿.
3. Going to the moon is no longer a ＿＿ idea.
4. Ted heard an animal ＿＿＿ past the tent.

Review: Spelling Spree

Word Clues   Write a Basic or Review Word for each clue.

1. a flower planted in fall
2. a small copy
3. a country or a people
4. worship
5. "Buy now, pay later."
6. fast
7. wicked
8. to like better
9. knowing
10. might be read for fun
11. a shaded area
12. It has one or two humps.
13. where a broom is kept
14. disappear
15. a machine with a "brain"
16. played on a phonograph
17. to fill with surprise

Proofreading   18-25. Find eight misspelled Basic or Review Words in this science article. Write each word correctly.

Modern Robots

The robot is no longer a novel machine. The early types were very basec. They could only reapeat the same actions over and over. Robots have undergone a totle change. The new robots are different in every ditail. They hardly look or behav like people. Most robots are designed to do rapid work and are of greatest vaule in factories. No humen can equel the speed of these machines at their tasks.

■ **Challenge Words**   Make a crossword puzzle. Use all of the Challenge Words and as many other words from this unit as you can. Write the answers on the back of your paper. Then trade puzzles with a classmate, and complete each other's puzzles.

Writing Application: A Want Ad   Imagine that you are a robot with special skills. You are tired of your job and want a change. Write an ad for yourself, telling what you do best. Try to use five words from the list on page 122.

19   Spelling Across the Curriculum

Science: *Robots*

Theme Vocabulary

assemble
operate
computer
mechanical
circuit
remote control
sensors
command

Using Vocabulary   Write the Vocabulary Words to complete the paragraph. Use your Spelling Dictionary.

A robot performs human tasks. Its "brain" is a __(1)__ that processes information. The information is stored in a tiny electronic __(2)__. A robot can __(3)__ in places where humans cannot go. A scientist can send a __(4)__ to the robot from a distance by using __(5)__. A robot with __(6)__ arms is used to explore the ocean floor. Its arms have __(7)__ that react to pressure changes. Robots may soon be used to build, or __(8)__, space stations.

Understanding Vocabulary   Write *yes* if the underlined word is used correctly. Write *no* if it is not.

9. <u>Sensors</u> can react to light and dark.
10. Thinking is a <u>mechanical</u> task.
11. Follow the instructions to <u>assemble</u> the robot.
12. Give the proper <u>command</u>, and the robot will work.

FACT FILE

Some robots inspect cars for flaws. They use a thin stream of light called a laser beam, which can measure distance more exactly than any mechanical tool can.

Enrichment   19

👨‍👩‍👧 *Robotalog*

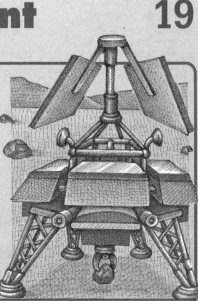

Some robots repair satellites; others collect minerals from the ocean bottom or rocks from the surface of Mars. With a classmate research the different types of robots. Then make a robot catalog. Draw each robot on a separate sheet of paper. Describe what it can do, using the words from the lists in this unit. Staple the pages together, and make a cover.

📖 *Writing*
Command Performance

Imagine that you have just built your first robot. It is now ready to be programmed. Choose one task that you would like your robot to do, such as vacuuming your room. Write clear step-by-step instructions for the task. Remember: The robot knows only what you tell it! Test your instructions on a class-mate. Try to use words from the lists in this unit. Be sure to proofread your instructions.

ROBOT PUPPET

Make a movable robot puppet. Using construction paper, cut out the parts for your robot. They can be any shape. Fasten the parts together with paper fasteners to form moving joints. Label each joint with a list word. Write one syllable of the word on each side of the paper fastener.

20 Words with -ed or -ing

LOOK

at each word.

SAY

each word.

Basic Words   ■ Challenge

1. directing
2. amusing
3. delivered
4. attending
5. offered
6. rising
7. deserved
8. supported
9. borrowed
10. freezing

11. awaiting
12. collapsed
13. providing
14. sheltered
15. resulting
16. arrested
17. damaged
18. seeking
19. squeezing
20. decided

21. rehearsing
22. portraying
23. dramatized
24. anticipated
25. entertaining

Star
Fire

THINK

about the words.

Each word is made up of a base word and an ending. A **base word** is a word to which endings can be added.

deserve + ed = deserv**ed**   offer + ed = offer**ed**
rise   + ing = ris**ing**   direct + ing = direct**ing**

• Look at the examples. Which words have a spelling change when the ending is added? What change occurs?

WRITE

the words.

Practice   Write the Basic Words to answer the questions.

A. In which **nine** words is the final *e* dropped when -*ed* or -*ing* is added?

CHECK

your spelling.

B. Which **eleven** words do not change spelling when -*ed* or -*ing* is added?

■ **Now write the five Challenge Words.** Circle the words in which the final *e* was dropped from the base word.

> **Spelling-Meaning Hint** *Supported* contains the word root *port*, meaning "to carry." A bridge is supported or "carried" by steel towers. Knowing the root *port* can also help you spell and understand the related words *transport* and *portable*.

sup**port**ed
trans**port**
portable

Independent Practice

Spelling-Meaning Look at the Spelling-Meaning Hint.

1-2. Write *portable*. Then write the Basic Word that has the same word root.

Word Analysis Write a Basic Word that has each base word.

3. decide   **5.** freeze   **7.** rise   **9.** arrest
4. await   **6.** damage   **8.** provide   **10.** direct

Context Sentences Write a Basic Word to complete each sentence.

11. We laugh when a movie is ____.
12. Return the movie you ____ from the library.
13. Tim Brown ____ an award for his role in *Raging Storm*.
14. Which letter carrier ____ mail to your house yesterday?
15. The old bridge ____ under the weight of the truck.

■ **Challenge Words** Write the Challenge Word that fits each clue. Use your Spelling Dictionary.

16. synonym for *expected*   **19.** synonym for *practicing*
17. opposite of *boring*   **20.** presented in a serious way
18. playing the part of

Summing Up

When a base word ends with *e*, the *e* is usually dropped when *-ed* or *-ing* is added. If a base word does not end with *e*, the ending *-ed* or *-ing* is usually added without a spelling change.

Basic

1. directing
2. amusing
3. delivered
4. attending
5. offered
6. rising
7. deserved
8. supported
9. borrowed
10. freezing
11. awaiting
12. collapsed
13. providing
14. sheltered
15. resulting
16. arrested
17. damaged
18. seeking
19. squeezing
20. decided

■ Challenge

21. rehearsing
22. portraying
23. dramatized
24. anticipated
25. entertaining

Review

1. dancing
2. landed
3. dared
4. traced
5. checking

Expanding Vocabulary

Exact Words for *damaged*   Suppose you have ordered a bike. It arrives in poor condition, so you call the store. Which sentence explains the problem more clearly?

> My bike arrived, but the frame is **damaged**.
> My bike arrived, but the frame is **dented**.

The second sentence explains the problem more clearly because *dented* tells exactly how the bike is damaged.

Practice   **Write the best word below to replace *damaged* in each sentence. Use your Thesaurus.**

> bruised   tattered   shattered   dented   scratched

1. Cold passed through the holes in the <u>damaged</u> coat.
2. Chris hammered the <u>damaged</u> fender back into shape.
3. The paint on the old car was badly <u>damaged</u>.
4. Before slicing apples, cut off the <u>damaged</u> spots.
5. Pieces of the <u>damaged</u> glass lay everywhere.

Dictionary

Base Words and Endings   A dictionary does not include a main entry for every form of a word. To find a word that ends with *-ed, -ing, -er,* or *-est,* look up the base word. The word forms follow the part of speech.

squeeze |skwēz| *v.* **squeezed, squeezing**
warm |wôrm| *adj.* **warmer, warmest**

Practice   **Write the base word that you would look up in the dictionary to find each word below.**

1. rising
2. sharpest
3. offered
4. collapsed
5. rarer
6. awaiting

Review: Spelling Spree

Meaning Match   Write a Basic or Review Word that has each meaning and ending below.

Example: entertain pleasantly + ing *amusing*

1. provide with cover + ed
2. to be in charge of + ing
3. bring to + ed
4. be present at + ing
5. make up one's mind + ed
6. supply + ing
7. go ashore + ed
8. move in time to music + ing
9. try to find + ing

10. be very cold + ing
11. wait for + ing
12. take prisoner + ed
13. harm + ed
14. examine + ing
15. take on loan + ed
16. press together + ing
17. follow the outline of
    a drawing + ed

Proofreading   **18-25.** Find eight misspelled Basic or Review Words in this movie ad. Write each word correctly.

Dancing in Borrowed Shoes

"Quite ammusing! I callapsed laughing!"—**Sue Critic**

"Teri Toon desirved an Oscar!"—**Ann E. Mation**

"Matt Kennett is a rizing actor. He suported the stars and offerd a new vision of today's teen."—**Ranton Rave**

"Mora Gags has daired to entertain us with two hours of nonstop fun, rezulting in a bad sideache."—**Marv L. Us**

■ **Challenge Words**   For each Challenge Word write a sentence about the movies, leaving a blank where the Challenge Word would go. Write your answers on the back of your paper. Trade papers with a classmate, and complete each other's sentences.

📖 *Writing Application:* A Movie Review   Write a review of a movie. What was the movie about? How well did the actors play their parts? Tell why you did or did not like the movie. Try to use five words from the list on page 128.

20 Spelling Across the Curriculum

Performing Arts: *Movies*

Theme Vocabulary

cinema
screenplay
matinee
soundtrack
projector
stunt
reel
documentary

Using Vocabulary Write the Vocabulary Words to complete the paragraph. Use your Spelling Dictionary.

Today I saw a __(1)__ on filmmaking. In the early 1900s a __(2)__, or script, was not written before a movie was made. A film had no speaking roles and no recorded __(3)__. An actor often had to perform his or her own __(4)__. The twenty-minute drama was made on one __(5)__ of film. At the __(6)__—or the nickelodeon, as the theater was called—a __(7)__ flashed pictures on the screen. A pianist played during the __(8)__ and the evening show.

Understanding Vocabulary Write *yes* if the underlined word is used correctly. Write *no* if it is not.

9. We attended a <u>matinee</u> last evening.
10. The actors read the new <u>screenplay</u>.
11. We saw a <u>documentary</u> on flood control.
12. The scenes were photographed with a new <u>projector</u>.

FACT FILE

Many scenes from early movies were filmed outdoors. Hollywood, California, became a film center because of its mild weather and variety of natural scenery.

Enrichment

20

👥 *Charades*

freezing

Players: 2 teams of 4-6 players **You need:** 25 cards with a Basic or Review Word on each card **How to play:** A player from Team 1 picks a card and pantomimes the word on the card for his or her team members. Team 1 has one minute to guess the word and spell it correctly. If the word is spelled correctly, Team 1 scores a point. Team 2 then takes a turn. The first team to score ten points wins.

LIGHTS, CAMERA, ACTION!

Create a silent movie for your class. Tape together several strips of construction paper. Draw frames on the paper. Illustrate scenes from your movie in each frame. Write dialogue for the characters in the frames. Try to use words from the lists in this unit. Roll each end of the paper around a stick. Show your movie by unrolling the paper.

📖 *Writing*
A Star Is Born

A biographical sketch tells about a person's life. Write a biographical sketch about your favorite actor. Tell where and when the actor was born, and include significant events in the actor's life. Describe the actor's appearance and personal qualities. Try to use words from the lists in this unit. Be sure to proofread your paper.

Theme: Cooking

21 More Words with -ed or -ing

LOOK
at each word.

SAY
each word.

Basic Words

1. whipped
2. skimmed
3. dripped
4. covered
5. gathering
6. bragging
7. visiting
8. planned
9. winning
10. mixed

11. stunned
12. hitting
13. begged
14. shipped
15. ordered
16. slammed
17. swimming
18. suffering
19. wandered
20. spotted

■ Challenge

21. catering
22. shredded
23. layered
24. scalloped
25. whirred

THINK
about the words.

Each word has -ed or -ing added to a base word. Each base word ends with a vowel and a consonant.

whip + ed = whip**ped**   cover + ed = cover**ed**

• How many syllables do you hear in the word *whip*? in the word *cover*? In which word is the final consonant doubled when -ed is added? How is the Elephant Word different?

WRITE
the words.

Practice   **Write the Basic Words to answer the questions.**

A. In which **thirteen** words is the final consonant doubled when -ed or -ing is added?

CHECK
your spelling.

B. In which **seven** words is the final consonant not doubled when -ed or -ing is added?

■ **Now write the five Challenge Words.** Underline the words in which the final consonant is doubled when -ed or -ing is added.

> ***Spelling-Meaning Hint*** Can you see *win* in *winner* and *winning*? Different endings can be added to base words to form new words that are related in spelling and meaning.

Independent Practice

Spelling-Meaning   Look at the Spelling-Meaning Hint.

1-2. Write *win*. Then write the Basic Word that is related in spelling and meaning to *win*.

Word Analysis   Write six Basic Words by combining each base word and ending.

3. visit + ing	**5.** beg + ed	**7.** skim + ed
4. slam + ed	**6.** mix + ed	**8.** hit + ing

Synonyms   Write the Basic Word that is a synonym for each word below.

9. located

10. boasting

11. collecting

12. commanded

13. dazed

14. roamed

15. sent

■ **Challenge Words**   Write the Challenge Word that fits each meaning. Use your Spelling Dictionary.

16. providing food for a party

17. baked with sauce

18. placed several thicknesses on top of each other

19. cut into small strips

20. moved quickly with a buzzing sound

Summing Up

When a one-syllable word ends with one vowel and a single consonant, the consonant is usually doubled when *-ed* or *-ing* is added. When a two-syllable word ends with one vowel and a single consonant, the consonant is often not doubled when *-ed* or *-ing* is added.

Basic

1. whipped
2. skimmed
3. dripped
4. covered
5. gathering
6. bragging
7. visiting
8. planned
9. winning
10. mixed
11. stunned
12. hitting
13. begged
14. shipped
15. ordered
16. slammed
17. swimming
18. suffering
19. wandered
20. spotted

■ Challenge

21. catering
22. shredded
23. layered
24. scalloped
25. whirred

Review

1. flipped
2. rubbing
3. snapping
4. dimmed
5. stripped

Expanding Vocabulary

Onomatopoeia In the sentence *Kate slammed the door*, the word *slammed* lets you hear what happened—it imitates the sound. *Sizzle* and *gurgle* also imitate sounds. The use of sound words is called **onomatopoeia**. Sound words help make stories and poems come to life.

Practice **Write the word below that best completes each sentence.**

sizzled   hissed   thumped   gurgled   slurped

1. The onions ____ when I put them in the hot oil.
2. A sack of grain ____ as it hit the barn floor.
3. The steam ____ from the living room radiator.
4. The thirsty cow ____ water from the trough.
5. Rust-colored water ____ out of the old pump.

Proofreading

Commas with Nouns in Direct Address Whenever you speak to a person by name, you are using a noun in direct address. Use a comma or commas to set off the noun.

Angie, are you hungry?   No, Bert, I just ate dinner.

Practice **Proofread this TV script. Find four misspelled words and three missing commas. Write the script correctly.**

Jo: Today we are visting with Chef Ada. She has been snaping peas for stew. I have always flipt over her stew. I see you have covered the mixt vegetables Ada. Is that part of a winning recipe?

Ada: No Jo I did not want to spill the beans!

Review: Spelling Spree

Crack the Code   Use the following code to find a Basic or Review Word in each item below. Write each word correctly.

CODE	z	y	x	w	v	u	t	s	r	q	p	o	j	i	h	g	f	e	d	c	b	a
LETTER	a	b	c	d	e	f	g	h	i	k	l	m	n	o	p	r	s	t	u	v	w	x

Example: widypvw   *doubled*

1. fegrhhvw
2. fjzhhrjt
3. fqroovw
4. bzjwvgvw
5. fduuvgrjt
6. oravw
7. sreerjt
8. igwvgvw
9. hpzjjvw
10. yvttvw
11. xicvgvw
12. fpzoovw
13. uprhhvw
14. fedjjvw
15. bsrhhvw

Book Titles   Write a Basic or Review Word to complete each funny book title. Remember to use capital letters.

16. *The Tale of the* _____ *Coat* by Leo Pard
17. *Where the Water* _____ by Lee Key Faucet
18. *Diving and* _____ *in the Ocean* by C. Otter
19. *Making a Fire by* _____ *Sticks Together* by Frick Shun
20. *Get Ahead by* _____ *About Your Achievements* by Bo Sting
21. *Is* _____ *Everything?* by Kaymen Last
22. *Finding and* _____ *Plants You Can Eat* by Herb Cole Ecter
23. *Where Were You When the Lights* _____*?* by Flash Bulb
24. *Shaped Up and* _____ *Out* by C. Goer
25. *Talking and* _____ *with the Queen* by Roy L. Guest

■ **Challenge Words**   Write five funny book titles and authors, using a Challenge Word in each title. Capitalize the first, last, and each important word. Underline each title. Share your titles.

📖 *Writing Application:* A Restaurant Review Imagine that you review restaurants for a newspaper. Write a review of your favorite place to eat, describing the best foods. Try to use five words from the list on page 134.

21 Spelling Across the Curriculum

Home Economics: *Cooking*

Theme Vocabulary

casserole
biscuit
herb
spicy
garlic
vinegar
onion
cinnamon

Using Vocabulary   Write the Vocabulary Words to complete the paragraph. Use your Spelling Dictionary.

Myles and I made a tuna-noodle __(1)__ for lunch. I sliced a round yellow __(2)__ and added it to the noodles and tuna for extra flavor. Myles added some basil, my favorite __(3)__, and pepper to make it __(4)__. I mixed a fresh green salad. Then I made a salad dressing by mixing a clove of __(5)__ with oil and __(6)__. We each had a fresh-baked buttermilk __(7)__ and a mug of hot cider with a __(8)__ stick. The lunch was delicious!

Understanding Vocabulary   Write *T* if the sentence is true. Write *F* if it is not.

9. You can grow an herb in a garden.
10. Water is normally very spicy.
11. Vinegar makes a salad dressing sweet.
12. A casserole is baked and served in the same dish.

FACT FILE

Most spices come from plants. For example, cinnamon comes from tree bark, and the mustard we spread on sandwiches comes from the seeds of the mustard plant.

Enrichment 21

👥 *Menu Magic*

Work with a classmate to create a menu for your own restaurant. Make your menu on a piece of construction paper. Divide the selections into appetizers, entrees, desserts, and beverages. Name and describe each item. Make up a lunch special for each day, and give every item a price. Try to use some words from the lists in this unit. Print the name of the restaurant on the menu. Illustrate the front and back covers.

📖 *Writing*
Lunch Lines

Write rhyming couplets about your favorite foods. Here are two to get you started:

This soup has a winning taste.
Don't let any go to waste!

I'm stunned to hear you
disagree,
But spinach is the food for me.

Try to use words from the lists in this unit. Be sure to proof-read your paper.

GAME MATS

Give your customers something to do while they wait to eat! Make a place mat on a piece of construction paper. Write your favorite puzzles, jokes, riddles, and games on the mat. Draw illustrations for your mat. Try to use words from the unit lists.

Theme: Mysteries

22 Words with Suffixes

Basic Words   ■ Challenge

1. dreadful	11. closeness	21. suspenseful
2. enjoyment	12. lately	22. suspiciously
3. safely	13. goodness	23. defenseless
4. watchful	14. retirement	24. seriousness
5. speechless	15. forgetful	25. contentment
6. paleness	16. basement	
7. breathless	17. softness	
8. government	18. delightful	
9. cheerful	19. settlement	
10. actively	20. countless	

THINK
about the words.

Each word has a base word and a **suffix,** a word part added to the end of a base word. A suffix adds meaning.

safe	+ ly	= safe**ly**	speech	+ less	= speech**less**
cheer	+ ful	= cheer**ful**	enjoy	+ ment	= enjoy**ment**
pale	+ ness	= pale**ness**			

- What suffixes do you see? Does each suffix begin with a vowel or a consonant? Does the spelling of the base word change when the suffix is added? What do you think each suffix means?

WRITE
the words.

CHECK
your spelling.

Practice   Write the Basic Words to answer the questions.

A. Which **three** words have the suffix -*ly*?
B. Which **nine** words have the suffix -*ment* or -*ness*?
C. Which **eight** words have the suffix -*ful* or -*less*?

■ **Now write the five Challenge Words.** Circle the suffixes.

Spelling-Meaning Hint Can you see *govern* in these words: *government, governor*? These words are all related in spelling and meaning. **Think of this:** The *government* could not *govern* without laws.

govern
government
governor

Independent Practice

Spelling-Meaning Look at the Spelling-Meaning Hint.

1-2. Write *govern*. Then write the Basic Word that is related in spelling and meaning to *govern*.

Word Analysis Complete the exercises with Basic Words.

3-6. Write the four words that have the |ā| sound spelled *a*-consonant-*e*.

7-10. Write the word that has the same base word as each word below.

    7. closely   **8.** speeches   **9.** settler   **10.** enjoyable

Antonyms Write the Basic Word that is an **antonym,** or a word that means the opposite, of each word below.

11. unhappy   **13.** wonderful   **15.** few

12. hardness   **14.** badness

watch ful

■ **Challenge Words** Write the Challenge Word that fits each meaning. Use your Spelling Dictionary.

16. helpless   **18.** full of uncertainty   **20.** happiness and

17. importance   **19.** distrustfully   satisfaction

Summing Up

A **suffix** is a word part added to the end of a base word. A suffix adds meaning to the word. The word parts *-ly, -ful, -ness, -less,* and *-ment* are suffixes. The spelling of the base word is usually not changed when the suffix begins with a consonant.

Basic

1. dreadful
2. enjoyment
3. safely
4. watchful
5. speechless
6. paleness
7. breathless
8. government
9. cheerful
10. actively
11. closeness
12. lately
13. goodness
14. retirement
15. forgetful
16. basement
17. softness
18. delightful
19. settlement
20. countless

■ Challenge

21. suspenseful
22. suspiciously
23. defenseless
24. seriousness
25. contentment

Review

1. fearful
2. movement
3. careless
4. lonely
5. powerful

Expanding Vocabulary

Regional Differences People from various regions of the United States call some things by different names. For example, the bottom floor of a house may be called the basement in one region and the cellar in another region. Many other words also change from region to region.

Practice **Write a word from the list below that has the same meaning as each numbered word. Use your Spelling Dictionary.**

goober	firefly
porch	attic
tap	drinking fountain

1. veranda
2. lightning bug
3. faucet
4. bubbler
5. garret
6. peanut

Dictionary

Suffixes Dictionaries list suffixes in alphabetical order among the entry words. A hyphen is shown before a suffix.

-ness A suffix that forms nouns and means "condition" or "quality." *Kindness* is the condition or quality of being kind.

You will not find a dictionary entry for every word with a suffix, but you can always look up the base word and the suffix separately. Then you can figure out their combined meaning.

Practice **Look up each base word and suffix below in your Spelling Dictionary. Write the meaning of each word below.**

1. quietly
2. useless
3. sweetness
4. swiftly

Review: Spelling Spree

Syllable Scramble   Rearrange the syllables to write a Basic or Review Word. One syllable in each item is extra.

Example: ful ion watch   *watchful*

1. tire al ment re
2. get for ous ful
3. less plore speech
4. er ence pow ful
5. ness able good
6. ment ern ly gov
7. pale re ness
8. ful fear tive
9. close ceed ness
10. tle ing set ment
11. ture ly lone
12. light sion ful de
13. ac ly tive ed
14. ness ure soft
15. cheer ic ful
16. joy ment tion en

Proofreading   17-25. Find nine misspelled Basic or Review Words in this detective's log. Write each word correctly.

Tuesday, March 12 *What a dredful assignment! I spend contless hours in the basment of this apartment building keeping a wachful eye on the residents. There has been a lot of movment in one of the apartments latly. I wait, brethless, because I can't afford to be carless. Powerful people may have their head-quarters here, and the government wants the criminals safly behind bars.*

■ **Challenge Words** Write five tongue twisters, using a Challenge Word in each one. Trade papers with a classmate, and read each other's tongue twisters aloud.

Example: Sam Sleuth surveyed the silly scene suspiciously.

Writing Application: A Biographical Note Imagine that you are an editor. Write a one-paragraph biographical note about the author of a new mystery novel for the book jacket. Try to use five words from the list on page 140.

Watchful Eyes

22 Spelling Across the Curriculum

Language Arts: *Mysteries*

Theme Vocabulary

mystery
suspect
baffle
solve
motive
weapon
guilty
evidence

Using Vocabulary Write the Vocabulary Words to complete the paragraph. Use your Spelling Dictionary.

Miss Jane Marple and Hercule Poirot are fictional detectives, creations of the famous __(1)__ writer Agatha Christie. No crime will ever __(2)__ these two! They always find the __(3)__ person. How do they __(4)__ a case? They examine every bit of __(5)__. They find out which __(6)__ was used to commit the crime. They question every __(7)__ to determine who had a __(8)__, or reason, for committing the crime.

Understanding Vocabulary Write *yes* if the underlined word is used correctly. Write *no* if it is not.

9. The prosecutor submitted the scarf as <u>evidence</u>.
10. The innocent person was <u>guilty</u>.
11. A <u>motive</u> was used to commit the crime.
12. The gun was the <u>weapon</u> found at the crime scene.

FACT FILE

The world's most famous detective is Sherlock Holmes. He is the creation of the writer Sir Arthur Conan Doyle. Holmes solves crimes by finding clues others have missed.

Enrichment

The Mystery Word Is . . .

This is so powerful that when you look through it you'll see the redness of Mars! It is a _____.

Write at least three of your own riddles that give clues about a mystery person or object. Try to use a list word in each riddle. Then have a quiz show, using the riddles. Divide into teams of two to four players. The teams take turns asking each other their riddles. The team that answers the most riddles correctly is the winner.

A BOOK JACKET

Create a book jacket for an imaginary mystery book. Draw a picture on the front. Print the title and the author's name. Write a few sentences for the jacket flap that tell the reader what the book is about. Try to use words from the unit lists.

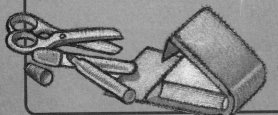

Clever Clara   Sneaky Pete

Writing
What's in a Name?

The characters in mysteries often have very descriptive names. Create a cast of humorous characters for a mystery novel. Try to use words from the lists in this unit. Be sure to proofread your paper.

Theme: Exploration

23 Final |n| or |ən|, |chər|, and |zhər|

LOOK
at each word.

SAY
each word.

Basic Words

1. mountain
2. treasure
3. culture
4. fountain
5. creature
6. captain
7. future
8. adventure
9. moisture
10. surgeon
11. lecture
12. curtain
13. pasture
14. measure
15. fixture
16. feature
17. furniture
18. pleasure
19. mixture
20. luncheon

■ Challenge

21. departure
22. leisure
23. architecture
24. texture
25. villain

THINK
about the words.

Each word has the final |n|, |ən|, |chər|, or |zhər| sounds:

	n	or	ən		capt**ain**
	chər		cul**ture**
	zhər		trea**sure**

- What is one pattern for the final |n| or |ən| sounds? What is one pattern for the final |chər| sounds? What is one pattern for the final |zhər| sounds? How are the |ən| sounds spelled in the Elephant Words?

WRITE
the words.

CHECK
your spelling.

Practice **Write the Basic Words to answer the questions.**

A. Which **six** words have the final |n| or |ən| sounds?
B. Which **eleven** words have the final |chər| sounds?
C. Which **three** words have the final |zhər| sounds?

■ **Now write the five Challenge Words.** Underline the patterns that spell the final |ən|, |chər|, and |zhər| sounds.

> *Spelling-Meaning Hint*   How can you remember to spell the |ch| sound in *moisture* with a *t*? Think of the *t* in the related word *moist*.

moisture
moist

Independent Practice

Spelling-Meaning   Look at the Spelling-Meaning Hint.

1-2. Write *moisture*. Then write the word that helps you remember how to spell the |ch| sound in *moisture*.

Word Analysis   Complete the exercises with Basic Words.

3-4. Write the two words that have the |ē| sound spelled *ea*.

5-7. Write the three words that have the |ĕ| sound spelled *ea*.

8-9. Write the two words that have the |ou| sound.

Analogies   Write a Basic Word to complete each analogy.

10. *Chicken* is to *meat* as *chair* is to ____.
11. *Morning* is to *breakfast* as *afternoon* is to ____.
12. *Day* is to *night* as *past* is to ____.
13. *Sew* is to *tailor* as *operate* is to ____.
14. *Lamp* is to *shade* as *window* is to ____.
15. *Airplane* is to *pilot* as *ship* is to ____.

■ **Challenge Words**   Write the Challenge Word that fits each clue. Use your Spelling Dictionary.

16. free time
17. antonym of *hero*
18. a style of building
19. antonym of *arrival*
20. the feel of a surface

Summing Up

The final |n| or |ən| sounds may be spelled with the pattern *ain*.
The final |chər| sounds are usually spelled with the pattern *ture*.
The final |zhər| sounds are usually spelled with the pattern *sure*.

Basic

1. mountain
2. treasure
3. culture
4. fountain
5. creature
6. captain
7. future
8. adventure
9. moisture
10. surgeon
11. lecture
12. curtain
13. pasture
14. measure
15. fixture
16. feature
17. furniture
18. pleasure
19. mixture
20. luncheon

■ Challenge

21. departure
22. leisure
23. architecture
24. texture
25. villain

Review

1. nature
2. picture
3. capture
4. bridge
5. climb

Expanding Vocabulary

Exact Words for *mixture* The words *jumble* and *blend* both mean "a mixture," but each describes a particular kind of mixture.

> **jumble**: a group of things mixed without any order
> **blend**: a mixture in which the parts are combined completely

Practice Write *blend* or *jumble* to replace *mixture*.

1. Mr. Ahn has a <u>mixture</u> of junk and treasures in his attic.
2. The sweet odor was a <u>mixture</u> of roses and lilacs.
3. The <u>mixture</u> of red and blue paint made purple.
4. My room is a <u>mixture</u> of toys, games, and books.
5. The wonderful flavor was a <u>mixture</u> of garlic and onions.

Proofreading

Quotation Marks Set off a speaker's exact words with quotation marks. Capitalize the first word of the quotation. Put end marks inside the quotation marks.

> Juan said, "The explorer Paul Cohen gave a talk."
> "What did he talk about?" asked Kim.

Practice Proofread this dialogue. Find four misspelled words, one word that needs a capital letter, and two missing quotation marks. Write the dialogue correctly.

Juan explained, "Mr. Cohen is the captian of an exploration team. He showed a picher of some tresure he found in a cave on a mountain."

What an adventure he had! said Nicole. "his talk did <u>capure</u> the thrill of the discovery."

Review: Spelling Spree

Jobs Match   Write a Basic or Review Word that names something each person makes or someone or something each person works with.

1. carpenter
2. chef
3. photographer
4. chemist
5. architect
6. tailor
7. nurse
8. zoo keeper
9. lieutenant

Word Clues   Write a Basic or Review Word to fit each clue.

10. This is where cows graze.
11. This is a speech that gives information about something.
12. You might see this hanging from the ceiling.
13. This is taller than a hill.
14. This is not the past or the present.
15. You must do this to get to the top of a cliff.
16. Trees, plants, and animals are part of this.
17. You will find this in a wet basement.
18. This is a feeling of happiness and delight.
19. This is a full-length film.
20. You do this to find out how tall a person is.
21. This is a good place to get a drink of water.
22. A sheriff must do this when a prisoner escapes.
23. This is an exciting, dangerous experience.
24. This is something that is valued highly.
25. Customs, beliefs, and ways of life are part of this.

■ **Challenge Words**   Look at the Word Clues activity. Write a clue for each Challenge Word. Write the answers on the back of your paper. Trade papers with a classmate, and answer each other's clues.

> 📖 *Writing Application:* Creative Writing   Imagine that you have discovered an unknown island in the South Pacific. Write a paragraph describing the people and their island. Try to use five words from the list on page 146.

23 Spelling Across the Curriculum

Social Studies: *Exploration*

Theme Vocabulary

Marco Polo
Leif Ericson
John Cabot
Sir Francis
  Drake
Ferdinand
  Magellan
Christopher
  Columbus
Robert Peary
Meriwether
  Lewis

Using Vocabulary Write a Vocabulary Word to complete each sentence. Use your Spelling Dictionary.

1. The Viking ___ reached America around A.D. 1000.
2. It was not until 1492 that ___ reached America.
3. In 1497 ___ claimed America for England.
4. A merchant who made trips to China was ___.
5. While trying to sail around the world, ___ died.
6. The English explorer ___ was also a naval hero.
7. The Pacific Northwest was explored by ___.
8. The North Pole was first reached by ___ in 1909.

Understanding Vocabulary Write a Vocabulary Word to match each clue.

9. He sailed for the Indies but found America instead.
10. He followed the caravan routes to China.
11. He made several Arctic expeditions.
12. He led the British navy under Queen Elizabeth I.

FACT FILE

In 1924–1925 Delia Akeley crossed undeveloped parts of Africa alone from east to west. During her trip she lived with and studied Pygmy tribes. She later published her studies.

Enrichment 23

👪 *Globetrotters*

Early explorers crisscrossed the globe, discovering faraway lands. With your classmates draw a large map of the world. Label the oceans and the continents. Then work in pairs to research the travels of famous explorers. Using a different colored marker for each explorer, draw on the world map the routes taken by the explorers. Label each route and the important landmarks of each expedition. Write the dates of the journey.

📖 *Writing*
The Final Frontier

Suppose that you are a modern explorer. You are given the opportunity to explore another planet and to begin a colony there. Write an essay explaining why you would or would not like to be a space colonist. Try to use words from the lists in this unit. Be sure to proofread your essay.

ADVENTURE, INC.

Imagine that you are hiring crew members for an exciting expedition. Design an ad that will encourage adventurers to sign up for the trip. Write captions for your pictures, describing the adventure. Try to use words from the lists in this unit.

24 Review: Units 19–23

Unit 19 VCV Pattern pp. 120-125

behave	rapid	equal	closet	robot
novel	aware	camel	shadow	record

Remember: To find the syllables of a VCV word, divide the word before or after the consonant. Note carefully the spelling of the unstressed syllable.

Each word below is missing a syllable. Write the word.

1. clos I _____
2. ro I _____
3. shad I _____
4. rap I _____
5. cam I _____
6. nov I _____

Write the word that fits each meaning.

7. the same
8. conscious of something
9. to act in a certain way
10. to set down in writing

Unit 20 Words with *-ed* or *-ing* pp. 126-131

delivered	amusing	directing	attending	deserved
resulting	squeezing	collapsed	providing	arrested

Remember: amuse − e + ing = amus**ing**
direct + ing = direct**ing**

Write the word that rhymes with each word below.

11. freezing
13. swerved
15. tested
12. shivered
14. consulting
16. mending

Write the word that is a synonym for each word below.

17. toppled
18. managing
19. supplying
20. entertaining

Half of the words from each unit are reviewed on these pages.
The rest are reviewed on pages 238–240.

Review **24**

Unit 21 More Words with *-ed* or *-ing* pp. 132-137

winning	gathering	covered	planned	mixed
ordered	suffering	begged	swimming	spotted

Remember: *one-syllable words:* spot + t + ed = spot**ted**
two-syllable words: cover + ed = cover**ed**

plan n ed

Write the word that completes each analogy.
21. *Zebra* is to *striped* as *leopard* is to _____.
22. *Polite* is to *courteous* as *hurting* is to _____.
23. *Finished* is to *incomplete* as *losing* is to _____.
24. *Court* is to *basketball* as *pool* is to _____.

Write the word that fits each meaning.
25. arranged in sequence   27. intended   29. blended
26. bringing together   28. pleaded   30. put over

Unit 22 Words with Suffixes pp. 138-143

actively	cheerful	paleness	government	speechless
softness	lately	countless	forgetful	settlement

Remember: A **suffix** is a word part added to the end of a base word.
These word parts are suffixes: **-ful, -ly, -less, -ment, -ness**.

watch ful

Write the word that fits each clue.
31. antonym of *few*   33. recently   35. unable to speak
32. antonym of *gloomy*   34. busily   36. lack of color

Write the word that completes each sentence.
37. The President is the highest _____ official.
38. Jamestown was the first permanent _____ in America.
39. Tina cannot remember anything. She is so _____.
40. Joseph stroked the kitten's fur, surprised by its _____.

24 Review

Unit 23 Final |n| or |ən|, |chər|, |zhər| pp. 144-149

culture   creature   mountain   treasure   surgeon
curtain   mixture   pleasure   furniture   luncheon

Remember: |n| or |ən| → **ain** |chər| → **ture** |zhər| → **sure**

Write the word that belongs in each group. Then circle the words that have the final |chər| sounds.

41. beast, animal, ____   44. river, valley, ____
42. joy, delight, ____   45. shade, blind, ____
43. blend, combination, ____

Write the word that fits each clue.

46. a way of life   49. a midday meal
47. a doctor   50. a precious object
48. chairs and tables

■ Challenge Words Units 19-23 pp. 120-149

module   entertaining   catering   anticipated
leisure   suspiciously   scalloped   architecture
nuisance   seriousness

Write the word that fits each meaning.

51. providing food and drink   54. relaxation
52. baked in a casserole with sauce 55. someone who is
53. the art of designing buildings   annoying

Write the word that fits each clue. Then circle the word in which a final *e* is dropped before *-ed* or *-ing* is added.

56. antonym of *humor*   59. antonym of
57. synonym for *amusing*   *trustfully*
58. antonym of *unexpected*   60. synonym for *unit*

Spelling-Meaning Strategy

Consonant Changes: The Sound of *t*

You know that some words in a word family often have the same spellings for different sounds. Read this paragraph.

> I love to **create** animals from things I find outdoors. Yesterday I made a funny **creature** from moss, leaves, and sticks.

create
creature

Think

- What does *create* mean? What does *creature* mean? How are they related in meaning?
- What sound does the letter *t* spell in each word?

Here are more related words in which the spelling remains the same even though the sound of the *t* changes.

depart	habit	fact
departure	habitual	factual

Apply and Extend

Complete these activities on a separate piece of paper.

1. Look up the meanings of the words in the word box above in your Spelling Dictionary. Then write six sentences, using one of the words in each sentence.
2. With a partner list as many words as you can that are related to *create, depart, habit,* and *fact.* Then look on page 270 of your Spelling-Meaning Index. Add any other words that you find in these families to your list.

Summing Up   The sound of a final *t* may change when an ending or a suffix is added. Thinking of a related word can help you remember that the Ichl sound can be spelled *t.*

Description

Rumi, a city child, is visiting a farm. Which of your five senses does this description appeal to?

The barn was nice and cool, and it smelled of fresh hay and animals. I looked for the mules and found them outside standing in the hot sun, swishing flies with their tails. I lured them over to the fence with some weeds I pulled from the ground, but when they got close and sniffed the weeds, they just bared their huge yellow teeth at me.

I finally found Rick, the old collie, lying in the shade of the walnut tree, and he gave me a friendly wag of his tail. His nose felt cool and wet even in all that heat, and when I scratched his head, he thumped his tail again.

I walked out a little way after that, right up to the edge of the vineyards. They looked as though they went on forever, curving clear around the entire world, and I could feel the sun beating down on them and on my head like a silent drum. There were no sounds of streetcars or rumbling delivery trucks. I felt as though somebody had put a huge glass bowl over my head that shut out all the sounds of the world.

from "A Zillion Stars" by Yoshiko Uchida

Think and Discuss

1. What **sense words**, such as *huge yellow teeth*, tell what Rumi saw, heard, smelled, and felt?
2. What **exact words** did the author use to name the dog, a tree, and the fields on the farm?
3. Does this description give the impression of a peaceful or a busy farm?

The Writing Process

The description on page 154 creates a clear picture of a peaceful farm. When you write a description, choose **details** to create an impression that supports your purpose. Use **sense words** to describe how something looks, smells, tastes, sounds, and feels. Use **exact words** to paint a clear mental picture for your readers.

Assignment: Write a Description

Step One: Prewriting

1. List some things you can describe. Discuss them with a classmate, and choose one idea to write about.
2. Make a cluster. Write your topic, and circle it. Then write words around your topic that describe it.

Step Two: Write a First Draft

1. Think about your purpose and your audience.
2. Do not worry about mistakes—just write!

Step Three: Revise

1. Did you appeal to at least three senses?
2. Where could you add exact words and details?
3. Use your Thesaurus to find exact words.
4. Read your description to a classmate. Make changes.

Step Four: Proofread

1. Did you use commas and end marks correctly?
2. Did you spell all words correctly? Copy any words that you misspelled into your Notebook for Writing.

Step Five: Publish

1. Copy your description neatly, and add a title.
2. Share your description by making a poster.

Composition Words

freezing
slammed
breathless
softness
watchful
shadow
amusing
vanish

Proofreading Marks

¶ Indent
∧ Add something
ℓ Take out something
≡ Capitalize
/ Make a small letter

(Theme: Travel)

25 Final |ĭj|, |ĭv|, and |ĭs|

LOOK
at each word.

SAY
each word.

Basic Words   ■ Challenge

1. voyage	11. captive	21. heritage
2. baggage	12. average	22. cooperative
3. luggage	13. justice	23. apprentice
4. native	14. bandage	24. superlative
5. language	15. message	25. primitive
6. postage	16. service	
7. notice	17. shortage	
8. creative	18. passage	
9. practice	19. detective	
10. knowledge	20. relative	

THINK
about the words.

Each word has the final |ĭj|, |ĭv|, or |ĭs| sounds:

|ĭj| voy**age** |ĭv| nat**ive** |ĭs| not**ice**

• What is one pattern for the final |ĭj| sounds? What is one pattern for the final |ĭv| sounds? What is one pattern for the final |ĭs| sounds? How is the Elephant Word different?

WRITE
the words.

Practice   Write the Basic Words to answer the questions.

A. Which **ten** words have the final |ĭj| sounds spelled *age*?

B. Which word has the final |ĭj| sounds spelled another way?

CHECK
your spelling.

C. Which **five** words have the final |ĭv| sounds spelled *ive*?

D. Which **four** words have the final |ĭs| sounds spelled *ice*?

■ **Now write the five Challenge Words.** Underline the patterns that spell the final |ĭj|, |ĭv|, and |ĭs| sounds.

> ***Spelling-Meaning Hint***   How can you remember how
> to spell the |s| sound in *practice*? Think of the related word
> *practical*. The sound of the *c* changes, but the spelling
> remains the same.

practice
practical

Independent Practice

Spelling-Meaning   Look at the Spelling-Meaning Hint.
1-2. Write *practice* and *practical*. Then underline the letter in
   practical that helps you spell the |s| sound in *practice*.

Word Analysis   Complete the exercise with Basic Words.
3-7. Write the words with these base words.

voy*age*

3. pass	**5.** detect	**7.** create
4. bag	**6.** relate	

Definitions   Write the Basic Word that fits each meaning.

  8. the charge for mailing
  9. a covering for a wound
10. facts and ideas
11. a person held prisoner
12. not enough or lack of
13. the act of helping others
14. the quality of being fair
15. to pay attention to

■ **Challenge Words**   Write the Challenge Word that completes
each sentence. Use your Spelling Dictionary.
16. The tourists explored the ruins of a ___ civilization.
17. We went to Jamestown to learn about our nation's ___ .
18. The actor received an award for his ___ performance.
19. To work well with others, you must be ___ .
20. Amelia, a carpenter's ___ , enjoys learning her new trade.

Summing Up

The final |ĭj| sounds are often spelled with the pattern *age*.
The final |ĭv| sounds are often spelled with the pattern *ive*.
The final |ĭs| sounds are often spelled with the pattern *ice*.

Basic

1. voyage
2. baggage
3. luggage
4. native
5. language
6. postage
7. notice
8. creative
9. practice
10. knowledge
11. captive
12. average
13. justice
14. bandage
15. message
16. service
17. shortage
18. passage
19. detective
20. relative

■ Challenge

21. heritage
22. cooperative
23. apprentice
24. superlative
25. primitive

Review

1. village
2. package
3. manage
4. cottage
5. marriage

Expanding Vocabulary

Meanings for *passage*   You can read a passage about a ship's passage through a narrow passage. *Passage* has many meanings!

> **pas·sage** |păs′ ĭj| *n., pl.* **passages 1.** The act or process of passing: *The river is deep enough for safe passage.* **2.** A journey. **3.** A narrow path or channel. **4.** Approval of law by a legislative body. **5.** A part of a written work or piece of music.

Practice   **Write 1, 2, 3, 4, or 5 to show which meaning of** *passage* **is used in each sentence.**

1. The underground passage was dark and scary.
2. The senator thinks that passage of the bill is certain.
3. Is this your first passage across the ocean?
4. Lynn was unaware of the passage of time.
5. Let me read you a passage from my favorite story.

Proofreading

Titles   A person's title is often abbreviated. The abbreviation begins with a capital letter and ends with a period. (See also page 247 in your Student's Handbook.)

Mister **Mr.**   Doctor **Dr.**   Junior **Jr.**

Practice   **Proofread Amanda's announcement. Find four misspelled words, two missing periods, and one missing capital letter. Write the announcement correctly.**

◆◆◆◆◆◆◆◆◆◆◆◆◆◆◆◆◆◆◆◆◆◆◆◆◆◆◆◆◆◆◆◆

   Mr John Kurt and his son, John Kurt, jr, will speak to the Travel Club about their voage to the African country of Ghana. They will share their knowlege of the native langue, the villige life, and the creative crafts of Ghana.

◆◆◆◆◆◆◆◆◆◆◆◆◆◆◆◆◆◆◆◆◆◆◆◆◆◆◆◆◆◆◆◆

Review: Spelling Spree

Picture Clues   Write a Basic or Review Word for each clue.

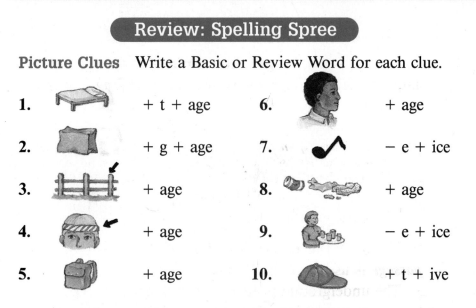

1.	+ t + age		6.	+ age	
2.	+ g + age		7.	− e + ice	
3.	+ age		8.	+ age	
4.	+ age		9.	− e + ice	
5.	+ age		10.	+ t + ive	

Ending Match   Write Basic or Review Words by matching word parts and endings. Be sure to write each ending correctly.

| ˅|ĭj| | ˂|ĭv| | ˃|ĭs| |

11. lugg ˃

12. relat ˂

13. creat ˂

14. just ˃

15. aver ˃

16. marri ˃

17. nat ˂

18. detect ˂

19. knowl ˃

20. short ˃

21. vill ˃

22. langu ˃

23. pract ˃

24. pass ˃

25. voy ˃

■ **Challenge Words**   Write messages for bumper stickers, using the Challenge Words. You can make the messages humorous or serious. They can be about yourself or something you believe in.
Example: Cooperative Drivers Are Safe Drivers

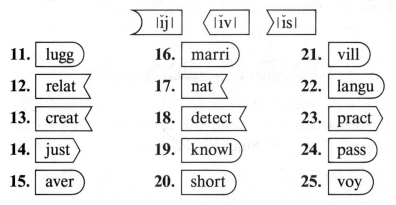

📖 *Writing Application:* Creative Writing   Imagine that you journey to a faraway land. One day a stranger hands you a message. What does the message tell you? Write the message. Try to use five words from the list on page 158.

25 Spelling Across the Curriculum

Social Studies: *Travel*

Theme Vocabulary

region
porter
customs
schedule
scenic
sightseer
berth
passport

Using Vocabulary Write the Vocabulary Words to complete the paragraph. Use your Spelling Dictionary.

The movement of the train woke me, and I sat up in my __(1)__ . My curiosity about new places made me an eager __(2)__ . I pulled aside the curtain to enjoy the __(3)__ countryside. I had never seen this __(4)__ of the world. We arrived at the Swiss border at 7:55 A.M.—right on __(5)__ . The train had to wait while the __(6)__ officer examined each person's __(7)__ . When I arrived in Bern, I found a __(8)__ to help carry my bags.

Understanding Vocabulary Write *yes* if the underlined word is used correctly. Write *no* if it is not.

9. Many artists have painted this <u>scenic</u> countryside.
10. Next summer we will tour the northern <u>berth</u>.
11. According to my <u>passport</u>, the train is late.
12. At the border you must pass a <u>customs</u> inspection.

FACT FILE

The Great Wall of China, built to prevent invasion, winds more than fifteen hundred miles across mountains and desert. Made by hand, it is the world's longest structure.

Enrichment 25

👪 *World Traveler Game*

Players: 4   **You need:** poster paper, game markers, colored pens, spinner numbered 1-6
How to play: With the other players, make a game board with a border of twenty squares. Write *Start/Finish* on one square. On each of the other squares, write a statement and a direction, such as *You have lost your passport. Move back two squares.* Use a word from the lists in this unit in each square. Players take turns spinning the spinner, moving their markers, and following the directions. The first player to move around the board wins.

POST CARD FROM ???

Create a new country in your imagination. Then make a big post card. Draw a colorful scene on the front. Write a message on the back, using some words from the lists in this unit. Draw a stamp in the upper right corner, giving the country's name and showing something special about the country.

📖 Writing
A Traveler's Tale

Imagine that you are the captain of an ocean liner that cruises around the world. Write a story based on an exciting event that happened on one of your voyages. Try to use words from the lists in this unit. Be sure to proofread your story.

26 Spelling Unstressed Syllables

LOOK
at each word.

SAY
each word.

Basic Words   ■ Challenge

1. pilgrim	11. wisdom	21. refuge
2. worship	12. crystal	22. charter
3. forbid	13. respond	23. somber
4. distance	14. program	24. exert
5. hidden	15. solid	25. adapt
6. repair	16. salute	
7. dozen	17. spinach	
8. destroy	18. ashamed	
9. carrot	19. blossom	
10. entry	20. neglect	

THINK
about the words.

Each two-syllable word has the VCCV, VCCCV, or VCV pattern. To help you spell these words, divide the words into syllables. Listen for the unstressed syllable, and note its spelling carefully. Spell the words by syllables.

re | **pair** | rĭ pâr′ | **pil** | grim | pĭl′ grĭm |

- Which words have an unstressed first syllable, as in *repair*? Which words have an unstressed second syllable, as in *pilgrim*? Why should you pay careful attention to the spelling of the unstressed syllables?

WRITE
the words.

CHECK
your spelling.

Practice   Write the Basic Words to answer the questions.

A. Which **seven** words have unstressed first syllables?

B. Which **thirteen** words have unstressed second syllables?

■ **Now write the five Challenge Words.** Underline the unstressed syllables.

> ***Spelling-Meaning Hint***   Did you know that the words *enter*, *entry*, and *entrance* are related in meaning? They all come from a Latin word meaning "within." **Think of this:** *Enter* the building through the *entry*.

enter
entry
entrance

Independent Practice

Spelling-Meaning   Look at the Spelling-Meaning Hint.

1-2. Write *enter*. Then write the Basic Word that is related to *enter*.

Word Analysis   Complete the exercises with Basic Words.

3-5. Write the three words that have double consonants.

6-10. Write the words that have the underlined syllables below.
    6. <u>for</u>get   **7.** <u>spin</u>ner   **8.** <u>worry</u>   **9.** <u>dis</u>like   **10.** <u>a</u>gree

Analogies   Write the Basic Word that completes each analogy.
11. *Two* is to *pair* as *twelve* is to ____ .
12. *Question* is to *ask* as *answer* is to ____ .
13. *Beautiful* is to *beauty* as *wise* is to ____ .
14. *Metal* is to *silver* as *glass* is to ____ .
15. *Reduce* is to *increase* as *break* is to ____ .

■ **Challenge Words**   Write the Challenge Word that fits each meaning. Use your Spelling Dictionary.
16. apply effort
17. serious
18. protection
19. to change for a certain purpose
20. a written formal document granting certain rights

Summing Up

To spell a two-syllable word, divide the word into syllables. Spell the word by syllables, noting carefully the spelling of the unstressed syllable.

Basic

1. pilgrim
2. worship
3. forbid
4. distance
5. hidden
6. repair
7. dozen
8. destroy
9. carrot
10. entry
11. wisdom
12. crystal
13. respond
14. program
15. solid
16. salute
17. spinach
18. ashamed
19. blossom
20. neglect

■ Challenge

21. refuge
22. charter
23. somber
24. exert
25. adapt

Review

1. harvest
2. honest
3. allow
4. whether
5. middle

Expanding Vocabulary

Antonyms   Suppose you try to repair a kite, but instead you accidentally destroy it. You have done the opposite of what you meant to do. The words *repair* and *destroy* are **antonyms**, or words that have opposite meanings.

Practice   Write the word below that is an antonym for each numbered word. Use your Spelling Dictionary.

hollow	proud	visible
ignorance	allow	exit

1. hidden   **3.** forbid   **5.** entry

2. solid   **4.** wisdom   **6.** ashamed

Proofreading

Titles   Capitalize the first, last, and all important words in a title. Underline the titles of books, magazines, newspapers, and movies. Put quotation marks around the titles of short stories, songs, articles, book chapters, and most poems.

BOOK: At Home in a New Land   POEM: "The Promise"

Practice   Proofread Eva's book report. Find four misspelled words, two missing capital letters, and two missing quotation marks. Write the book report correctly.

Title: a Salute to america
Author: Beth Ray
About the Book: This book includes a dosen stories about the American Colonies. One story titled The Harvest is about an English girl who sails the long distants to America in the midle of winter. Bad storms almost distroy the ship.

Review: Spelling Spree

Finding Words   Each word below is hidden in a Basic or Review Word. Write the Basic or Review Word.

Example: is *wisdom*

1. pond	**4.** bid	**7.** pin	**10.** ship
2. vest	**5.** hid	**8.** grim	**11.** pair
3. gram	**6.** nest	**9.** lid	**12.** shame

Questions   Write the Basic or Review Word that answers each question.

13. What do military officers do when they meet?

14. What helps you make good decisions?

15. Which word rhymes with *together*?

16. What could cause a garden to fill up with weeds?

17. What does a yardstick measure?

18. What is a stronger word for *damage*?

19. What is a solid with a regular pattern, such as a snowflake?

20. What is halfway between two points?

21. What is another word for a flower?

22. What does every room have?

23. What is a set of twelve called?

24. What is a synonym for *permit*?

25. What is a vegetable that is popular with rabbits?

■ **Challenge Words**   Make a Word Square puzzle. Write each Challenge Word across, down, or diagonally. Then fill in the square with Basic Words or other letters. Trade papers with a partner. Find and circle the Challenge and Basic Words in each other's puzzles.

Writing Application: A Description The year is 1630, and you are an English settler in America. You have made a clearing in the woods, built a cabin, and planted a garden. Write a paragraph describing your new surroundings. Try to use five words from the list on page 164.

26 Spelling Across the Curriculum

Social Studies: *The Pilgrims*

Theme Vocabulary

freedom
Mayflower
Puritans
Plymouth
hardships
governor
treaty
prosper

Using Vocabulary Write the Vocabulary Words to complete the paragraph. Use your Spelling Dictionary.

The Pilgrims belonged to a religious group known as the __(1)__. Seeking religious __(2)__, the Pilgrims sailed to America on the __(3)__ and settled __(4)__ Colony. John Carver was the first __(5)__ of the colony. During the first winter the Pilgrims suffered many __(6)__. In the spring they signed a peace __(7)__ with the Wampanoag Indians. The Wampanoags showed the Pilgrims where to fish and how to grow crops, and the colony started to __(8)__.

Understanding Vocabulary Write *yes* if the underlined word is used correctly. Write *no* if it is not.

9. The Pilgrims came to America on <u>hardships</u>.
10. The Pilgrims chose a <u>governor</u> to lead the colony.
11. A <u>treaty</u> was served at the harvest feast.
12. The Pilgrims worked hard in order to <u>prosper</u>.

FACT FILE

According to legend, the first thing the Pilgrims stepped on when they landed in America was Plymouth Rock. This rock is on display in Plymouth, Massachusetts.

Enrichment 26

A Pilgrim Time Line

In a small group research information about the Pilgrims. Divide the research into three parts: (1) the reasons for leaving England, (2) the voyage to America, and (3) life in Plymouth Colony. Write down important dates and events. Then make a wall-length time line. Mark off the date of each major event. Draw a picture, and write a sentence describing the event. Try to use words from the lists in this unit.

1608 SEPARATISTS LEFT ENGLAND.

1620 PILGRIMS FOUNDED PLYMOUTH COLONY.

1621 FIRST THANKSGIVING

Writing
A Diary

If you could live one day as a Pilgrim, which day would it be? Would it be a day on the *Mayflower*? Would it be the day that the Pilgrims sighted land? Write a diary entry, describing your day. Include your thoughts and feelings. Try to use words from the lists in this unit. Be sure to proofread your diary.

SEAL OF APPROVAL

Imagine that you are an artist living in Plymouth Colony. On construction paper design a flag and an official seal to present to the governor of the colony. Write a slogan for the seal. Try to use words from the lists in this unit.

Theme: The *Titanic*

27 Words with Prefixes

LOOK

at each word.

SAY

each word.

Basic Words   ■ **Challenge**

1. disaster   11. insult   21. inquiry
2. unknown   12. regard   22. unfortunate
3. discover   13. install   23. unnecessary
4. unable   14. dismiss   24. inflate
5. inform   15. relax   25. responsible
6. increase   16. unaware
7. report   17. disagree
8. dispute   18. unskilled
9. insist   19. revenge
10. remind   20. display

THINK

about the words.

Each word begins with a prefix. A **prefix** is a word part added to the beginning of a base word or a word root. It adds meaning to a word. Find the prefix and the base word or the word root to help you spell the word.

PREFIX	BASE WORD			PREFIX	WORD ROOT	
un	+ able	=	**un**able	in	+ sist	= **in**sist
dis	+ agree	=	**dis**agree	re	+ port	= **re**port

• What four prefixes do you see?

WRITE

the words.

Practice   **Write the Basic Words to answer the questions.** Underline the prefix in each word.

CHECK

your spelling.

A. Which **nine** words have the prefix *re-* or *un-*?

B. Which **eleven** words have the prefix *dis-* or *in-*?

■ **Now write the five Challenge Words.** Underline the prefix in each word.

insist
assist
resist
consist

> *Spelling-Meaning Hint* *Insist* contains the Latin word root *sist*, meaning "to stand." To *insist* is to "stand on" your wish or request. Other words with this root are *assist*, *resist*, and *consist*.

Independent Practice

Spelling-Meaning Look at the Spelling-Meaning Hint.
1-2. Write *resist*. Then write the Basic Word that also has the word root *sist*.

Word Analysis Complete the exercise with Basic Words.
3-7. Write five words by changing the underlined prefixes.
  3. <u>im</u>port **4.** <u>dis</u>able **5.** <u>re</u>cover **6.** <u>re</u>sult **7.** <u>de</u>crease

Definitions Write the Basic Word that fits each meaning.

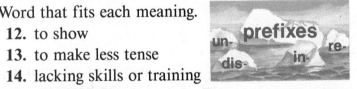

  8. to send away
  9. to fail to agree
  10. to cause to remember
  11. not familiar
  12. to show
  13. to make less tense
  14. lacking skills or training
  15. to argue or debate

■ **Challenge Words** Write the Challenge Word that completes each sentence. Use your Spelling Dictionary.
  16. The boating accident was due to ____ circumstances.
  17. Strong winds and high waves were ____ for the accident.
  18. The passengers were able to ____ their life raft.
  19. Would the Coast Guard conduct an ____?
  20. As no other boat was involved, an investigation is ____.

Summing Up

A **prefix** is a word part added to the beginning of a base word or a word root. A prefix adds meaning. *Un-, in-, dis-,* and *re-* are prefixes. Find the prefix and the base word or the word root. Spell the word by parts.

Expanding Vocabulary

Meanings for *report* The word *report* has several meanings. What does *report* mean in this headline?

Special **Report**! Students **Report** for School in July

> **re·port** |rĭ pôrt′| *n., pl.* **reports 1.** A spoken or written description: *weather report.* **2.** A formal account of the activities of a group. *v.* **reported, reporting 1.** To provide an account for publication. **2.** To present oneself.

Practice How is *report* used in each sentence? Write the abbreviation for the part of speech and the number of the correct meaning.

1. The fire department received a report of a fire.
2. The newspapers will report the signing of the treaty.
3. Team members must report for practice on time.
4. The committee presented its monthly report on Tuesday.

Dictionary

Word History English has borrowed words from many languages. As words pass from one language to another, they often change in meaning. Read the history of *disaster*.

> **Disaster** goes back to the Italian word *disastro*, which was formed from the Latin prefix *dis-*, meaning "away from," and the Greek word *ast*, meaning "star." *Disastro* meant "bad luck brought by the stars." When *disaster* came into English, it meant simply "something that causes destruction."

Practice Read the history of each word below in your Spelling Dictionary. Write the earlier form of the word, the language it came from, and what it meant.

1. robot   2. clue

Review: Spelling Spree

Alphabet Puzzler   Write the Basic or Review Word that fits alphabetically between the two words in each group.

1. unpack, ____, unsound
2. inside, ____, inspect
3. under, ____, unit
4. reason, ____, recover
5. displace, ____, dispose
6. reject, ____, relay
7. dimple, ____, disappear
8. disk, ____, dismay
9. remember, ____, rent
10. inspire, ____, instead
11. disobey, ____, disorganize
12. instrument, ____, interest
13. dispose, ____, dissolve
14. rest, ____, review
15. umbrella, ____, unarmed
16. repair, ____, rescue
17. unsteady, ____, untie

Proofreading   18-25. Find eight misspelled Basic Words in this report. Write each word correctly.

The captain of the *Titanic* was not unawear that ice lay in his path. More than one report had been sent to imform him of this danger. The reason is unnown, but something caused the captain to desmiss the warnings and, in fact, to incress his speed. Had he shown more reguard for the safety of those on board, he might have prevented the dizaster. Once he did descover how serious the danger was, he was unable to save the ship.

■ **Challenge Words**   Write five newspaper headlines about a disaster, such as a shipwreck, using a Challenge Word in each headline. Capitalize the first, last, and each important word.

📖 *Writing Application:* A News Report Imagine that you are a TV newscaster. A disaster has just occurred. Write a paragraph about the event for the evening news. Try to use five words from the list on page 170.

27 Spelling Across the Curriculum

Social Studies: *The Titanic*

Theme Vocabulary

iceberg
passengers
luxury
survivors
lifeboat
emergency
Atlantic Ocean
unsinkable

Using Vocabulary Write the Vocabulary Words to complete the paragraph. Use your Spelling Dictionary.

The *Titanic* was so well built that it was thought to be __(1)__. It featured every kind of __(2)__ for the pleasure of its __(3)__. No one could have imagined that the *Titanic* would strike a floating body of ice, or __(4)__, and sink into the __(5)__ on its first voyage. An SOS—the __(6)__ signal for help—was sent, but the rescuing ship arrived too late. Some people managed to escape by __(7)__, but those who died far outnumbered the __(8)__.

Understanding Vocabulary Write *yes* if the underlined word is used correctly. Write *no* if it is not.

9. Lianne put an <u>iceberg</u> in her juice.
10. The siren alerted everyone to the <u>emergency</u>.
11. The diamond necklace was a <u>luxury</u>.
12. The accident's <u>survivors</u> had been frightened.

FACT FILE

Icebergs are huge bodies of ice that float in the sea. About one-tenth of an iceberg is visible. The rest lies below the water. Icebergs are very dangerous to ships.

Enrichment 27

👪 *SOS!*

With a partner write and exchange messages using the International Flag Code. This is the code used by ships from all nations for some short-distance communications. Write your message by drawing pictures of the flags that represent the letters you want to use. Decode and write each other's messages. Try to use some words from the lists in this unit.

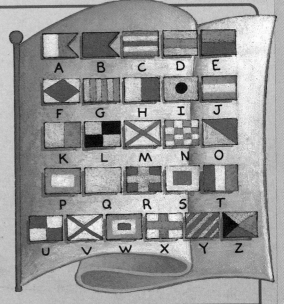

SUN SIGNS

Make Sun Signs to illustrate words with the prefixes *un-*, *in-*, *dis-*, and *re-*. Draw a sun with rays around it. Then write a prefix in the center of the sun. Along each ray write a base word or a word root that can be combined with the prefix to form a word from the lists in this unit. You may want to add other familiar base words or word roots.

📖 *Writing*
The Lost Ship

Imagine that you are a scientist who explores the ocean. You have just discovered a ship that disappeared mysteriously long ago. Write an article for *Explorer's Journal*, describing what you found. What happened to the ship? Try to use words from the unit lists. Be sure to proofread your article.

(Theme: The American Revolution)

28 Changing Final y to i

LOOK
at each word.

SAY
each word.

Basic Words

			■ Challenge
1. liberties	11. pitied	21. unified
2. victories	12. ladies	22. levied
3. countries	13. busier	23. colonies
4. spied	14. duties	24. rivalries
5. enemies	15. lilies	25. strategies
6. armies	16. worthiness	
7. scariest	17. tiniest	
8. dirtier	18. emptiness	
9. happiness	19. replies	
10. abilities	20. dizziness	

THINK
about the words.

Each word has an ending or a suffix added to a base word.
Each base word ends with a consonant and *y*.

army + es = arm**ies**   scary + est = scar**iest**
spy + ed = sp**ied**   happy + ness = happ**iness**
dirty + er = dirt**ier**

- How does the spelling of each base word change when an ending or a suffix is added? Is the next-to-the-last letter in each base word a vowel or a consonant?

WRITE
the words.

CHECK
your spelling.

Practice **Write the Basic Words to answer the questions.**

A. Which **twelve** words end with -*es* or -*ed*?
B. Which **four** words end with -*er* or -*est*?
C. Which **four** words end with -*ness*?

■ **Now write the five Challenge Words.** Underline the ending or the suffix in each word.

Spelling-Meaning Hint How can you remember how to spell the schwa sound in *abilities*? Think of the |ā| sound in the related word *able*. **Think of this:** If you are *able* to draw, you have artistic *abilities*.

a|bilities
a|ble

Independent Practice

Spelling-Meaning   Look at the Spelling-Meaning Hint.

1-2. Write *able*. Then write the Basic Word that is related to *able* in spelling and meaning.

Word Analysis   Complete the exercises with Basic Words.

3-6. Write the plural of each word below.

    3. duty   **4.** army   **5.** enemy   **6.** liberty

7-9. Write the three words that have the |ī| sound.

Making Inferences   Write a Basic Word to fit each clue.

10. These appear on a map.
11. A winning team has these.
12. Your mother and aunt are examples of these.
13. This is what you feel when you get an *A* on a test.
14. People often experience this after spinning around.
15. You might find some of these in a field or a garden.

s p y

■ **Challenge Words**   Write the Challenge Word that fits each definition. Use your Spelling Dictionary.

    16. settled territories   **19.** ordered something to be paid
    17. made into a whole   **20.** fierce competitions
    18. plans of action

Summing Up

If a word ends with a consonant and *y*, change the *y* to *i* when adding *-es, -ed, -er, -est,* or *-ness*.

Basic

1. liberties
2. victories
3. countries
4. spied
5. enemies
6. armies
7. scariest
8. dirtier
9. happiness
10. abilities
11. pitied
12. ladies
13. busier
14. duties
15. lilies
16. worthiness
17. tiniest
18. emptiness
19. replies
20. dizziness

■ Challenge

21. unified
22. levied
23. colonies
24. rivalries
25. strategies

Review

1. cities
2. easier
3. families
4. studied
5. angriest

Expanding Vocabulary

Exact Words for *small* Mr. Rudolph complained, "I ordered a *small* steak, but this one is *tiny*!" Using the exact word *tiny* helped the customer make his point clearly.

Practice Write the best word below to replace *small* in each sentence. Use your Thesaurus.

tiny   minor   stunted   microscopic   miniature

1. Jess carved a <u>small</u> model of a soldier.
2. The <u>small</u> infant was one hour old.
3. The human eye cannot see the <u>small</u> red blood cells.
4. The plan was perfect except for one <u>small</u> problem.
5. The plants were <u>small</u> this year because of dry weather.

Proofreading

Punctuating Business Letters Use a colon after the greeting in a business letter. Use a comma after the closing.

Dear Mr. Armando<u>:</u>   Sincerely<u>,</u>

Practice Proofread this letter. Find four misspelled words, one incorrect comma, and one missing comma. Write the letter correctly.

Dear Ms. Kaplan,

Welcome to your new dutys at the American History Museum. I hope you find happiness in your work here. I am busyer than ever, but your abbilities will make my job easer.

Sincerely

Paul Martinez

Paul Martinez

American History Museum

Review: Spelling Spree

Syllable Rhymes   Write the Basic or Review Word that has a first syllable that rhymes with each word below.

1. ham
2. rib
3. slap
4. mud
5. when
6. tic
7. quiz
8. peas
9. star
10. shirt

Puzzle Play   Write a Basic or Review Word to fit each clue. Circle the letter that would appear in the box. Write the circled letters in order. They will spell three mystery words that are a nickname for the United States flag.

11. nations _ _ _ _ _ _ _ _☐
12. very large towns _ _☐_ _ _
13. the most angry ☐_ _ _ _ _ _ _
14. answers ☐_ _ _ _ _ _
15. most frightening _ _ _ _ _ _☐_
16. women _☐_ _ _ _
17. value _ _ _ _ _ _☐_ _
18. watched secretly _ _ _ _ _☐
19. trumpet-shaped flowers _ _ _ _ _ _☐
20. felt sorry for _ _☐_ _ _
21. having more to do _ _ _ _ _☐
22. the smallest _☐_ _ _ _ _
23. nothing inside _ _☐_ _ _ _ _
24. skills _ _ _ _ _ _ _☐_
25. responsibilities _ _ _ _ _☐

■ **Challenge Words**   Write your own Puzzle Play, using the Challenge Words and any Basic Words that you need to form a mystery word. Write the answers to the clues and the mystery word on the back of your paper. Trade puzzles with a classmate.

Writing Application: A Speech   Imagine that you are living in one of the American Colonies. Write a speech, urging the Colonies to fight for their freedom from England. Try to use five words from the list on page 176.

28 Spelling Across the Curriculum

Social Studies: *The American Revolution*

Theme Vocabulary

revolution
rebel
boycott
battleground
patriot
taxation
allegiance
independence

Using Vocabulary Write the Vocabulary Words to complete the paragraph. Use your Spelling Dictionary.

By 1773 many American colonists felt no __(1)__ to Britain. When the British decided to tax tea and other basic products, the colonists thought that this __(2)__ was unfair. They chose to __(3)__ these products rather than pay the tax. These taxes and other problems led the colonists to __(4)__ and declare their __(5)__ from Britain. This caused a __(6)__, which turned America into a __(7)__. Every __(8)__ fought for the new country.

Understanding Vocabulary Write *yes* if the underlined word is used correctly. Write *no* if it is not.

9. The colonists stopped buying tea as part of a <u>boycott</u>.
10. The government pays <u>taxation</u> to the people.
11. A <u>patriot</u> supports and protects his or her country.
12. He showed his <u>allegiance</u> by fighting for his country.

FACT FILE

Powerful speeches helped spark the American Revolution. One of the most powerful was given by Patrick Henry, a Virginian, who said, "Give me liberty, or give me death."

Enrichment

28

👥 For or Against?

Imagine that you are an American colonist. With a small group plan a debate on whether to declare independence from Great Britain. First, break your group into those who will argue in favor of independence and those who will argue against it. Then research information about the Revolution to support both points of view. Present your arguments in class, and let your classmates decide who is most convincing.

📖 *Writing*

"If I had my way . . ."

Imagine that you have the opportunity to settle a new country. You are responsible for choosing the type of government for the country and creating its laws. Write an essay that explains your plan for your new country. Try to use words from the lists in this unit. Be sure to proofread your essay.

PAINTING THE PAST

Paint or draw three scenes from United States history. You may want to show events from the American Revolution or perhaps something important that happened as recently as yesterday. Write titles for your artwork. Try to use words from the unit lists.

WASHINGTON CROSSING THE DELAWARE (Detail),
Emanuel Gottlieb Leutze

Theme: Television

29 Adding -ion

LOOK

at each word.

SAY

each word.

Basic Words   ■ **Challenge**

1. televise	11. react	21. animate
2. television	12. reaction	22. animation
3. act	13. tense	23. fascinate
4. action	14. tension	24. fascination
5. regulate	15. populate	
6. regulation	16. population	
7. locate	17. convict	
8. location	18. conviction	
9. elect	19. correct	
10. election	20. correction	

THINK

about the words.

Each pair of words is made up of a verb and a noun. The verb in each pair is the base word. The noun is formed when the suffix *-ion* is added to the verb.

VERB: elect   locat**e**
NOUN: elect**ion**   locat**ion**

• In which pair of example words does a spelling change occur when *-ion* is added? What change occurs?

WRITE

the words.

CHECK

your spelling.

Practice   **Write the Basic Words to answer the questions.**

A. In which **five** pairs of words is the spelling of the verb not changed when *-ion* is added?

B. In which **five** pairs of words is the final *e* dropped when *-ion* is added to the verb?

■ **Now write the four Challenge Words.** Underline the letter that is dropped from each verb when *-ion* is added.

regulation
regulate

> **Spelling-Meaning Hint**   To remember how to spell the |sh| sound in *regulation*, think of the *t* in *regulate*. The *t* is kept in *regulation* even though the sound changes.

Independent Practice

Spelling-Meaning   Look at the Spelling-Meaning Hint.

1-2. Write *regulate* and *regulation*. Underline the letter in *regulate* that helps you spell the |sh| sound in *regulation*.

Word Analysis   Complete the exercises with Basic Words.

3-4. Write the word pair with the prefix *con-*.

5-8. Write *act* and *action*. Then write the word pair that has a prefix added to *act* and *action*.

9-10. Write the two words that have double consonants.

Context Sentences   Write a Basic Word to complete each sentence.

11. Our local station will ____ the high school football game.
12. The show was filmed on ____ in Quebec, Canada.
13. How many hours of ____ do you watch every week?
14. If you are old enough, you should vote in every ____ .
15. I cannot seem to ____ Tim's street on the map.
16. During the last five years the town's ____ has increased.

■ **Challenge Words**   Write the Challenge Word that has each verb definition. Then write the noun form of the verb. Use your Spelling Dictionary.
17-18. to attract the interest of   **19-20.** to bring to life

Summing Up

The suffix *-ion* can change verbs into nouns. When a verb ends with *e*, drop the *e* before adding *-ion*.

Basic

1. televise
2. television
3. act
4. action
5. regulate
6. regulation
7. locate
8. location
9. elect
10. election
11. react
12. reaction
13. tense
14. tension
15. populate
16. population
17. convict
18. conviction
19. correct
20. correction

■ Challenge

21. animate
22. animation
23. fascinate
24. fascination

Review

1. camera
2. movie
3. famous
4. minute
5. question

Expanding Vocabulary

The Greek Word Part *tele* When the Greek word part *tele* is combined with other word parts, its meaning is included in the meaning of the new word.

ROOT	MEANING	WORD
tele	far off, distant	televise

Televise means "to see images broadcast from a distance."

Practice **Write the word that completes each sentence. Use your Spelling Dictionary.**

telephone   telegram   telecast   telescope   television

1. Peter looked at the North Star through a ____ .
2. Every Sunday I talk on the ____ to my grandmother.
3. Eva's favorite ____ program is shown on Tuesday.
4. Contact someone far away quickly by sending a ____ .
5. The dolphin show was ____ live from the aquarium.

Dictionary

Primary and Secondary Stress You know that the syllables in a word are said with different levels of stress.

pop·u·late |pŏp′ yə lāt′|

The first syllable in *populate* is shown in dark print with a dark accent mark ('). It has **primary stress** and is said more strongly. The last syllable has **secondary stress**. It has a light accent mark (') and is said with less stress.

Practice **Write each word below in syllables. Underline the syllable with primary stress. Circle the syllable with secondary stress. Use your Spelling Dictionary.**

1. regulate
2. regulation
3. population
4. imitation
5. televise
6. decoration

Review: Spelling Spree

Syllable Scramble   Rearrange the syllables to write a Basic or Review Word. One syllable in each item is extra.

1. re er act
2. ness vict con
3. la reg al u tion
4. ly lect e
5. vic tion ex con
6. ic ac tion
7. lo de cate
8. cor tion rec less

9. late u en pop
10. e ful vise tel
11. cor er rect
12. sion ten vent
13. pre fa mous
14. reg u ist late
15. lec val e tion
16. u pop pro la tion

Proofreading   17-25. Find nine misspelled Basic or Review Words in this interview. Write each word correctly.

☆ ☆

Reporter: I know that you've been asked this qustion before, Tillie. How does it feel to be a famous star?

Tillie Burbanks: I love the riaction of my adoring fans. They won't leave me alone for a minite.

Reporter: You will soon begin filming a moovie for telavision. What's it about? Are you tenss?

Tillie: It's a Western. The action will take place in New Mexico, and most scenes will be shot on loction. I can't wait to akt in front of the camra again!

☆ ☆

■ **Challenge Words**   Write five tongue twisters, using a Challenge Word in each one. Trade papers with a classmate, and read each other's tongue twisters aloud.

📖 *Writing Application:* A TV Schedule   Write a television schedule of shows for one evening. Include the times, the channels, the names of the shows, and one sentence for each show that tells what the program is about. Try to use five words from the list on page 182.

29 Spelling Across the Curriculum

Performing Arts: *Television*

Theme Vocabulary

broadcast
network
sponsor
channel
commercial
series
video
episode

Using Vocabulary Write the Vocabulary Words to complete the paragraph. Use your Spelling Dictionary.

NBS is the national TV __(1)__ for action-packed shows this season. *Cat Man* has surprised everyone with its success. The show is so popular that each __(2)__ pays a fortune to air a thirty-second __(3)__. *Cat Man* is __(4)__ every Monday at 8:00 P.M. Check TV listings for the NBS __(5)__ in your area. The last __(6)__ of the ten-part __(7)__ will air in April. If you missed any parts, a __(8)__ of the entire program will soon be available.

Understanding Vocabulary Write *yes* if the underlined word is used correctly. Write *no* if it is not.

9. CBC is producing a four-part <u>episode</u> on whales.
10. The parade scene had a <u>broadcast</u> of many people.
11. Feline Feast will <u>sponsor</u> the animal program.
12. The <u>commercial</u> advertised a new breakfast cereal.

FACT FILE

The Nielsen Survey helps a network keep track of a show's popularity. The viewing choices of the 1200 families who participate supposedly reflect the choices of the nation.

Enrichment 29

Today's Special Guest Is . . .

With a partner present a TV talk show. Decide what kind of personality the host will have and who the guest will be. Is the guest an actor? a doctor? an inventor? Write the host's questions, and make notes for the guest's answers. Try to use words from the lists in this unit. Rehearse your questions and answers, and present your talk show to a small group.

TV MAGAZINE

You are the art director for a magazine about television. Create a cover for this month's issue. Give the magazine a title. Make up titles for three articles in the magazine that will make people want to buy this issue. Try to use words from the lists in this unit. Your cover illustration should have something to do with one of the articles.

Writing
Viewer's Choice

Think about your two favorite television shows. Are they comedies or dramas? What kinds of subjects do the shows cover? What are the main characters like? Write paragraphs that compare and contrast the shows. Try to use words from the lists in this unit. Remember to proofread your paper.

30 **Review:** Units 25–29

Unit 25 Final |ij|, |iv|, and |is| pp. 156-161

voyage

| creative | baggage | notice | language | knowledge |
| justice | service | average | relative | detective |

Remember: |ij| → **age** |iv| → **ive** |is| → **ice**

Write the word that fits each clue.

1. ordinary
2. English or Spanish
3. used when traveling
4. facts and ideas
5. inventive
6. to pay attention to

Write the word that completes each sentence.

7. The courts make sure that _____ is carried out.
8. Rosa Martinez, the new _____, solved the crime.
9. My cousin Sammy is my favorite _____.
10. We thanked the waiter for his excellent _____.

Unit 26 Unstressed Syllables pp. 162-167

blos som

| dozen | worship | pilgrim | forbid | repair |
| salute | crystal | neglect | respond | spinach |

Remember: To spell a two-syllable word, divide the word into syllables. Note carefully the spelling of the unstressed syllable. Spell the word by syllables.

Write the word that fits each meaning.

11. to mend
12. a set of twelve
13. to honor and love
14. a traveler to a sacred place
15. to fail to care for
16. to order not to do something

Write the word that completes each group.

17. answer, reply, _____
18. silver, china, _____
19. cabbage, lettuce, _____
20. handshake, wave, _____

Half of the words from each unit are reviewed on these pages.
The rest are reviewed on pages 241–243.

Review **30**

Unit 27   Words with Prefixes   pp. 168-173

| dispute | insist | increase | discover | unknown |
| install | dismiss | regard | unskilled | revenge |

Remember: A **prefix** is a word part added to the beginning of a base word or a word root. These are prefixes: **dis-, re-, in-, un-.**

prefixes
un-   re-
dis-   in-

Write the word that fits each meaning.

21. to place in service   **23.** to argue   **25.** to demand

22. to think highly of   **24.** to get even   **26.** growth

Write the word that completes each analogy.

27. *Ordinary* is to *unusual* as *familiar* is to _____ .

28. *Melt* is to *dissolve* as *release* is to _____ .

29. *Perfect* is to *imperfect* as *skilled* is to _____ .

30. *Observe* is to *see* as *learn* is to _____ .

Unit 28   Changing Final *y* to *i*   pp. 174-179

| abilities | happiness | dirtier | scariest | spied |
| dizziness | tiniest | pitied | replies | busier |

Remember: If a word ends with a consonant and **y**, change the **y** to **i** when adding an ending or a suffix.

s p y

Write the word formed by adding each base word to the ending or suffix.

31. dizzy + ness   **33.** pity + ed   **35.** spy + ed

32. reply + es   **34.** scary + est   **36.** dirty + er

Write the words that complete the paragraph.

  Ice-skating keeps Anna __(37)__ than most children, and it brings her great __(38)__ . She practices hard to improve her __(39)__ . Even the __(40)__ improvement takes hours of work.

30 Review

televise   elect   locate   react   populate
television   election   location   reaction   population

Remember: If a verb ends with **e**, drop the **e** before adding **-ion**. If a verb does not end with **e**, just add **-ion**.

Write the noun that fits each meaning.

41. the number of people who live in a particular place
42. a device that receives and reproduces sounds and images

43. selection by vote
44. a position
45. a response

Write the verb form of each noun.

46. reaction
47. location
48. television
49. population
50. election

■ Challenge Words   Units 25-29   pp. 156-185

cooperative   charter   strategies   fascinate
unfortunate   refuge   apprentice   fascination
responsible   unified

Write the word that fits each meaning. Circle the word that begins with the |yo͞o| sound.

51. joined
52. to attract
53. plans of action

54. a person who is learning a job
55. having a certain obligation
56. a strong attraction

Write the word that completes each group. Circle the word that has the base word *operate*.

57. document, contract, ____
58. protection, shelter, ____

59. unlucky, unhappy, ____
60. willing, helpful, ____

188

Spelling-Meaning Strategy

The Greek Word Part *ast*

Did you know that *disaster*, *asterisk*, and *astronomer* are related in meaning? Each word has the Greek word part *ast*, meaning "star." A Greek word part affects the meaning of each word that contains it. You have learned that many years ago *disaster* meant "bad luck brought by the stars." An asterisk is a symbol shaped like a star. An astronomer is someone who studies the stars. Knowing the meaning of *ast* can help you spell and understand other words with this same word part.

Here is a list of words that contain the Greek word part *ast*.

asterisk	**astronomer**	**astronomy**
aster	**asteroid**	**astronaut**

Think
* Look up each word above in your Spelling Dictionary. How does the word part *ast* affect the meaning of each word?

Apply and Extend

Complete these activities on a separate piece of paper.
1. Write six sentences, using one word from the word box above in each sentence. Can you make the words' meanings clear?
2. With a partner list as many other words as you can that include the word part *ast*. Then look on page 274 of your Spelling-Meaning Index. Add any other words that you find with this word part to your list.

Summing Up The Greek word part *ast* means "star." Words that have the same Greek word part are often related in spelling and meaning. Knowing the meaning of the word part can help you understand and spell the words in that family.

disaster
asterisk

Persuasive Letter

Rachel's grandfather has the same problem as the grandfather in Gramp *by Joan Tate. Rachel wrote this business letter to her building manager. What does she ask him to do?*

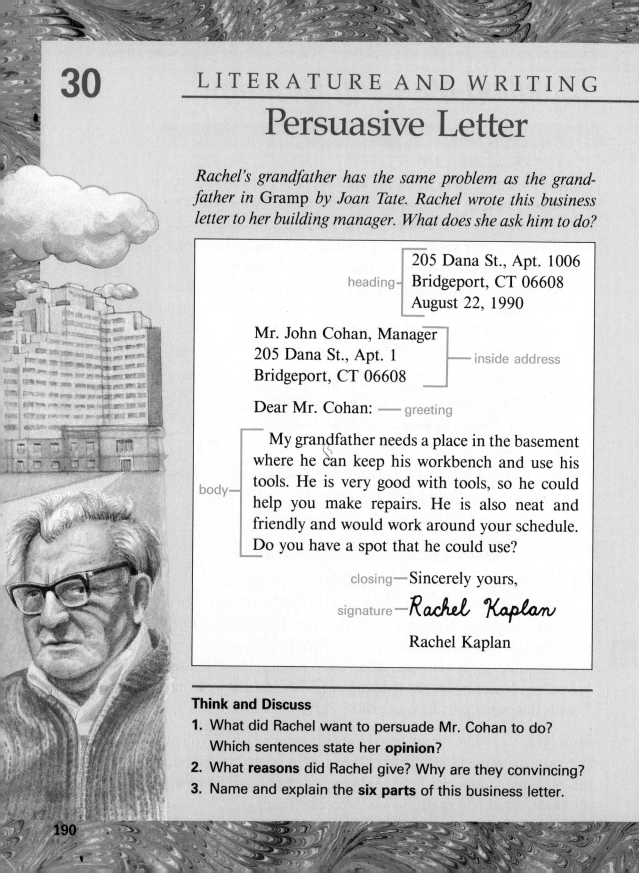

heading —
205 Dana St., Apt. 1006
Bridgeport, CT 06608
August 22, 1990

Mr. John Cohan, Manager
205 Dana St., Apt. 1 — inside address
Bridgeport, CT 06608

Dear Mr. Cohan: — greeting

body —
My grandfather needs a place in the basement where he can keep his workbench and use his tools. He is very good with tools, so he could help you make repairs. He is also neat and friendly and would work around your schedule. Do you have a spot that he could use?

closing — Sincerely yours,

signature — *Rachel Kaplan*

Rachel Kaplan

Think and Discuss

1. What did Rachel want to persuade Mr. Cohan to do? Which sentences state her **opinion**?
2. What **reasons** did Rachel give? Why are they convincing?
3. Name and explain the **six parts** of this business letter.

The Writing Process

The letter on page 190 was written to persuade Mr. Cohan to set aside space for a workbench. When you write a persuasive letter, state your **opinion** clearly in your topic sentence. Support your opinion with strong **reasons** that will appeal to your audience. Order your reasons—most to least important, for example—in the best way to convince your audience. Restate your opinion at the end.

Assignment: Write a Persuasive Letter

Step One: Prewriting

1. What would you like to persuade someone to do? Make a list. Discuss your ideas with a classmate. Choose one.
2. List strong reasons to support your opinion.

Step Two: Write a First Draft

1. Think about your purpose and your audience.
2. Do not worry about mistakes—just write!

Step Three: Revise

1. Did you use reasons that will convince your audience?
2. Use your Thesaurus to find exact words.
3. Read your letter to a classmate. Make other changes.

Step Four: Proofread

1. Did you use proper format?
2. Did you punctuate correctly?
3. Did you spell all words correctly? Copy any words that you misspelled into your Notebook for Writing.

Step Five: Publish

1. Copy your letter neatly.
2. Address and stamp an envelope, and mail the letter.

Composition Words

repair
respond
action
notice
neglect
inform
disagree
regulate

Proofreading Marks

¶ Indent
∧ Add something
ℓ Take out something
≡ Capitalize
/ Make a small letter

(Theme: Pollution)

31 More Words with -ion

Basic Words **■ Challenge**

1. pollute   11. promote   21. contaminate
2. pollution   12. promotion   22. contamination
3. protect   13. imitate   23. irritate
4. protection   14. imitation   24. irritation
5. inspect   15. decorate
6. inspection   16. decoration
7. impress   17. confess
8. impression   18. confession
9. migrate   19. express
10. migration   20. expression

THINK
about the words.

Each pair of words is made up of a verb and a noun. The noun is formed by adding the suffix *-ion* to the verb.

VERB:	impress	pollut**e**
NOUN:	impress**ion**	pollut**ion**

- Look at the examples. Does the spelling of *impress* change when *-ion* is added? How does the spelling of *pollute* change when *-ion* is added?

WRITE
the words.

Practice **Write the Basic Words to answer the questions.**

A. In which **five** pairs of words is the spelling of the verb not changed when *-ion* is added?

CHECK
your spelling.

B. In which **five** pairs of words is the final *e* dropped when *-ion* is added to the verb?

■ **Now write the four Challenge Words.** Underline the letter that is dropped from each verb when *-ion* is added.

> ***Spelling-Meaning Hint*** *Inspect* and *inspection* share the word root *spect*, meaning "to look." To inspect is to look at closely. Knowing the root *spect* will help you spell and understand the related words *spectacle* and *spectator*.

inspect
inspect**ion**
spectacle
spectator

Independent Practice

Spelling-Meaning Look at the Spelling-Meaning Hint.

1-2. Write *inspect* and *inspection*. Underline the root in each word.

Word Analysis Complete the exercise with Basic Words.

3-9. Add *-ion* to each verb to write a Basic Word.

3. pollute   7. imitate
4. protect   8. impress
5. promote   9. express
6. confess

Definitions Write the Basic Word that fits each definition.

10. an ornament
11. to make dirty or impure
12. to copy the actions of
13. to move from one region to another
14. to keep safe from harm
15. to put into words
16. to furnish with something attractive

■ **Challenge Words** Write the Challenge Word that fits each meaning. Use your Spelling Dictionary.

17. an impurity
18. to annoy
19. an annoyance
20. to make impure

Summing Up

The suffix *-ion* can change verbs to nouns. When a verb ends with *e*, drop the *e* when adding *-ion*. If a verb does not end with *e*, just add *-ion*.

Basic

1. pollute
2. pollution
3. protect
4. protection
5. inspect
6. inspection
7. impress
8. impression
9. migrate
10. migration
11. promote
12. promotion
13. imitate
14. imitation
15. decorate
16. decoration
17. confess
18. confession
19. express
20. expression

■ Challenge

21. contaminate
22. contamination
23. irritate
24. irritation

Review

1. garbage
2. health
3. dirty
4. ocean
5. awful

Expanding Vocabulary

Easily Confused Words   Did the Europeans who settled in America *emigrate* or *immigrate*? Actually, they did both.

> **emigrate**: to leave a country to settle in another
> **immigrate**: to come into a foreign country to live

The prefix *e-* means "away." The prefix *im-* means "in."

Practice   Write *emigrate* or *immigrate* to complete each sentence.
1. Mr. Chang planned to ___ from his homeland.
2. My aunt will ___ to this country next year.
3. How many people will ___ from Italy this year?
4. Do you plan to ___ to America, or will you just visit?

Proofreading

Commas in Letter Headings   Use a comma between the city and the state and between the day and the year.

> Columbus, OH   43229   October 12, 1991

Practice   Proofread Lavinia's letter for four misspelled words and two missing commas. Write the letter correctly.

> 1414 Tidewater Dr.
> Baton Rouge LA 70811
> April 10 1990
>
> Dear Ms. Sanchez,
>
>   I want to exspress my thanks to you for coming to my helth class. Your talk about polution and the protection of wildlife made a strong impreshion on me.

Review: Spelling Spree

Syllable Addition   Combine the first syllable of the first word with the final syllable of the second word to write a Basic or Review Word.

1. excellent + compress =
2. provide + demote =
3. open + crustacean =
4. garden + cabbage =
5. important + depress =
6. increase + respect =
7. provide + detect =
8. continue + profess =
9. dirtier + tasty =
10. minor + integrate =

Book Titles   Write a Basic or Review Word to complete each funny book title. Begin each word with a capital letter.

11. *Don't Dirty or _____ Our Water*   by Crystal Kleer
12. *How to _____ a Fancy Cake*   by F. Ross Ting
13. *Bird _____*   by Duck E. Overhead
14. *How to Make a Positive _____*   by Look N. Goode
15. *Physical Fitness and Your _____*   by Bea Vita Min
16. *How to _____ Bird Calls*   by Ma Kingbird
17. *The Terrible, Horrible, _____ Day*   by Mona Growner
18. *A Criminal's _____*   by Gil T. Pardee
19. *How to Speak with Enthusiasm and _____*   by Hammett Up
20. *How to Earn a _____ to a Higher Position*   by Getta Head
21. *The Care and _____ of Your Belongings*   by Lock N. Keye
22. *Apartment Design and _____*   by D. Zina Pad
23. *Cleaning Up Environmental _____*   by Ernest Scrubber
24. *How to Get Your Car to Pass _____*   by Fussy Checker
25. *Making _____ Pearls Look Real*   by Kop E. Kat

■ **Challenge Words**   What situation might involve an irritation? What situation might involve contamination? Write sentences, using all of the Challenge Words, to answer the questions.

📖 *Writing Application:* An Essay   Write an essay, explaining three ways you might help stop pollution. Try to use five words from the list on page 194.

31 Spelling Across the Curriculum

Health: *Pollution*

Theme Vocabulary
chemicals
recycle
toxic
environment
waste
litter
smog
fumes

Using Vocabulary Write the Vocabulary Words to complete the paragraph. Use your Spelling Dictionary.

Keeping our __(1)__ clean is important. We try not to __(2)__ public areas with bottles and paper, but more care is required. Laws now regulate the use of acids and other __(3)__ because they are __(4)__, or poisonous. New auto exhaust systems reduce the __(5)__ from cars, which contribute to __(6)__ in the air. Rather than bury or dump leftover __(7)__ materials, some companies __(8)__ them for use in other products. How can *you* help?

Understanding Vocabulary Write *yes* if the underlined word is used correctly. Write *no* if it is not.

9. <u>Smog</u> blanketed the city of Los Angeles.
10. The desert is a dry <u>environment</u>.
11. The fresh, unpolluted air was <u>toxic</u> to my health.
12. The <u>fumes</u> filled the room with a pleasant odor.

FACT FILE

The Air Quality Index tells the amount of harmful particles and chemicals in the air. An index above 100 indicates unhealthy air. An index above 400 indicates a health emergency.

Enrichment 31

👪 *Spaceship Earth*

With a small group research one pollution problem, such as acid rain, the "greenhouse effect," garbage disposal, or water pollution. How is this problem affecting plants and animals? What is being done to solve the problem? Take notes on index cards. Then present your information to the class. Explain the problem. You may want to use pictures, charts, or graphs to illustrate your talk. Try to use words from the lists in this unit.

📖 *Writing*
Pollution Solution

Imagine that a lake near your home is being polluted by chemical waste from a factory. Write a letter to the editor of a local newspaper. Explain why a better way should be found to dispose of the waste. Support your opinion with strong reasons. Try to use words from the lists in this unit. Be sure to proofread your letter.

MOBILE MESSAGES

A bumper sticker conveys a message using a few well-chosen words, such as "Grime is a crime! Stop pollution!" Design bumper stickers for a campaign to clean up the environment. Illustrate each sticker. Try to use words from the lists in this unit.

(Theme: Making Laws)

32 More Words with Prefixes

LOOK
at each word.

SAY
each word.

Basic Words   ■ Challenge

1. propose   11. extend   21. enactment
2. convince   12. prefix   22. procedure
3. concern   13. engage   23. convene
4. enforce   14. pronoun   24. preamble
5. compare   15. consist   25. concise
6. excuse   16. enclose
7. conduct   17. consent
8. preserve   18. proverb
9. contain   19. compound
10. excite   20. exchange

THINK
about the words.

Each word is made up of a prefix and a base word or a word root:

com + pare = **com**pare   ex + cite = **ex**cite
con + vince = **con**vince   pre + serve = **pre**serve
en + force = **en**force   pro + pose = **pro**pose

• What six prefixes do you see? *Com-* is a form of the prefix *con-*. Before which letter is *con-* spelled *com*?

WRITE
the words.

CHECK
your spelling.

Practice   Write the Basic Words to answer the questions.

A. Which **seven** words have the prefix *en-* or *ex-*?
B. Which **eight** words have the prefix *com-* or *con-*?
C. Which **five** words have the prefix *pre-* or *pro-*?

■ **Now write the five Challenge Words.** Underline the prefix in each word.

> *Spelling-Meaning Hint*   How can you remember how
> to spell the first schwa sound in *proposition*? Think of the
> |ō| sound in the related word *propose*.

propo|**sition**
propo|**se**

Independent Practice

Spelling-Meaning   Look at the Spelling-Meaning Hint.

1-2. Write *propose* and *proposition*. Underline the letter in
propose that helps you spell the schwa sound in *proposition*.

Word Analysis   Complete the exercises with Basic Words.

3-6. Write the four words with the |s| sound spelled *c* or *ce*.

7-8. Write the word that rhymes with each word below.

    7. spare   **8.** pretend

Synonyms   Write the Basic Word that is a synonym for each
word below.

  9. protect   **13.** permission
10. trade   **14.** surround
11. behavior   **15.** pardon
12. hold

com-
con-
en-
ex-
pre-
pro-

■ **Challenge Words**   Write the Challenge Word that fits each
meaning. Use your Spelling Dictionary.

16. a way of doing something   **19.** passage of a law
17. to come together   **20.** brief and to
18. an introduction to   the point
    a document

Summing Up

En-, ex-, com-, con-, pre-, and *pro-* are prefixes. To spell a word
with a prefix, find the prefix and the base word or the word root.
Spell the word by parts.

Basic

1. propose
2. convince
3. concern
4. enforce
5. compare
6. excuse
7. conduct
8. preserve
9. contain
10. excite
11. extend
12. prefix
13. engage
14. pronoun
15. consist
16. enclose
17. consent
18. proverb
19. compound
20. exchange

■ Challenge

21. enactment
22. procedure
23. convene
24. preamble
25. concise

Review

1. compose
2. exact
3. exit
4. common
5. expert

Expanding Vocabulary

Building Words   Words are like building blocks. New words can be created by using different prefixes with the same word root. The meaning of the new word is taken from the meanings of the prefix and the word root.

pro-   + pose   = **pro**pose
("before")   ("put")   ("to suggest or put forth")

Practice   **Add a prefix below to the word root** *pose* **to write a word for each meaning. Use your Spelling Dictionary.**

op- against   *trans-* change
ex- out   *com-* together, with

1. to put in a new order
2. to put together
3. to be against
4. to put out in the open

Dictionary

Different Pronunciations   Some words have different pronunciations when used as different parts of speech. *Excuse* is pronounced with a final |z| sound when used as a verb and with a final |s| sound when used as a noun.

ex·cuse |ĭk skyo͞oz′| *v.* **excused, excusing 1.** To forgive: *Please excuse me for what I did.* **2.** To release from a duty or promise. |ĭk skyo͞os′| *n., pl.* **excuses** Something given as a reason for excusing: *a written excuse for an absence.*

Practice   **Write the part of speech for each underlined word. Use your Spelling Dictionary.**

1. Lauren has a good <u>excuse</u> for being late.
2. Mr. Stern will <u>excuse</u> David from gym today.
3. Please <u>excuse</u> me for interrupting you.
4. Ushers in theaters <u>conduct</u> people to their seat.
5. Ms. Yazzi praised the team for their good <u>conduct</u>.

Review: Spelling Spree

Changing Prefixes Change the underlined prefix in each word to write a Basic or Review Word.

1. <u>pre</u>pare
2. <u>in</u>tend
3. <u>ac</u>cuse
4. <u>dis</u>close
5. <u>re</u>act
6. <u>de</u>serve
7. <u>in</u>sist
8. <u>re</u>sent
9. <u>im</u>pound
10. <u>de</u>tain
11. <u>dis</u>cern
12. <u>re</u>cite
13. <u>suf</u>fix
14. <u>de</u>duct
15. <u>inter</u>change

Proofreading **16-25.** Find ten misspelled Basic or Review Words in this speech. Write each word correctly.

A provirb says, "Actions speak louder than words." Our comman sense tells us that now is the time for action! *We*—I emphasize the pronun—must preserve our historic buildings. We have to convience Congress to pass and inforce a law to protect these landmarks. I. M. A. Saver, an expirt on colonial architecture, will compos a bill. She will also ingage Senator Hy Rise in debate. I perpose that everyone support her efforts. Near the exsit you will find more information about the debate.

■ **Challenge Words** Write five analogies, using one Challenge Word in each analogy. The analogy should compare two pairs of synonyms or two pairs of antonyms.

Example: *Depart* is to *leave* as *brief* is to *concise.*

📖 *Writing Application:* An Essay Imagine that you are president of the United States. Write one or two paragraphs telling about some of the changes you want to make. What laws would you pass? Why? Try to use five words from the list on page 200.

32 Spelling Across the Curriculum

Social Studies: *Making Laws*

Theme Vocabulary
legislation
amendment
veto
majority
statute
bill
lobbyist
filibuster

Using Vocabulary Write the Vocabulary Words to complete the paragraph. Use your Spelling Dictionary.

How does a __(1)__ become a law? First, it is debated in Congress. If a member of Congress wants to make changes, he or she attaches an __(2)__ or stages a __(3)__ to delay passage. Often a __(4)__ for a special-interest group will try to influence votes. If a __(5)__ of the members vote for the proposed law, it is sent to the President, who can sign the piece of __(6)__ or __(7)__ it. Once the President signs the proposal, it becomes a __(8)__ .

Understanding Vocabulary Write *yes* if the underlined word is used correctly. Write *no* if it is not.

9. Congress quickly passed the <u>filibuster</u>.
10. The <u>statute</u> on auto insurance never became law.
11. The President may <u>veto</u> any bill.
12. The <u>majority</u> of senators, 75 to 25, voted *yes*.

FACT FILE

The first ten amendments to the Constitution are known as the Bill of Rights. They guarantee such basic rights as freedom of speech and freedom of religion.

Enrichment 32

👪 The Prefix Game

Players: 4 **You need:** 20 cards with the word root or the base word of one of the Basic Words on each card; 3 cards for each of the prefixes *com-*, *con-*, *en-*, *ex-*, *pre-*, and *pro-*

How to play: Place the prefix cards in a pile. Each player gets five of the other cards. Players take turns choosing a prefix card. If the prefix makes a spelling word with a word root or a base word in his or her hand, the player lays down those cards. If the cards do not make a spelling word, the prefix card is put at the bottom of the pile. The first player to lay down all of his or her cards wins.

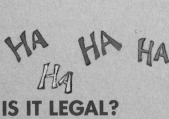

IS IT LEGAL?

Did you know that in one state you may not giggle uncontrollably? Some laws were written long ago and are no longer enforced. Write some of your own unusual laws, and illustrate each one. Try to use words from the unit lists.

📖 Writing
Safety First

Write a discussion between Ms. Stat S. Quo, who supports the existing speed limit, and Ms. Revette Upp, who wants a higher limit. Try to use words from the lists in this unit. Be sure to proofread your discussion.

33 Words with -ent, -ant; -able, -ible

LOOK
at each word.

SAY
each word.

Basic Words   ■ Challenge

1. fashionable   11. absent   21. elegant
2. comfortable   12. vacant   22. prominent
3. different   13. servant   23. extravagant
4. suitable   14. valuable   24. durable
5. merchant   15. accident   25. reversible
6. profitable   16. horrible
7. student   17. honorable
8. possible   18. reasonable
9. resident   19. remarkable
10. terrible   20. laughable

THINK
about the words.

The suffixes *-ent* and *-ant* and the suffixes *-able* and *-ible* sound alike but are spelled differently. Each word has one of these suffixes. Because these suffixes begin with a schwa sound, their spellings must be remembered.

|ənt| stud**ent**, merch**ant** |ə bəl| suit**able**, poss**ible**

• What are two spelling patterns for the suffix |ənt|? What are two patterns for the suffix |ə bəl|?

WRITE
the words.

CHECK
your spelling.

Practice   Write the Basic Words to answer the questions.

A. Which **five** words have |ənt| spelled *-ent*?
B. Which **three** words have |ənt| spelled *-ant*?
C. Which **nine** words have |ə bəl| spelled *-able*?
D. Which **three** words have |ə bəl| spelled *-ible*?

■ **Now write the five Challenge Words.** Underline the suffix in each word.

> *Spelling-Meaning Hint*   *Resident* and *reside* have different vowel sounds but are related in spelling and meaning. **Think of this:** You must *reside* within the Tampa city limits to be a *resident* of Tampa.

resident
reside

Independent Practice

Spelling-Meaning   Look at the Spelling-Meaning Hint.
1-2. Write *reside.* Then write the Basic Word that is related in spelling and meaning to *reside.*

Word Analysis   Complete the exercise with Basic Words.
3-8. Write the Basic Word that has each base word below.

   3. profit   **5.** differ   **7.** honor
   4. fashion   **6.** laugh   **8.** value

Word Clues   Write the Basic Word that fits each clue.

  9. at ease   **13.** an unexpected event
10. not occupied   **14.** sensible
11. extraordinary **15.** capable of being done
12. proper

■ **Challenge Words**   Write the Challenge Word that fits each meaning. Use your Spelling Dictionary.
  16. wasteful
  17. able to take hard wear
  18. marked by good taste
  19. widely known
  20. able to be worn or used with either side out

Summing Up

The suffixes *-ent* and *-ant* and the suffixes *-able* and *-ible* sound alike but are spelled differently. The spellings of these suffixes have to be remembered.

Basic

1. fashionable
2. comfortable
3. different
4. suitable
5. merchant
6. profitable
7. student
8. possible
9. resident
10. terrible
11. absent
12. vacant
13. servant
14. valuable
15. accident
16. horrible
17. honorable
18. reasonable
19. remarkable
20. laughable

■ Challenge

21. elegant
22. prominent
23. extravagant
24. durable
25. reversible

Review

1. current
2. important
3. moment
4. silent
5. parent

Expanding Vocabulary

The Latin Root *vac* A vacant house is not occupied. A vacuum has nothing in it. *Vacant* and *vacuum* each have the root *vac*.

ROOT	MEANING	WORDS
vac	empty	**vac**ant, **vac**uum

Practice **Write the word that completes each sentence. Underline the Latin root. Use your Spelling Dictionary.**

vacate   vacuum   vacancy   evacuate   vacant

1. We played baseball on a ____ lot.
2. There is nothing in a ____ , not even air.
3. We must either sign a lease or ____ our apartment.
4. The residents had to ____ the burning building.
5. We could not stay at the hotel because it had no ____ .

Proofreading

Using *I* and *me* Use *I* as the subject of a sentence or after forms of *be*. Use *me* after action verbs or prepositions. When using *I* or *me* with nouns or other pronouns, name yourself last.

Pat and I bought jeans.   These jeans look good on me.

Practice **Proofread this ad. Find four misspelled words and three errors in using *I* and *me*. Write the ad correctly.**

I am Mike Mars, speaking for Jax jeans. You and me are no diffrent when it comes to jeans. It's importent for I and you to be comfortable and fashonable. Try these remarkable jeans now!

Syllable Scramble   Rearrange the syllables to write a Basic or Review Word. One syllable in each item is extra.

1. ri hor pre ble
2. a son ble en rea
3. tant cap por im
4. ble fort ion a com
5. u ble trans a val
6. ment cre mo
7. cant pre va

8. a hon tion or ble
9. ble fer pos si
10. a suit de ble
11. in re a ble mark
12. ble ate ri ter
13. ci dent com ac

Suffix Clues   Write the Basic or Review Word that fits each clue.

14. What *ent* word studies hard?
15. What *ent* word is not the same as something else?
16. What *ent* word is part of the present?
17. What *able* word is very funny?
18. What *ent* word has no sound?
19. What *ant* word will serve you?
20. What *ent* word lives in a particular place?
21. What *ant* word sells goods?
22. What *ent* word has children?
23. What *ent* word is not present?
24. What *able* word makes money?
25. What *able* word is never out of style?

■ **Challenge Words**   Look at the Suffix Clues activity. Write five similar questions that can be answered with the Challenge Words. Write the answers on the back of your paper. Trade papers with a classmate, and answer each other's questions.

Writing Application: Creative Writing A shoe company is making a fancy new sneaker. Name the sneaker, and write the words for a catchy song for the product. Try to use five words from the list on page 206.

33 Spelling Across the Curriculum

Business: *Fashion*

Theme Vocabulary

fad
tailor
garment
designer
fabric
boutique
modeling
alteration

Using Vocabulary Write the Vocabulary Words to complete the paragraph. Use your Spelling Dictionary.

How is a dress, a suit, or any stylish __(1)__ made? A fashion __(2)__ creates the style. He or she also chooses the type of __(3)__ from which to make a sample. The sample is sewn by a __(4)__ , who may suggest a change, or __(5)__ , in the design. The next step is __(6)__ the sample in a fashion show. If the buyers at the show like the sample, you may soon see the style in a clothing store or a __(7)__ . If the style is popular, it may start a __(8)__ !

Understanding Vocabulary Write the Vocabulary Word that fits each clue.

9. This job may be done in front of a camera.
10. Expensive perfumes might be sold here.
11. This is chosen for its pattern and texture.
12. This is here today but gone tomorrow.

FACT FILE

Long ago in Japan a belted robe called a kimono was the fashion for both men and women. Today kimonos are worn mainly for special events and ceremonies, such as weddings.

Enrichment 33

👪 *Changing Fashions*

Did you know that Greeks and Romans used to wear togas or that it was once fashionable for women to weave birds' nests into their hair? Divide your class into small groups. With your group research the fashions worn during a particular period in history. On separate sheets of paper, draw pictures of and describe the clothing worn during that period. Try to use some words from the unit lists. Staple the pages together to make a fashion magazine.

📖 *Writing*
A Fashion Guide

Write a fashion guide of do's and don't's for young people. Describe the kind of clothing you consider proper and stylish for different occasions, such as school, parties, or special events. Then describe styles you would *not* recommend. Use a separate sheet of paper for each occasion. Try to use words from the lists in this unit. Be sure to proofread your guide.

FUTURE FASHIONS

What will people wear in the future? Will cloth change its color to match its surroundings? Will sports clothes glow in the dark for safety? Design some clothing for the twenty-first century. Then write an ad for your clothing. Try to use some words from the lists in this unit.

(Theme: National Parks)

34 Three-Syllable Words

LOOK
at each word.

SAY
each word.

Basic Words   ■ **Challenge**

1. wilderness
2. vacation
3. president
4. popular
5. memory
6. monument
7. educate
8. general
9. regular
10. avenue

11. canary
12. potato
13. energy
14. deposit
15. period
16. industry
17. uniform
18. condition
19. romantic
20. attention

21. *majestic*
22. *reverence*
23. *astonish*
24. *stimulate*
25. *obvious*

THINK
about the words.

Each word has three syllables. To help you spell the words, divide them into syllables. Look for familiar patterns. Note the spelling of the two syllables that are unstressed or have secondary stress. Spell the words by syllables.

va | ca | tion |vā kā′ shən| **ed | u | cate** |ĕj′ə kāt′|

• Where is each word divided into syllables? What familiar patterns do you see?

WRITE
the words.

Practice   Write the Basic Words to answer the questions. Underline the unstressed syllables in each word. Use your Spelling Dictionary.

CHECK
your spelling.

A. Which **thirteen** words have a stressed first syllable?

B. Which **seven** words have a stressed second syllable?

■ **Now write the five Challenge Words.** Underline the unstressed syllables.

> *Spelling-Meaning Hint*   How can you remember how
> to spell the final |ər| sounds in *regular*? Think of the |ăr|
> sounds in the related word *regularity*.

regular
regular ity

Independent Practice

Spelling-Meaning   Look at the Spelling-Meaning Hint.

1-2. Write *regular* and *regularity*. Then underline the two letters
in *regularity* that help you remember how to spell the final
|ər| sounds in *regular*.

Word Analysis   Complete the exercises with Basic Words.

3-6. Write the four words that end with the |ē| sound spelled *y*.

7-9. Write the three words that end with the suffix *-ion*.

Analogies   Write the Basic Word that completes each analogy.

10. *Doctor* is to *heal* as *teacher* is to ____ .
11. *Navy* is to *admiral* as *army* is to ____ .
12. *Fruit* is to *apple* as *vegetable* is to ____ .
13. *Team* is to *captain* as *government* is to ____ .
14. *Keen* is to *sharp* as *well-liked* is to ____ .
15. *Actor* is to *costume* as *police officer* is to ____ .

■ **Challenge Words**   Write the Challenge Word that fits each
meaning. Use your Spelling Dictionary.

16. deep respect   **18.** easy to see   **20.** to surprise
17. to make active   **19.** stately

Summing Up

A three-syllable word has one stressed syllable and two syllables
with less stress. To help you spell the word, divide the word into
syllables. Note the spelling of the syllables that have less stress.
Spell the word by syllables.

Basic

1. wilderness
2. vacation
3. president
4. popular
5. memory
6. monument
7. educate
8. general
9. regular
10. avenue
11. canary
12. potato
13. energy
14. deposit
15. period
16. industry
17. uniform
18. condition
19. romantic
20. attention

■ Challenge

21. majestic
22. reverence
23. astonish
24. stimulate
25. obvious

Review

1. beautiful
2. remember
3. library
4. another
5. enemy

Expanding Vocabulary

Synonyms What synonym can replace *regular* in this sentence?

>   Alan makes **regular** visits to the dentist.

Your Thesaurus gives two synonyms for *regular*: *common* and *routine*. The definitions and example sentences show that *routine* would be the better synonym to replace *regular*.

Practice **Find each underlined word in your Thesaurus. Write the synonym that can replace each word.**

1. The large wrench helped the plumber to <u>join</u> the pipes.
2. We took three <u>different</u> cars to the football game.
3. The rancher's son had little <u>knowledge</u> of city life.
4. Heidi liked the <u>taste</u> of the colorful vegetable.
5. The admiral decided to change an important <u>order</u>.
6. Cara saw the dinosaur <u>display</u> at the Science Museum.

Dictionary

Prefixes Dictionaries list prefixes in alphabetical order among the entry words. A hyphen follows the prefix.

> **uni-** A prefix that means "one, single": *unicycle.*

You will not find a dictionary entry for every word with a prefix, but you can look up the base word and the prefix separately. Then you can combine their meanings.

Practice **Look up the prefix and the base word of each word below in your Spelling Dictionary. Then write the meaning of each word listed below.**

1. preboard   3. inexact
2. reship   4. dissimilar

Review: Spelling Spree

Hidden Words   Write the Basic or Review Word that is hidden in each row of letters. Don't let the other words fool you!

Example: c a m p e r i o d d l y *period*

1. g a m e m o r y o l e
2. l i p o t a t o m i c
3. w i n d u s t r y o u t
4. t r o p i c a n a r y e
5. l i m p o p u l a r g e
6. f u n i f o r m a l l y
7. w h e n e r g y r o
8. f a r e m e m b e r b
9. e c o n d i t i o n y
10. r e d u c a t e r i n
11. m e n e m y p u m
12. h e r o m a n t i c h
13. t a n o t h e r m o s
14. c r a v e n u e t t a
15. d r e g u l a r v a
16. s p r e s i d e n t i

Proofreading   **17-25.** Find nine misspelled Basic or Review Words in this article. Write each word correctly.

▲▲▲▲▲▲▲▲▲▲▲▲▲▲▲▲▲▲▲▲▲▲▲▲▲▲▲▲▲▲▲▲▲▲

Visitors to the Dinosaur Quarry, a popular national monewment and vakation spot, can watch workers dig up dinosaur fossils from an ancient time peroid. Dinosaur skeletons in perfect condition have been found in this beutiful wildaness, which is located in Colorado and Utah. The quarry, with its amazing deposite of fossils, has drawn attenshun from scientists and the genaral public. Books about the area are available in any libary.

▼▼▼▼▼▼▼▼▼▼▼▼▼▼▼▼▼▼▼▼▼▼▼▼▼▼▼▼▼▼▼▼▼▼

■ **Challenge Words**   Make a mini-thesaurus. Find one synonym for each Challenge Word. Write the Challenge Word and its synonym. Write a definition and a sample sentence for every word. Use your Spelling Dictionary and a class dictionary.

📖 *Writing Application:* A Personal Narrative   Write a story about a visit you made to a national park or another park. What did you see there? What did you do? Try to use five words from the list on page 212.

Crystal Lake

34 Spelling Across the Curriculum

Social Studies: *National Parks*

Theme Vocabulary
Everglades
Yosemite
Grand Canyon
Yellowstone
Glacier
Shenandoah
Badlands
Acadia

Using Vocabulary Write the Vocabulary Words to complete the paragraph. Use your Spelling Dictionary.

Explore our national parks. See the colored, mile-deep walls of the _(1)_. Admire the Blue Ridge Mountains in Virginia's _(2)_ National Park. Walk the Maine coast in _(3)_ National Park. See fossils in the cliffs of South Dakota's _(4)_. Explore Florida's _(5)_, a vast swamp. Walk on rivers of ice in _(6)_ National Park. Time the eruptions of Old Faithful in _(7)_. Don't forget the spectacular waterfalls in _(8)_!

Understanding Vocabulary Write the Vocabulary Word that fits each clue.

9. The Colorado River runs through this park.
10. This park lies in Montana and borders Canada.
11. Established in 1872, this was the first national park.
12. Granite mountains line the seashores of this park.

FACT FILE

Petrified Forest National Park in Arizona contains the stonelike fossil remains of thousands of trees. These giant trees lived about one hundred and fifty million years ago.

Enrichment

America's Wonderlands

With a partner research one of our national parks. An encyclopedia will give a complete list of the parks. To get more information you can write to the National Park Service as well as do research in the library. Prepare a presentation for your class. Tell where the park is located, how big it is, when it was founded, and what the sights are. If possible, bring in maps and photographs to make your talk more interesting.

A PARK OF YOUR OWN

If you could design your own park, what would it look like? Draw a map of your park. Show the locations of the scenic spots, roads, and information centers as well as any recreational areas. Label each feature of your park. Share your map with your classmates.

Writing
A Tame Talk

Imagine that you are going to interview Wilderness Willy, a ranger with the National Park Service. Write a list of questions to ask him. Then write an interview between you and Willy, using your questions and supplying his answers. Try to use words from the lists in this unit. Be sure to proofread your interview.

(Theme: Summer Olympic Games)

35 More Three-Syllable Words

LOOK
at each word.

SAY
each word.

Basic Words   ■ **Challenge**

1. champion
2. stadium
3. history
4. dangerous
5. slippery
6. favorite
7. personal
8. continue
9. division
10. apartment

11. violet
12. emotion
13. typical
14. imagine
15. grocery
16. consider
17. property
18. festival
19. companion
20. sensitive

21. Olympics
22. muscular
23. amateur
24. spectator
25. ovation

THINK
about the words.

Each word has three syllables. One syllable is stressed. The other syllables are unstressed. To help you spell each word, divide the word into syllables. Look for familiar spelling patterns. Note the spelling of the unstressed syllables.

cham | pi | on |chăm′ pē ən| **di | vi | sion** |dĭ vĭzh′ ən|

• Where is each word divided into syllables? What familiar spelling patterns do you see?

WRITE
the words.

Practice **Write the Basic Words to answer the questions.** Underline the unstressed syllables in each word. You may want to use your Spelling Dictionary.

CHECK
your spelling.

A. Which **thirteen** words have a stressed first syllable?

B. Which **seven** words have a stressed second syllable?

■ **Now write the five Challenge Words.** Underline the unstressed syllables.

> ***Spelling-Meaning Hint*** How can you remember how to spell the schwa sound in *history*? Think of the |ôr| sounds in the related word *historical*.

hist◻ry
hist◻◻ical

Independent Practice

Spelling-Meaning Look at the Spelling-Meaning Hint.
  1-2. Write *historical*. Then write the Basic Word that is related to *historical*.

Word Analysis Complete the exercises with Basic Words.

  3-4. Write the two words that begin with the prefix *con-*.

5-10. Write the Basic Word that is formed from each base word below.

5. slip	**8.** sense
6. favor	**9.** danger
7. person	**10.** image

Classifying Write the Basic Word that belongs in each group.
11. rose, lily, ＿＿   **14.** shop, market, ＿＿
12. friend, buddy, ＿＿   **15.** addition, subtraction, ＿＿
13. house, cabin, ＿＿

■ **Challenge Words** Write the Challenge Word that fits each clue. Use your Spelling Dictionary.
16. someone in the audience   **19.** antonym of *professional*
17. having strong muscles   **20.** athletic competition
18. a big round of applause   originating in Greece

Summing Up

To help you spell a three-syllable word, divide the word into syllables. Look for familiar spelling patterns. Note carefully the spelling of the unstressed syllables, and spell the word by syllables.

Expanding Vocabulary

The Suffix -ous "Danger! Thin Ice!" These words warn skaters that a lake is a dangerous, or unsafe, place to skate. *Dangerous* has the base word *danger* and the suffix *-ous*, meaning "full of" or "having."

danger + ous = danger**ous**   "full of danger"
fame   + ous = fam**ous**   "having fame"
vary   + ous = vari**ous**   "having variety"

The spelling of the base word may change when *-ous* is added.

Practice   **Add -ous to each base word to write a word that fits each meaning. Use your Spelling Dictionary.**

space   mystery   harmony   mountain   fury

1. having mountains   **3.** having harmony   **5.** full of fury
2. full of mystery   **4.** having space

Proofreading

Contractions   A **contraction** is a shortened form of two words, usually a verb and *not* or a pronoun and a verb. An apostrophe replaces the dropped letters. (See page 250 in your Student's Handbook for other contractions.)

would not = wouldn't   cannot = can't   she is = she's

Practice   **Proofread this notice for four misspelled words and two missing apostrophes. Write the notice correctly.**

The track events start tomorow and continnue all week. Its your personel responsibility to get to the stadium on time. Dont be late. Have a companion remind you of your schedule.

Review: Spelling Spree

Puzzle Play   Write a Basic or Review Word to fit each clue. Circle the letter that would appear in the box. Write these letters in order to spell three mystery words that name an award.

Example: risky _ _ _ _ _☐_ _ _ *dangerous*

1. like best _☐_ _ _ _ _ _

2. sore _ _ _☐_ _ _ _ _

3. keep up _ _ _ _☐_ _ _

4. slick _☐_ _ _ _ _ _

5. 10 ÷ 5 _ _☐_ _ _ _ _

6. think of _ _ _ _ _ _☐_

7. with _ _ _ _ _ _ _☐

8. pretend _☐_ _ _ _ _ _

9. feeling ☐_ _ _ _ _ _ _

10. arena _ _ _☐_ _ _ _

11. pal _ _ _ _☐_ _ _ _

12. ordinary _ _ _ _ _ _☐

Using Clues   Write a Basic or Review Word to fit each clue.

13. This is another name for land or real estate.

14. The things sold here are canned, frozen, or fresh.

15. Doctors and nurses work here.

16. This is a school subject.

17. This is the day after today.

18. This is the day before today.

19. These kinds of thoughts might be written in a diary.

20. This publication may contain articles and short stories.

21. You get this color when you mix red and blue.

22. This is another name for a winner.

23. This usually has a bedroom, a bathroom, and a kitchen.

24. Driving over the speed limit is this.

25. This might include a parade and special foods.

■ **Challenge Words**   Look at the Using Clues activity. Write a clue for each Challenge Word. Write your answers on the back of your paper. Have a classmate answer your clues.

📖 *Writing Application:* A Character Sketch   Does a champion always have to win? Should a champion be sensitive? Write a description of the ideal champion. Try to use five words from the list on page 218.

35 Spelling Across the Curriculum

Recreation: *Summer Olympic Games*

Theme Vocabulary

gymnastics
marathon
discus
javelin
fencing
decathlon
vault
kayak

Using Vocabulary Write the Vocabulary Words to complete the paragraph. Use your Spelling Dictionary.

The Summer Olympic Games include a variety of events, such as paddling a __(1)__ over a 1000-meter course, __(2)__ with a sword, running a 26-mile __(3)__ , and performing acrobatic tricks in __(4)__ . The toughest event is the __(5)__ , which actually includes ten events. As part of this contest an athlete must use a pole to __(6)__ over a high crossbar, throw a spear called a __(7)__ , hurl a round __(8)__ , and compete in track events.

Understanding Vocabulary Write *yes* if the underlined word is used correctly. Write *no* if it is not.

9. The runners were exhausted after the <u>marathon</u>.
10. An athlete gripped the <u>decathlon</u> with his fingers.
11. The <u>kayak</u> cut through the water like a knife.
12. The pointed tip of the <u>discus</u> pierced the earth.

FACT FILE

The Olympic Games began in ancient Greece as a festival to honor the Greek god Zeus. The word *Olympic* comes from Mount Olympus, where Zeus was believed to live.

Enrichment 35

👪 *Olympic Games Chart*

The Summer Olympic Games include archery, cycling, field hockey, swimming, basketball, and many track and field events. With a classmate make a chart of the games. List at least ten events, and write a brief description of each one. Try to use words from the lists in this unit. Then draw pictures or find photographs in magazines and newspapers to illustrate some of the games.

📖 *Writing*
Olympic Champion

You have just won a gold medal in an Olympic event! Imagine standing on the winner's platform while the band plays your national anthem. How did you achieve this success? Describe the years of training and the day of the contest. Try to use words from the lists in this unit. Be sure to proofread your story.

SYLLABILITY

Make a puzzle, using a full-page magazine picture. Paste the picture on heavy paper. Draw six squares across the picture and ten squares down. Write two Basic Words across each row of the puzzle, one syllable to a square. Cut out the squares, and mix them up. Have a classmate put your puzzle together.

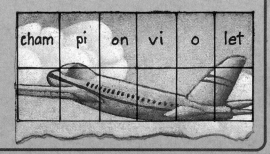

cham | pi | on | vi | o | let

36 Review: Units 31–35

Unit 31   More Words with *-ion*   pp. 192-197

pollute **-ion**
pollution

| impress | pollute | migrate | express | imitate |
| impression | pollution | migration | expression | imitation |

Remember: If a verb ends with **e**, drop the **e** when **-ion** is added. If a verb does not end with **e**, just add **-ion**.

Write the verb that fits each clue.
1. to have an effect on
2. to make known
3. what car fumes do
4. what many birds do
5. to copy

Write the noun form of each verb.
6. migrate
7. imitate
8. pollute
9. impress
10. express

Unit 32   More Words with Prefixes   pp. 198-203

com-
con-
en-
ex-
pre-
pro-

| concern | excite | preserve | enforce | propose |
| compound | consent | prefix | enclose | extend |

Remember: Com-, con-, en-, ex-, pre-, and **pro-** are prefixes. To spell a word with a prefix, find the prefix and the base word or word root. Spell the word by parts.

Write the word that belongs in each group.
11. spread, expand, ____
12. suggest, present, ____
13. agree, approve, ____
14. worry, trouble, ____

Write the word that fits each clue.
15. rhymes with *suffix*
16. a word such as *baseball*
17. to surround
18. to freeze, can, or pickle
19. to make others obey
20. rhymes with *ignite*

Half of the words from each unit are reviewed on these pages.
The rest are reviewed on pages 244–246.

Review **36**

Unit 33   *-ent, -ant; -able, -ible*   pp. 204-209

| terrible | comfortable | different | merchant | resident |
| absent | horrible | reasonable | laughable | vacant |

Remember: |ənt| → **-ent, -ant** |ə bəl| → **-able, -ible**

suit **able**
poss **ible**

Write the words to complete the sentences.

21. In our neighborhood we have a ____ lot for playing ball.

22. Tammy has been a ____ of Georgia for two years.

23. Lila loves to curl up in a ____ chair and read a book.

24. A local ____ is having a sale on blue jeans.

25. John is ____ from school today.

Write the words that are forms of the words below.

26. terror   **28.** laugh   **30.** differ

27. horror   **29.** reason

Unit 34   Three-Syllable Words   pp. 210-215

| popular | memory | vacation | wilderness | monument |
| potato | canary | industry | condition | energy |

Remember: A three-syllable word has one stressed syllable
and two syllables with less stress or no stress.

va   ca   tion

Write the words to complete the sentences.

31. Coal mining is an important ____ in West Virginia.

32. Elk living in the ____ travel in herds.

33. This summer we will spend our ____ in the mountains.

34. In honor of the soldiers, the town built a ____ .

Write the word that fits each meaning.

35. well-liked   **37.** the ability to remember   **39.** a songbird

36. power   **38.** working order   **40.** a vegetable

36 Review

Unit 35   More Three-Syllable Words   pp. 216-221

stadium	division	slippery	champion	dangerous
emotion	property	grocery	typical	companion

cham pi **on**

Remember: A three-syllable word has one stressed syllable and two syllables with less stress or no stress.

Write the word that completes each analogy.

41. *Numerous* is to *few* as *unusual* is to ____ .
42. *Hockey* is to *rink* as *football* is to ____ .
43. *Safe* is to *secure* as *risky* is to ____ .
44. *Sandpaper* is to *rough* as *oil* is to ____ .

Write the word that fits each clue.

45. love, sorrow, joy   47. a hero   49. a market
46. possessions   48. separation   50. friend

■ Challenge Words   Units 31-35   pp. 192-221

enactment	astonish	contaminate	extravagant
reversible	muscular	contamination	procedure
spectator	stimulate		

Write the word that fits each clue.

51. excite 52. strong 53. impurity 54. viewer 55. amaze

Write a word that can replace each underlined word or phrase.

56. This jacket is <u>wearable on both sides</u>.
57. This outfit is much too <u>expensive</u> for me to buy.
58. Control the fumes so that they do not <u>pollute</u> the air.
59. To assemble the tent, follow this simple <u>series of steps</u>.
60. The <u>passage</u> of the new law will change the length of the school year.

Spelling-Meaning Strategy

The Latin Word Root *spect*

Did you know that *inspect* and *spectator* are related in meaning? Each word has the Latin word root *spect*, meaning "to look." When you inspect something, you look at it carefully. A spectator is someone who looks at an event. Knowing the meaning of *spect* can help you spell and understand other words with this same word root.

Here is a list of words that contain the Latin word root *spect*.

in**spect**	**spect**ator	su**spect**
spectrum	in**spect**or	**spect**acle

in**spect**
spectator

Think

- Look up each word in the word box above in your Spelling Dictionary. How does the word root *spect* affect the meaning of each word?

Apply and Extend

Complete these activities on a separate piece of paper.

1. Write six sentences, using one word from the word box above in each sentence. Can you make the meaning of each word clear?
2. With a partner list as many other words as you can that include the Latin root *spect*. Then look on page 274 of your Spelling-Meaning Index. Add any other words that you find with this word root to your list.

Summing Up The Latin word root *spect* means "to look." Words that have the same Latin word root are related in spelling and meaning. Knowing the meaning of the word root *spect* can help you understand and spell the words in that family.

LITERATURE AND WRITING

Research Report

Electric eels have unusual abilities. What part of the electric eel produces electricity?

The electric eel uses its electricity in several ways. When it swims, a small "battery" in its tail sends out weak electric pulses at a rate of twenty to fifty a second. The eel uses these electric pulses to find its way. They bounce off objects and come back to special pits in the eel's head. The eel uses electricity in much the same way that bats use sound to find their way around. Scientists think that the electric eel may also use electricity to communicate with other eels.

from Nature's Champions *by Alvin and Virginia Silverstein*

Think and Discuss

1. What part of the electric eel sends out electric pulses?
2. What is the **main idea** of this paragraph? What is the **topic sentence**?
3. What **facts** did you learn about how the electric eel uses its electricity?

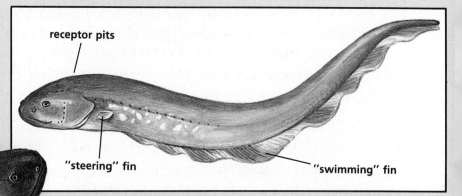

receptor pits

"steering" fin

"swimming" fin

The Writing Process

The paragraph on page 226 gives **facts** about electric eels. When you write a research report, include only facts, not opinions, about your topic. Each paragraph should have a **topic sentence** that states the **main idea**. The other sentences should give **details** that support the main idea.

Assignment: Write a Research Report

Steps One and Two: Prewriting and Planning

1. Make a list of topics you would like to learn about. Discuss them with a classmate, and choose one.
2. Write five questions to answer in your report.
3. Find facts to answer your questions. Take notes.
4. Organize your notes into an outline.

Step Three: Write a First Draft

1. Follow your outline as you write.
2. Think about your purpose and your audience.
3. Do not worry about mistakes—just write!

Step Four: Revise

1. Does each paragraph have a topic sentence and supporting details? Are the facts explained clearly?
2. Use your Thesaurus to help you find exact words.
3. Read your report to a classmate. Make other changes.

Step Five: Proofread

1. Did you capitalize and punctuate correctly?
2. Did you spell all words correctly? Copy any words that you misspelled into your Notebook for Writing.

Step Six: Publish

Copy your report neatly. Display it with related books.

Composition Words

protection
president
pollution
different
remarkable
popular
history
dangerous

Proofreading Marks

¶ Indent
∧ Add something
ℓ Take out something
≡ Capitalize
/ Make a small letter

Student's Handbook

Extra Practice and Review   Cycle 1

Unit 1   Short Vowels   pp. 12-17

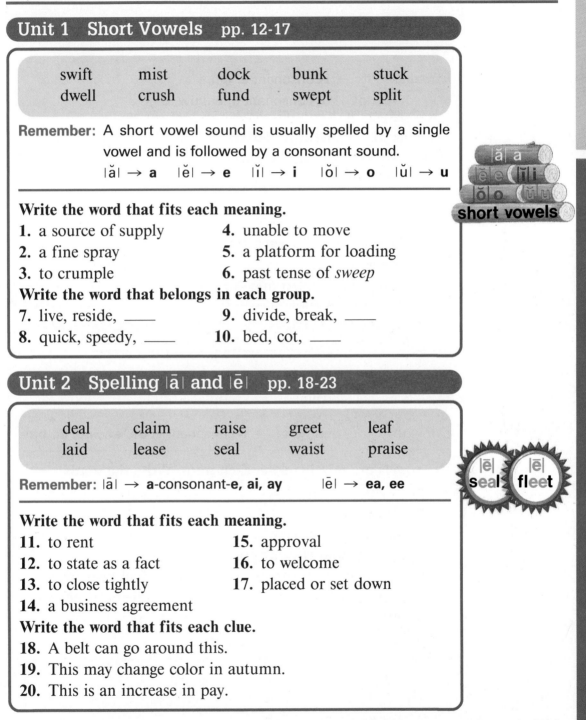

| swift | mist | dock | bunk | stuck |
| dwell | crush | fund | swept | split |

Remember: A short vowel sound is usually spelled by a single vowel and is followed by a consonant sound.

|ă| → **a** |ĕ| → **e** |ĭ| → **i** |ŏ| → **o** |ŭ| → **u**

short vowels

Write the word that fits each meaning.

1. a source of supply
2. a fine spray
3. to crumple
4. unable to move
5. a platform for loading
6. past tense of *sweep*

Write the word that belongs in each group.

7. live, reside, ____
8. quick, speedy, ____
9. divide, break, ____
10. bed, cot, ____

Unit 2   Spelling |ā| and |ē| pp. 18-23

| deal | claim | raise | greet | leaf |
| laid | lease | seal | waist | praise |

Remember: |ā| → **a-consonant-e, ai, ay** |ē| → **ea, ee**

|ē| seal |ē| fleet

Write the word that fits each meaning.

11. to rent
12. to state as a fact
13. to close tightly
14. a business agreement
15. approval
16. to welcome
17. placed or set down

Write the word that fits each clue.

18. A belt can go around this.
19. This may change color in autumn.
20. This is an increase in pay.

Cycle 1

Unit 3   Spelling |ī| and |ō| pp. 24-29

thrown	strike	sign	stole	boast
code	slope	slight	flow	hose

Remember: |ī| → **i-consonant-e, igh, i**

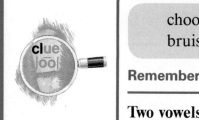

o-consonant-e

|ō| → **o-consonant-e, oa, ow, o**

Combine the underlined letters in the first word with the underlined letters in the second word. Write the new word.

21. <u>str</u>aw + b<u>ike</u>
22. <u>fl</u>ing + m<u>ow</u>
23. <u>sl</u>im + h<u>ope</u>
24. <u>st</u>em + m<u>ole</u>
25. <u>thr</u>ee + sh<u>own</u>
26. <u>sl</u>ick + n<u>ight</u>

Write the word that fits each clue.

27. stockings or socks
28. what a proud person may do
29. secret writing
30. to write one's name

Unit 4   Spelling |o͞o| and |yo͞o| pp. 30-35

choose	proof	route	troop	rule
bruise	rude	scoop	flute	loop

Remember: |o͞o| and |yo͞o| → **u-consonant-e, ue, ew, oo, ui, ou**

Two vowels are missing from each word. Write the words.

31. pr __ __ f
32. br __ __ se
33. r __ __ te
34. sc __ __ p
35. ch __ __ se

Write the word that fits each meaning.

36. not considerate of others
37. a group of soldiers
38. a circular path or pattern
39. a musical instrument
40. a statement or principle that controls behavior

Unit 5 Spelling |ou|, |ô|, and |oi| pp. 36-41

Cycle 1

hawk	tower	bald	claw	prowl
coward	haunt	drown	fault	royal

Remember: |ou| → **ou, ow** |ô| → **aw, au, a** before **l**

     |oi| → **oi, oy**

|ô|

aw au a+l

Change the underlined letter in each word to a different letter. Write the new word.

41. b<u>o</u>ld   **43.** g<u>a</u>wk   **45.** <u>v</u>ault   **47.** <u>f</u>law

42. <u>b</u>rown   **44.** <u>p</u>ower   **46.** <u>l</u>oyal

Write the word that completes each sentence.

48. At night cats like to ____ around my neighborhood.

49. Choosing not to fight does not mean one is a ____ .

50. Kay loved to win, but a defeat would ____ her for days.

■ Challenge Words Units 1-5 pp. 12-41

nominate	reproach	plight	presume	trek
campaign	pursuit	mascot	awkward	site
intrude	grouse	poise	rustic	cease

Write the word that fits each meaning.

51. the act of chasing

52. countrylike

53. a slow, hard journey

54. not graceful

55. organized activity to gain a goal

56. to suppose to be true

57. blame or disapproval

58. to select as a candidate

59. a position or a location

60. someone or something believed to bring good luck

Write the word that belongs in each group.

61. trespass, invade, ____

62. problem, difficulty, ____

63. sureness, confidence, ____

64. stop, halt, ____

65. turkey, quail, ____

Cycle 2

flare flair

|ār|

Unit 7 Spelling |ôr|, |âr|, and |är| pp. 48-53

hare	scar	lord	sore	torch
tore	flare	fare	rare	barge

Remember: |ôr| → **or, ore, oar** |âr| → **are, air** |är| → **ar**

Write a word by changing the underlined letter in each word.
  1. blare   **2.** porch   **3.** star   **4.** large
Write the word that completes each analogy.
  5. *Ordinary* is to *common* as *unusual* is to ____ .
  6. *Wear* is to *wore* as *tear* is to ____ .
  7. *Burro* is to *donkey* as *jack rabbit* is to ____ .
  8. *Puffy* is to *swollen* as *painful* is to ____ .
  9. *Museum* is to *fee* as *bus* is to ____ .
  10. *Boss* is to *chief* as *nobleman* is to ____ .

Unit 8 Spelling |ûr| and |îr| pp. 54-59

blur	squirm	nerve	early	worth
term	steer	thirst	stern	hurl

Remember: |ûr| → **er, ir, ur, ear, or** |îr| → **eer, ear**

squirt

|ûr|

Two letters are missing from each word. Write the words.
  11. n __ __ ve   **14.** bl __ __
  12. th __ __ st   **15.** squ __ __ m
  13. h __ __ l   **16.** w __ __ th
Write the word that completes each sentence.
  17. The governor was elected to a second ____ in office.
  18. We left before sunrise to get an ____ start on our hike.
  19. The propeller of a boat is in the ____ , or rear.
  20. Try to ____ your bicycle away from potholes.

Unit 9 Compound Words pp. 60-65

Cycle 2

basketball cheerleader weekend everybody grandparent
highway shipyard daytime turnpike household

Remember: A compound word may be written as one word, as two or more words joined by hyphens, or as separate words.

daytime

Write the compound word that fits each clue.

21. Saturday and Sunday
22. a home and its activities
23. one who leads a cheering section
24. where boats are built
25. a wide road that drivers pay a toll to use

Write the compound word that contains part of each word below.

26. baseball
27. grandchild
28. nighttime
29. everyone
30. highlight

Unit 10 Homophones pp. 66-71

poll   main   loan   heal   pore
pole   mane   lone   heel   pour

Remember: Homophones are words that sound alike but have different spellings and meanings.

berry   bury

Write the word that completes each sentence.

31. I asked my sister to ____ me one of her sweaters.
32. Al stumbled when he caught his ____ on a root.
33. The only shade on the farm came from a ____ cottonwood.
34. A good scrubbing cleans every ____ of your skin.

Write the word that is a synonym for each word below.

35. rod
36. flow
37. chief
38. survey
39. mend
40. hair

Cycle 2

Unit 11 Final |ər| pp. 72-77

theater
actor
lunar

actor	powder	humor	anger	banner
matter	flavor	clover	burglar	tractor

Remember: The final |ər| sounds are often spelled **er, or,** or **ar** in words of more than one syllable.

Two letters are missing from each word. Write the words.

41. ang __ __   **44.** clov __ __

42. powd __ __   **45.** matt __ __

43. flav __ __

Write the word that belongs in each group.

46. stage, script, ____   **49.** plow, thresher, ____

47. comedy, joke, ____   **50.** robber, thief, ____

48. flag, sign, ____

■ Challenge Words Units 7-11 pp. 48-77

self-assured	unicorn	ordeal	clamor	canvas
quick-witted	scholar	emerge	yearn	canvass
limelight	chamber	career	hoard	

Write the word that belongs in each group.

51. uproar, racket, ____   **55.** collect, save, ____

52. arise, appear, ____   **56.** desire, want, ____

53. attention, publicity, ____   **57.** trial, hardship, ____

54. employment, occupation, ____

Write the word that fits each clue.

58. This person studies.   **63.** This is a synonym

59. An artist paints on this.   for *self-confident.*

60. People who take polls do this.   **64.** A bedroom or a

61. This is a synonym for *clever.*   living room is

62. This animal is not real.   one.

Unit 13   More Compound Words   pp. 84-89

Cycle 3

flashlight   classmate   baby-sit   sweetheart
touchdown   watermelon   masterpiece   whereabouts
worthwhile   part of speech

Remember: A compound word may be written as one word, as two or more words joined by hyphens, or as separate words.

Write the compound word that has each underlined part below.
1. <u>down</u>town
2. time<u>piece</u>
3. <u>part</u>-time
4. sit-<u>up</u>
5. <u>room</u>mate
6. water<u>fall</u>

Write the compound word that belongs in each group.
7. place, location, ____
8. lamp, lantern, ____
9. valuable, useful, ____
10. darling, valentine, ____

Unit 14   Final |l| or |əl| pp. 90-95

sparkle   angle   single   legal   angel
level   gentle   label   puzzle   ankle

Remember: The final |l| or |əl| sounds in a two-syllable word are often spelled **le, el,** or **al.**

Write the word that means the opposite of each word below.
11. illegal   12. harsh   13. married   14. tilted   15. devil

Write the word that completes each sentence.
16. Leah put gold paint on her valentine to make it ____.
17. Would you like to help me put together this jigsaw ____?
18. The contents of this box are listed on the ____.
19. A high-top sneaker supports your ____.
20. The view of the canyon is best from this ____.

Cycle 3

Unit 15   VCCV Pattern   pp. 96-101

| pattern | tunnel | collect | arrive | traffic |
| essay | publish | furnish | empire | sorrow |

Remember: To find the syllables of a VCCV word, divide the word between the two consonants.

Each word below is missing a syllable. Write the words.

21. tun I _____   23. em I _____   25. _____ I rive
22. _____ I lect   24. traf I _____   26. pub I _____

Write the word that is a synonym for each underlined word.

27. A store offered to <u>supply</u> the team with uniforms.
28. The fabric had a bright red polka dot <u>design</u>.
29. Kris proofread her <u>composition</u> about her trip.
30. A play about <u>sadness</u> is called a tragedy.

Unit 16   VCCCV Pattern   pp. 102-107

| improve | simply | explain | address | district |
| partner | monster | complex | mischief | orphan |

Remember: When two different consonants in a VCCCV word spell one sound or form a cluster, divide the word into syllables before or after the consonants.

Write the word that has each underlined syllable below.

31. <u>cor</u>ner   33. am<u>ply</u>
32. <u>ex</u>cite   34. <u>mis</u>take

Write the word that fits each clue.

35. synonym for *area*   38. a child without parents
36. 217 Baker Street   39. a frightening imaginary creature
37. to become better   40. difficult to understand

Unit 17   VV Pattern   pp. 108-113

giant	cruel	usual	idea	area
riot	diet	trial	lion	liar

Remember: When the two vowels in a VV pattern spell two vowel sounds, divide the word into syllables between the vowels.

v
cre

v
ate

Write the word that completes each analogy.
41. *Irregular* is to *strange* as *regular* is to ____ .
42. *Classroom* is to *lesson* as *courtroom* is to ____ .
43. *Mild* is to *harsh* as *kind* is to ____ .
44. *Small* is to *little* as *huge* is to ____ .
Two vowels are missing from each word. Write the words.
45. l _ _ r   **47.** r _ _ t   **49.** d _ _ t
46. id _ _   **48.** ar _ _   **50.** l _ _ n

■ Challenge Words   Units 13-17   pp. 84-113

appreciate	outspoken	extreme	abstain	vital
starry-eyed	exceed	Congress	neutral	mosaic
collide	mineral	awestruck	option	variety

Write the word that fits each meaning.
51. not to do   **54.** go beyond   **57.** to be thankful for
52. important   **55.** full of awe   **58.** not taking sides
53. farthest   **56.** crash   **59.** bold in speech
Write the word that completes each sentence.
60. The Romans mined copper, a ____ with many uses.
61. The President spoke to both houses of ____ .
62. Jo had the ____ of seeing three different movies.
63. The artist used colorful stone chips to form the ____ .
64. A salad can include a ____ of different vegetables.
65. Chen had youthful hope and confidence. He was ____ .

Cycle 4   Unit 19   VCV Pattern   pp. 120-125

evil	detail	value	repeat	nation
vanish	credit	prefer	adore	tulip

Remember: To find the syllables of a VCV word, divide the word before or after the consonant. Note carefully the spelling of the unstressed syllable.

Each word below is missing a syllable. Write the word.

1. tu l _____   **3.** e l _____   **5.** _____ l fer

2. van l _____   **4.** _____ l dore   **6.** na l _____

Write the word that fits each meaning.

7. to say or do again

8. what something is worth

9. a small part of a whole

10. belief or confidence in the truth of something

Unit 20   Words with -ed or -ing   pp. 126-131

borrowed	rising	supported	offered	freezing
awaiting	sheltered	seeking	decided	damaged

Remember: rise − e + ing = ris**ing**

shelter + ed = shelter**ed**

Write the word that fits each clue.

11. expecting   **13.** very cold   **15.** injured

12. kept from falling   **14.** volunteered   **16.** going up

Write the word that completes each sentence.

17. The jury finally _____ that the man on trial was innocent.

18. The doghouse Toni made _____ her pet comfortably.

19. I hope Klaus finds the kind of job he is _____.

20. Dana wore a baggy shirt she had _____ from her brother.

Unit 21   More Words with *-ed* or *-ing* pp. 132-137

Cycle 4

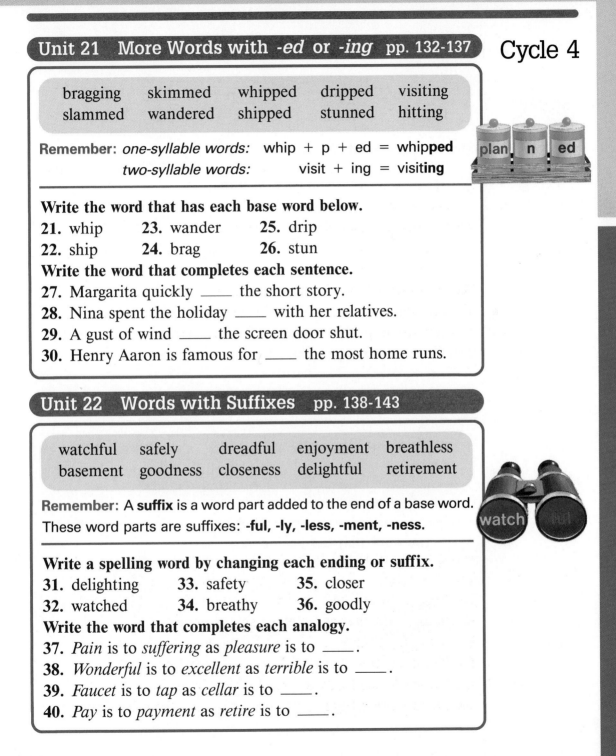

bragging skimmed whipped dripped visiting
slammed wandered shipped stunned hitting

Remember: *one-syllable words:* whip + p + ed = whip**ped**
           two-syllable words: visit + ing = visit**ing**

Write the word that has each base word below.
21. whip   23. wander   25. drip
22. ship   24. brag   26. stun

Write the word that completes each sentence.
27. Margarita quickly ____ the short story.
28. Nina spent the holiday ____ with her relatives.
29. A gust of wind ____ the screen door shut.
30. Henry Aaron is famous for ____ the most home runs.

Unit 22   Words with Suffixes   pp. 138-143

watchful safely dreadful enjoyment breathless
basement goodness closeness delightful retirement

Remember: A **suffix** is a word part added to the end of a base word.
These word parts are suffixes: **-ful, -ly, -less, -ment, -ness**.

Write a spelling word by changing each ending or suffix.
31. delighting   33. safety   35. closer
32. watched   34. breathy   36. goodly

Write the word that completes each analogy.
37. *Pain* is to *suffering* as *pleasure* is to ____ .
38. *Wonderful* is to *excellent* as *terrible* is to ____ .
39. *Faucet* is to *tap* as *cellar* is to ____ .
40. *Pay* is to *payment* as *retire* is to ____ .

Cycle 4

cul

Unit 23 Final |n| or |ən|, |chər|, |zhər| pp. 144-149

| adventure | captain | moisture | fountain | future |
| lecture | feature | pasture | fixture | measure |

Remember: |n| or |ən| → **ain** |chər| → **ture** |zhər| → **sure**

Write the word that fits each meaning.

41. the time that is to come
42. something that stays in place
43. one of the parts of the face
44. dampness
45. leader of a group
46. to find the size of

Write the word that completes each sentence.

47. The dentist gave Pepe a _____ about brushing his teeth.
48. I often get a drink of cool water at the _____.
49. A cow and her calf were grazing in the green _____.
50. Kate's camping trip in Alaska was a great _____.

■ Challenge Words   Units 19-23   pp. 120-149

contentment	departure	rehearsing	shredded	device
portraying	laser	suspenseful	villain	layered
dramatized	whirred	defenseless	logic	texture

Write the word that fits each clue.

51. acted out
52. uncertain
53. hummed
54. light beam
55. practicing
56. torn in strips
57. arranged in sheets
58. clear reasoning
59. playing the part of

Write the word that completes each analogy.

60. *Sadness* is to *gloominess* as *satisfaction* is to _____.
61. *Yo-yo* is to *toy* as *can opener* is to _____.
62. *Loud* is to *sound* as *rough* is to _____.
63. *Safe* is to *secure* as *unprotected* is to _____.
64. *Greeting* is to *arrival* as *farewell* is to _____.
65. *Good* is to *hero* as *evil* is to _____.

Unit 25 Final |ĭj|, |ĭv|, and |ĭs| pp. 156-161

Cycle 5

practice	native	luggage	postage	voyage
bandage	message	captive	shortage	passage

Remember: |ĭj| → **age** |ĭv| → **ive** |ĭs| → **ice**

Write the word that fits each clue.

1. This covers a wound.
2. This is a scarcity.
3. A ship or an airplane can take you on this.
4. This is a communication.
5. This is shown by a stamp.
6. This includes suitcases.

Write the word that belongs in each group. Underline the letters that spell the final |ĭv| sounds.

7. resident, citizen, _____
8. path, channel, _____
9. rehearsal, training, _____
10. trapped, imprisoned, _____

Unit 26 Unstressed Syllables pp. 162-167

carrot	hidden	entry	destroy	distance
blossom	ashamed	program	wisdom	solid

Remember: To spell a two-syllable word, divide the word into syllables. Note carefully the spelling of the unstressed syllable. Spell the word by syllables.

Write the word that has each underlined syllable.

11. milli<u>gram</u>   12. gar<u>den</u>   13. par<u>rot</u>   14. pan<u>try</u>

Write the word that fits each meaning.

15. feeling guilt
16. to bloom
17. strong and firm
18. to ruin completely
19. intelligence and good judgement
20. the amount of space between two places

Cycle 5

Unit 27   Words with Prefixes   pp. 168-173

report	unable	inform	remind	disaster
unaware	disagree	relax	display	insult

Remember: A **prefix** is a word part added to the beginning of a base word or a word root. These are prefixes: **dis-, re-, in-, un-**.

prefixes
un-
dis-
in-
re-

Add a prefix to each base word or word root. Write the words.

21. ____ l lax   23. ____ l form   25. ____ l aware

22. ____ l aster   24. ____ l port   26. ____ l sult

Write the word that completes each sentence.

27. Since I sprained my ankle, I am ____ to run very fast.

28. Tomas saw the book he wanted in the window ____.

29. These photos from last summer ____ me of the fun we had.

30. I will not vote for Smith because I ____ with his views.

Unit 28   Changing Final *y* to *i*   pp. 174-179

enemies	victories	armies	liberties	countries
ladies	emptiness	duties	lilies	worthiness

Remember: If a word ends with a consonant and **y**, change the **y** to **i** when adding an ending or a suffix.

Write the word formed by adding each base word and ending or suffix below.

31. empty + ness   33. enemy + es   35. worthy + ness

32. army + es   34. lily + es

Write the word that is a synonym for each word below.

36. nations   39. responsibilities

37. successes   40. freedoms

38. women

Unit 29 Adding *-ion* pp. 180-185

regulate	act	correct	tense	convict
regulation	action	correction	tension	conviction

Remember: If a verb ends with **e**, drop the **e** before adding **-ion**. If a verb does not end with **e**, just add **-ion**.

Write the word that completes each sentence.

41. The hero came on stage in the second ____ of the play.

42. My paper will have no errors after I make this ____.

43. Rather than complain, Jo took ____ to solve the problem.

44. Facts proved the man's innocence, so there was no ____.

Write the word that fits each meaning.

45. accurate   **47.** criminal   **49.** a rule

46. stress   **48.** anxious   **50.** to control

■ Challenge Words Units 25-29 pp. 156-185

superlative	primitive	levied	exert	animate
unnecessary	colonies	adapt	inflate	animation
rivalries	heritage	inquiry	somber	

Write the word that belongs in each group.

51. change, adjust, ____   **53.** simple, crude, ____

52. brighten, energize, ____   **54.** dark, gloomy, ____

Write the word that fits each clue.

55. synonym for *settlements*   **61.** synonym for *apply*

56. antonym of *needed*   **62.** synonym for *competitions*

57. synonym for *liveliness*   **63.** to fill with gas and expand

58. being the very best

59. imposed a tax   **64.** something handed down from earlier generations

60. the act of asking in order to find out

Cycle 6

Unit 31 More Words with *-ion* pp. 192-197

inspect	protect	promote	confess	decorate
inspection	protection	promotion	confession	decoration

Remember: If a verb ends with **e**, drop the **e** when **-ion** is added. If a verb does not end with **e**, just add **-ion**.

Write a word by changing each underlined prefix.

1. respect
2. detect
3. profession
4. remote

Write the word that fits each clue.

5. synonym for *admit*
6. an official examination
7. something put up for a party or a celebration
8. synonym for *beautify*
9. advancement in rank
10. what a guard provides

Unit 32 More Words with Prefixes pp. 198-203

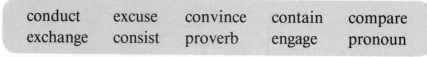

conduct	excuse	convince	contain	compare
exchange	consist	proverb	engage	pronoun

Remember: *Com-, con-, en-, ex-, pre-,* and *pro-* are prefixes. To spell a word with a prefix, find the prefix and the base word or word root. Spell the word by parts.

Write the word that fits each clue.

11. needed if you are late
12. synonym for *persuade*
13. takes the place of a noun
14. to swap
15. "Better late than never," for example

Write the word that rhymes with each word below.

16. insist
17. retain
18. prepare
19. deduct
20. enrage

Unit 33 *-ent, -ant; -able, -ible* pp. 204-209

Cycle 6

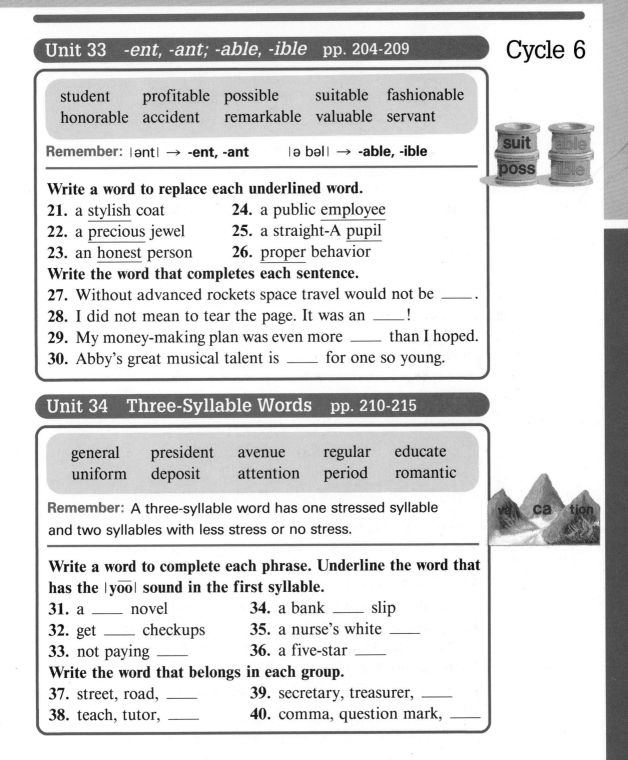

student   profitable   possible   suitable   fashionable
honorable   accident   remarkable   valuable   servant

Remember: |ənt| → **-ent, -ant** |ə bəl| → **-able, -ible**

Write a word to replace each underlined word.

21. a <u>stylish</u> coat
22. a <u>precious</u> jewel
23. an <u>honest</u> person
24. a public <u>employee</u>
25. a straight-A <u>pupil</u>
26. <u>proper</u> behavior

Write the word that completes each sentence.

27. Without advanced rockets space travel would not be ____ .
28. I did not mean to tear the page. It was an ____ !
29. My money-making plan was even more ____ than I hoped.
30. Abby's great musical talent is ____ for one so young.

Unit 34   Three-Syllable Words pp. 210-215

general   president   avenue   regular   educate
uniform   deposit   attention   period   romantic

Remember: A three-syllable word has one stressed syllable and two syllables with less stress or no stress.

Write a word to complete each phrase. Underline the word that has the |yōō| sound in the first syllable.

31. a ____ novel
32. get ____ checkups
33. not paying ____
34. a bank ____ slip
35. a nurse's white ____
36. a five-star ____

Write the word that belongs in each group.

37. street, road, ____
38. teach, tutor, ____
39. secretary, treasurer, ____
40. comma, question mark, ____

Cycle 6 Unit 35 More Three-Syllable Words pp. 216-221

cham pi on

| continue | personal | favorite | apartment | history |
| sensitive | consider | festival | violet | imagine |

Remember: A three-syllable word has one stressed syllable and two syllables with less stress or no stress.

Write a word by adding two syllables to each syllable below.

41. ___ l sid l ___   **43.** his l ___ ___   **45.** fa l ___ ___

42. ___ l mag l ___   **44.** ___ l tin l ___   **46.** sen l ___ ___

Write the word that completes each analogy.

47. *Fruit* is to *strawberry* as *flower* is to ____.

48. *Lone* is to *single* as *private* is to ____.

49. *Gathering* is to *meeting* as *celebration* is to ____.

50. *Fare* is to *airplane* as *rent* is to ____.

■ Challenge Words Units 31-35 pp. 192-221

preamble	Olympics	convene	durable	irritate
reverence	majestic	ovation	obvious	irritation
prominent	concise	elegant	amateur	

Write the word that is a synonym for each word below.

51. sturdy   **53.** respect   **55.** annoy   **57.** applause

52. brief   **54.** dignified   **56.** assemble

Write the word that completes each sentence.

58. The purpose of a document may be stated in the ____.

59. The new principal is a ____citizen.

60. Speed skating is my favorite event of the Winter ____.

61. Buzzing mosquitoes were a constant ____ on the hike.

62. Unlike a professional athlete, an ____ is not paid.

63. The decorations for the party were tasteful and ____.

64. I found an ____ spelling error in my essay.

Writer's Resources

Capitalization and Punctuation Guide

Abbreviations

	Abbreviations are shortened forms of words. Most abbreviations begin with a capital letter and end with a period. Use abbreviations only in special kinds of writing, such as addresses and lists.
Titles	Mr. *(Mister)* Mr. Juan Albano Sr. *(Senior)* John Helt, Sr. Mrs. *(Mistress)* Mrs. Frances Wong Jr. *(Junior)* John Helt, Jr. Ms. Leslie Clark Dr. *(Doctor)* Dr. Janice Dodd Note: *Miss* is not an abbreviation and does not end with a period.
Words used in addresses	St. *(Street)* Blvd. *(Boulevard)* Pkwy. *(Parkway)* Rd. *(Road)* Rte. *(Route)* Mt. *(Mount or Mountain)* Ave. *(Avenue)* Apt. *(Apartment)* Expy. *(Expressway)* Dr. *(Drive)*
Words used in business	Co. *(Company)* Inc. *(Incorporated)* Corp. *(Corporation)* Ltd. *(Limited)*
Other abbreviations	**Some abbreviations are written in all capital letters, with a letter standing for each important word.** P.D. *(Police Department)* P.O. *(Post Office)* J.P. *(Justice of the Peace)* R.N. *(Registered Nurse)*

The United States Postal Service uses two capital letters and no period in each of its state abbreviations.

AL *(Alabama)*	IA *(Iowa)*	NH *(New Hampshire)*
AK *(Alaska)*	KS *(Kansas)*	NJ *(New Jersey)*
AZ *(Arizona)*	KY *(Kentucky)*	NM *(New Mexico)*
AR *(Arkansas)*	LA *(Louisiana)*	NY *(New York)*
CA *(California)*	ME *(Maine)*	NC *(North Carolina)*
CO *(Colorado)*	MD *(Maryland)*	ND *(North Dakota)*
CT *(Connecticut)*	MA *(Massachusetts)*	OH *(Ohio)*
DE *(Delaware)*	MI *(Michigan)*	OK *(Oklahoma)*
FL *(Florida)*	MN *(Minnesota)*	OR *(Oregon)*
GA *(Georgia)*	MS *(Mississippi)*	PA *(Pennsylvania)*
HI *(Hawaii)*	MO *(Missouri)*	RI *(Rhode Island)*
ID *(Idaho)*	MT *(Montana)*	SC *(South Carolina)*
IL *(Illinois)*	NE *(Nebraska)*	SD *(South Dakota)*
IN *(Indiana)*	NV *(Nevada)*	TN *(Tennessee)*

(continued)

Abbreviations (continued)

Other abbreviations (continued)			
	TX *(Texas)*	VA *(Virginia)*	WI *(Wisconsin)*
	UT *(Utah)*	WA *(Washington)*	WY *(Wyoming)*
	VT *(Vermont)*	WV *(West Virginia)*	

Initials are abbreviations that stand for a person's first or middle name. Some names have both a first and a middle initial.

E.B. White *(Elwyn Brooks White)*
T. James Carey *(Thomas James Carey)*
Mr. John M. Gordon *(Mister John Morris Gordon)*

Titles

Underlining	**The important words and the first and last words in a title are capitalized. Titles of books, magazines, TV shows, movies, and newspapers are underlined.**

<u>Oliver Twist</u> *(book)*   <u>Treasure Island</u> *(movie)*

<u>Cricket</u> *(magazine)*   <u>The Phoenix Express</u> *(newspaper)*

<u>Nova</u> *(TV show)*

Quotation marks with titles	**Titles of short stories, songs, articles, book chapters, and most poems are set off by quotation marks.**

"The Necklace" *(short story)*   "The Human Brain" *(chapter)*

"Home on the Range" *(song)*   "Deer at Dusk" *(poem)*

"Three Days in the Sahara" *(article)*

Quotations

Quotation marks with commas and periods	**Quotation marks are used to set off a speaker's exact words. The first word of a quotation begins with a capital letter. Punctuation belongs *inside* the closing quotation marks. Commas separate a quotation from the rest of the sentence.**

"Where," asked the stranger, "is the post office?"

"Please put away your books now," said Mr. Emory.

Linda whispered, "What time is it?"

"It's late," replied Bill. "Let's go!"

Capitalization

Rules for capitalization

Capitalize the first word of every sentence.

What an unusual color the roses are!

Capitalize the pronoun *I*.

What should I do next?

Capitalize proper nouns. If a proper noun is made up of more than one word, capitalize each important word.

Emily G. Messe   District of Columbia   Lincoln Memorial

Capitalize titles or their abbreviations when used with a person's name.

Governor Bradford   Senator Smith   Dr. Ling

Capitalize proper adjectives.

We ate at a French restaurant.

She is French.

That is a North American custom.

Capitalize the names of days, months, and holidays.

My birthday is on the last Monday in March.

We watched the parade on the Fourth of July.

Capitalize the names of buildings and companies.

Empire State Building

Central School

Able Supply Company

Capitalize the first, last, and all important words in a title. Do not capitalize words such as *a, in, and, of,* and *the* unless they begin or end a title.

From Earth to the Moon   "The Rainbow Connection"

The New York Times   "Growing Up"

(continued)

Capitalization (continued)

Rules for capitalization (continued)	**Capitalize the first word of each main topic and subtopic in an outline.**
	
	I. Types of libraries
	   A. Large public library
	   B. Bookmobile

	Capitalize the first word in the greeting and the closing of a letter. Dear Marcia, Yours truly,

Punctuation

End marks	**There are three end marks. A *period (.)* ends a declarative or imperative sentence. A *question mark (?)* follows an interrogative sentence. An *exclamation point (!)* follows an exclamatory sentence.** The scissors are on my desk. *(declarative)* Look up the spelling of that word. *(imperative)* How is the word spelled? *(interrogative)* This is your best poem so far! *(exclamatory)*
Apostrophe	**To form the possessive of a singular noun, add an apostrophe and *s*.** doctor's teacher's grandmother's family's
	For a plural noun that ends in *s*, add only an apostrophe. sisters' families' Smiths' hound dogs'
	For a plural noun that does not end in *s*, add an apostrophe and *s*, to form the plural possessive. women's mice's children's geese's
	Use an apostrophe in contractions in place of dropped letters. Do not use contractions in formal writing. isn't *(is not)* don't *(do not)* wasn't *(was not)* can't *(cannot)* won't *(will not)* we're *(we are)*

(continued)

Punctuation *(continued)*

Apostrophe *(continued)*	it's *(it is)* they've *(they have)* could've *(could have)* I'm *(I am)* they'll *(they will)* would've *(would have)*
Colon	**Use a colon after the greeting in a business letter.** Dear Mrs. Trimby: Dear Realty Homes:
Comma	**A comma tells your reader where to pause. For words in a series, put a comma after each item except the last. Do not use a comma if only two items are listed.** Clyde asked if we had any apples, peaches, or grapes.
	Use commas to separate two or more adjectives that are listed together unless one adjective tells how many. The fresh, ripe fruit was placed in a bowl. One red apple was especially shiny.
	Use a comma before the conjunction in a compound sentence. Some students were at lunch, but others were studying.
	Use commas after introductory words such as *yes, no, oh,* and *well* when they begin a sentence. Well, it's just too cold out. No, it isn't six yet.
	Use a comma to separate a noun in direct address. Jean, help me fix this tire. How was your trip, Grandpa? Can you see, Joe, where I left my glasses?
	Use a comma between the names of a city and a state. Chicago, Illinois Miami, Florida
	Use a comma after the greeting in a friendly letter. Dear Deena, Dear Uncle Rudolph,
	Use a comma after the closing in a letter. Your nephew, Sincerely yours,

Friendly Letter

Use correct letter format, capitalization, and punctuation in a friendly letter. A friendly letter has five parts.

- The **heading** contains your complete address and the date.
- The **greeting** usually includes the word *Dear* and the name of the person to whom you are writing.
- The **body** is the main part of the letter. It includes all the information that you want to tell your reader.
- The **closing** says "good-by." Use closings such as *Your friend* or *Love*.
- The **signature** is your first name. Sign it under the closing.

Study this model.

Heading

1201 Ridge Road
Austin, TX 78768
October 5, 1990

Greeting

Dear Jerry,

Body

It seems funny to be writing to you instead of just running next door. I hope you feel at home in your new school by now. Make lots of new friends, but don't forget your old friends in Austin!

Nina and I have great plans for the class trip, but we miss your neat ideas. Write soon and tell us about Iowa!

Closing

Your friend,

Signature

Tony

Business Letter

Use correct letter format, capitalization, and punctuation in a business letter. A business letter has six parts.

- The **heading** is the same as in a friendly letter.
- The **inside address** includes the name and address of the person or business that will receive the letter.
- The **greeting** follows the inside address. If you do not know whom to address, use *Dear Sir or Madam* or the company's name. Use a colon (:) after the greeting.
- The **body** is your message. Be direct and polite.
- The **closing** is formal. Use *Yours truly,* for example.
- The **signature** is your full name. Write it under the closing. Print or type your name under your signature.

Study this model.

Heading	38 Spruce Street East Lansing, MI 48823 September 28, 1990
Inside Address	Royal Stamp Company 2102 North Avenue Chicago, IL 60607
Greeting	Dear Sir or Madam:
Body	I would like to be on your mailing list. I want to collect stamps from around the world that mark the birthdays of famous people. Please send me any of your catalogs that list this kind of stamp.
Closing	Sincerely,
Signature	*Daniel Hayes* Daniel Hayes

How to Use This Thesaurus

Use this Thesaurus to make your writing more exact and more interesting. Suppose you write this sentence:

A hot, dry climate is *perfect* for a cactus.

You decide that you want to replace the word *perfect* with another, more exact word. Turn to your Thesaurus Index to help you find words to use in place of *perfect*.

Using the Thesaurus Index The Thesaurus Index lists all the words in the Thesaurus in alphabetical order. Follow these steps to use the Thesaurus Index:

1. Look up your word in the Thesaurus Index under the letter it begins with. For example, look up *perfect* under *P*.
2. Note the main entry word in blue print. Look up the main entry word in the Thesaurus.

main entry word → **perfect** *adj.*

Suppose you already have the word *excellent* in mind to replace *perfect*. In the Thesaurus Index you will find

excellent **perfect** *adj.*

The slanted print shows you that you will find the word *excellent* under the main entry word *perfect* in the Thesaurus.

The Thesaurus Index also lists antonyms, or opposites, of words. They are shown like this:

faulty **perfect** *adj.*

The regular print shows you that *faulty* is the opposite of the main entry word *perfect*.

Using the Thesaurus Entry The main entry words in the Thesaurus are listed in alphabetical order. Study this entry for the main entry word *perfect*.

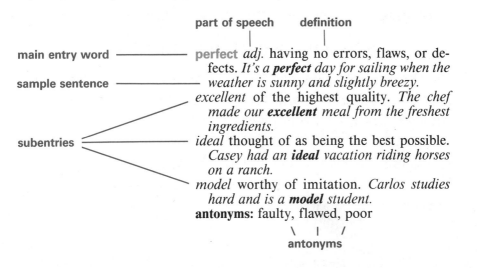

part of speech   definition

main entry word —————— perfect *adj.* having no errors, flaws, or defects. *It's a **perfect** day for sailing when the*
sample sentence ————— *weather is sunny and slightly breezy.*
excellent of the highest quality. *The chef made our **excellent** meal from the freshest ingredients.*
subentries ————— ideal thought of as being the best possible. *Casey had an **ideal** vacation riding horses on a ranch.*
model worthy of imitation. *Carlos studies hard and is a **model** student.*
antonyms: faulty, flawed, poor

antonyms

Notice that the entry gives three subentries, or words that you can use in place of *perfect: excellent, ideal,* and *model.* To help you choose one, the Thesaurus gives you
1. a meaning for each subentry, and
2. a sample sentence to show you how to use each word.

Now you can choose the most exact word for your sentence.

A hot, dry climate is *ideal* for a cactus.

Practice Look up each word below in the Thesaurus Index. Write the main entry word for each word.
1. spotless   **2.** haul   **3.** alarming   **4.** hurl   **5.** effect

Use the Thesaurus to choose a more exact word to replace each underlined word. Rewrite each sentence, using the new word.
  6. It was a <u>normal</u> spring day.
  7. I decided to <u>walk</u> to a nearby park.
  8. A small crowd had <u>gathered</u> near the bandstand.
  9. I stopped and heard two performers telling <u>funny</u> stories.
10. I did not <u>think</u> that I could laugh so hard!

Thesaurus Index

A

abnormal normal *adj.*
accept give *v.*
acceptable good *adj.*
accumulate gather *v.*
acquire get *v.*
active lively *adj.*
address speech *n.*
adept good *adj.*
adequate good *adj.*
admirable good *adj.*
admirable worthy *adj.*
admiration praise *n.*
agitated peaceful *adj.*
agreeable angry *adj.*
alarm warning *n.*
alarming scary *adj.*
alert warning *n.*
amusing funny *adj.*
angry *adj.*
antiseptic dirty *adj.*
anxious peaceful *adj.*
approval praise *n.*
arrangement order *n.*
assemble gather *v.*
average normal *adj.*
aware educated *adj.*
awareness knowledge *n.*
awful good *adj.*

B

bad good *adj.*
believe think *v.*
blend mixture *n.*
blossom grow *v.*
boast *v.*
bored eager *adj.*
boring *adj.*
brag boast *v.*
bruised damaged *adj.*
bunch gather *v.*
bury hide *v.*
buy get *v.*

C

calm angry *adj.*
calm peaceful *adj.*
careful adj.
cast throw *v.*
cause effect *n.*
caution warning *n.*
cautious careful *adj.*
changeable faithful *adj.*
cheer happiness *n.*
chief *adj.*
chipper lively *adj.*
choose decide *v.*
chuck throw *v.*
clean dirty *adj.*
cluster gather *v.*
collect gather *v.*
comforting scary *adj.*
comical funny *adj.*
command order *n.*
common regular *adj.*
competent good *adj.*
conceal hide *v.*
connect join *v.*
consequence effect *n.*
consider think *v.*
constant faithful *adj.*
contaminated dirty *adj.*
cover hide *v.*
create *v.*
criticism praise *n.*
cross angry *adj.*
crow boast *v.*

D

damaged *adj.*
dangerous *adj.*
decency justice *n.*
decide *v.*
decline grow *v.*
decrease increase *v.*
delight happiness *n.*
demolish create *v.*

E

demonstration display *n.*
dented damaged *adj.*
deposit put *v.*
depression happiness *n.*
deserve *v.*
design create *v.*
desirable good *adj.*
destroy create *v.*
determine decide *v.*
develop grow *v.*
devoted faithful *adj.*
different *adj.*
different same *adj.*
dingy dirty *adj.*
dirty *adj.*
disapproval praise *n.*
disinfected dirty *adj.*
disloyal faithful *adj.*
display *n.*
display hide *v.*
dissimilar same *adj.*
distressed peaceful *adj.*
double-crossing faithful
     adj.
drag pull *v.*
dreadful good *adj.*
dream think *v.*
dreary boring *adj.*
dry boring *adj.*
dull boring *adj.*
dull lively *adj.*
dusty dirty *adj.*
dwindle grow *v.*

E

eager *adj.*
earn deserve *v.*
earn get *v.*
earnest funny *adj.*
edgy peaceful *adj.*
educated *adj.*
effect *n.*
endanger protect *v.*
energetic lively *adj.*
enjoyment happiness *n.*

enlarge increase *v.*
enormous small *adj.*
enthusiastic eager *adj.*
equal same *adj.*
equality justice *n.*
establish create *v.*
excellent perfect *adj.*
exciting boring *adj.*
exhibit display *n.*
exhibit hide *v.*
expand increase *v.*
expose hide *v.*
extend increase *v.*
extraordinary normal *adj.*

F

fairness justice *n.*
faithful adj.
faithless faithful *adj.*
false faithful *adj.*
fast quick *adj.*
faulty perfect *adj.*
filthy dirty *adj.*
fine good *adj.*
fire throw *v.*
flavor taste *n.*
flawed perfect *adj.*
fling throw *v.*
flip throw *v.*
flourish grow *v.*
foolhardy careful *adj.*
forbidding scary *adj.*
forfeit get *v.*
forgiving angry *adj.*
frightening scary *adj.*
frisky lively *adj.*
funny *adj.*
furious angry *adj.*
furnish give *v.*

G

gather *v.*
general normal *adj.*
get *v.*

giant small *adj.*
give v.
good adj.
grave funny *adj.*
grimy dirty *adj.*
grow v.
grungy dirty *adj.*
guard protect *v.*

H

happiness n.
harmless dangerous *adj.*
harmonious peaceful *adj.*
hasty quick *adj.*
haul pull *v.*
hazardous dangerous *adj.*
heave throw *v.*
heedful careful *adj.*
hide *v.*
honorable worthy *adj.*
horrible good *adj.*
huge small *adj.*
humorous funny *adj.*
hurl throw *v.*
hygienic dirty *adj.*

I

ideal perfect *adj.*
identical same *adj.*
idle lively *adj.*
ignorant educated *adj.*
ignore see *v.*
imagine think *v.*
immaculate dirty *adj.*
impure dirty *adj.*
inactive lively *adj.*
increase *v.*
indifferent eager *adj.*
inequality justice *n.*
inferior good *adj.*
informed educated *adj.*
injustice justice *n.*
interesting boring *adj.*
invent create *v.*

J

join *v.*
jumble mixture *n.*
justice *n.*

K

keen eager *adj.*
knowledge *n.*
knowledgeable educated
    adj.

L

laughable funny *adj.*
launch throw *v.*
lay put *v.*
lay put *v.*
lazy lively *adj.*
leading chief *adj.*
learned educated *adj.*
lecture speech *n.*
leisurely quick *adj.*
lifeless lively *adj.*
limp walk *v.*
lively *adj.*
lively boring *adj.*
lob throw *v.*
locate put *v.*
lose get *v.*
loyal faithful *adj.*

M

magnify increase *v.*
main chief *adj.*
major chief *adj.*
major small *adj.*
march walk *v.*
marvelous good *adj.*
mask hide *v.*
menace protect *v.*
merit deserve *v.*
messy dirty *adj.*
microscopic small *adj.*
miniature small *adj.*

minor chief *adj.*
minor small *adj.*
misery happiness *n.*
miss see *v.*
mixture *n.*
model perfect *adj.*
monotonous boring *adj.*
morality justice *n.*
muddy dirty *adj.*
murky dirty *adj.*

N

neglectful careful *adj.*
nervous peaceful *adj.*
normal *adj.*
notice see *v.*

O

observe see *v.*
obtain get *v.*
offer give *v.*
order *n.*
outcome effect *n.*
outstanding good *adj.*
overhauled damaged *adj.*
overlook see *v.*

P

participate join *v.*
patched damaged *adj.*
peaceful *adj.*
pelt throw *v.*
perfect *adj.*
perilous dangerous *adj.*
place put *v.*
placid peaceful *adj.*
pleased angry *adj.*
pleasure happiness *n.*
polluted dirty *adj.*
ponder think *v.*
poor good *adj.*
poor perfect *adj.*
praise *n.*
preference taste *n.*

present give *v.*
principal chief *adj.*
produce create *v.*
propel throw *v.*
protect *v.*
provide give *v.*
pull *v.*
pure dirty *adj.*
push pull *v.*
put *v.*

Q

quick *adj.*
quiet peaceful *adj.*

R

rapid quick *adj.*
rare normal *adj.*
rate deserve *v.*
reason effect *n.*
reassuring scary *adj.*
receive give *v.*
reckless careful *adj.*
reduce increase *v.*
regard see *v.*
regular *adj.*
regular normal *adj.*
relaxed peaceful *adj.*
remarkable normal *adj.*
remove put *v.*
repaired damaged *adj.*
resentful angry *adj.*
resolve decide *v.*
restful peaceful *adj.*
restless peaceful *adj.*
result effect *n.*
reveal hide *v.*
risky dangerous *adj.*
routine regular *adj.*

S

sadness happiness *n.*
safe dangerous *adj.*
same *adj.*

sanitary dirty *adj.*
satisfactory good *adj.*
scary *adj.*
scatter gather *v.*
scorn praise *n.*
scratched damaged *adj.*
second-rate good *adj.*
secure dangerous *adj.*
see *v.*
separate different *adj.*
separate gather *v.*
serene peaceful *adj.*
serious funny *adj.*
set put *v.*
settle decide *v.*
shattered damaged *adj.*
shield protect *v.*
shoddy good *adj.*
shoot throw *v.*
shove pull *v.*
show hide *v.*
shrink increase *v.*
signal warning *n.*
slack quick *adj.*
sling throw *v.*
slow quick *adj.*
sluggish lively *adj.*
small *adj.*
smudged dirty *adj.*
soiled dirty *adj.*
soothing peaceful *adj.*
soothing scary *adj.*
sooty dirty *adj.*
sorrow happiness *n.*
source effect *n.*
speech *n.*
speedy quick *adj.*
spirited lively *adj.*
splendid good *adj.*
spot see *v.*
spotless dirty *adj.*
sprout grow *v.*
stained dirty *adj.*
sterile dirty *adj.*
strange normal *adj.*
stride walk *v.*
stroll walk *v.*
stunt grow *v.*
stunted small *adj.*

substandard good *adj.*
suffering happiness *n.*
sufficient good *adj.*
suitable good *adj.*
superb good *adj.*
supply give *v.*
swift quick *adj.*

T

take give *v.*
take away put *v.*
tarnished dirty *adj.*
taste *n.*
tattered damaged *adj.*
tense peaceful *adj.*
terrible good *adj.*
terrific good *adj.*
terrifying scary *adj.*
think *v.*
threaten protect *v.*
throw *v.*
thrust pull *v.*
tiny small *adj.*
tiptoe walk *v.*
tolerable good *adj.*
toss throw *v.*
tow pull *v.*
tranquil peaceful *adj.*
treacherous dangerous
  adj.

tremendous small *adj.*
troubled peaceful *adj.*
true faithful *adj.*
tug pull *v.*
typical normal *adj.*

U

unaware educated *adj.*
unclean dirty *adj.*
undeserving worthy *adj.*
undisturbed peaceful *adj.*
undo create *v.*
uneasy peaceful *adj.*
unenthusiastic eager *adj.*
uniform same *adj.*
unimportant chief *adj.*
unimportant worthy *adj.*
uninterested eager *adj.*
unlike same *adj.*
unruffled peaceful *adj.*
unsanitary dirty *adj.*
unschooled educated *adj.*
unsettled peaceful *adj.*
unsterile dirty *adj.*
unthreatening dangerous
  adj.
untroubled peaceful *adj.*
unusual different *adj.*
unusual normal *adj.*
upset angry *adj.*

upset peaceful *adj.*
upshot effect *n.*
useless worthy *adj.*
usual normal *adj.*

V

valuable worthy *adj.*
varied boring *adj.*
view see *v.*

W

walk *v.*
wander walk *v.*
warning *n.*
wary careful *adj.*
washed dirty *adj.*
watchful careful *adj.*
win get *v.*
wisdom knowledge *n.*
witness see *v.*
wonderful good *adj.*
worried peaceful *adj.*
worthless worthy *adj.*
worthy *adj.*
worthy good *adj.*
wrong justice *n.*

Thesaurus

A

angry *adj.* feeling or showing displeasure. *I was **angry** when I broke my shoelace.*

cross in a bad mood; grumpy. *I get **cross** if I don't get enough sleep.*

furious feeling or showing rage. *After missing his train, Ted was so **furious** that he tore up his ticket.*

resentful feeling or showing anger or bitterness over something that is thought to be unfair. *Beth was **resentful** when no one thanked her for her help.*

upset sad or worried. *Joy was **upset** until her lost cat returned.*

antonyms: agreeable, calm *adj.*, forgiving *adj.*, pleased *adj.*

B

boast *v.* to praise oneself, one's belongings, or one's actions. *Sara always **boasts** about how fast she can run.*

brag to speak with too much pride about oneself in an attempt to show off. *Leroy **bragged** to everyone about his new bike.*

crow to utter a cry of delight or victory. *We all smiled when Pat **crowed**, "I won! I won!"*

boring *adj.* not interesting. *The television program was so **boring** that I fell asleep.*

dreary boring; dull. *Cleaning my room was a **dreary** task.*

dry tiresome. *It was hard to finish reading the long, **dry**, government report.*

dull lacking excitement. *Neither team scored during the **dull** soccer match.*

monotonous not interesting because of being always the same. ***Monotonous** songs just repeat the same words over and over.*

antonyms: exciting *adj.*, interesting *adj.*, lively, varied *adj.*

C

careful *adj.* using caution or care. *Looking for clues, the detective made a **careful** search of the room.*

cautious not taking chances. *Kim is too **cautious** to try the dangerous climb to the top.*

heedful paying close attention. *The campers were **heedful** of the forest ranger's warnings about campfires.*

wary on one's guard against danger. *He was **wary** of skiing down such a steep and icy slope.*

watchful on the lookout; alert. *The **watchful** dog barked at every passer-by.*

antonyms: foolhardy, neglectful, reckless

chief *adj.* highest in rank or importance. *My sister was appointed **chief** architect for her company.*

leading most important. *Paris, France, is one of the **leading** cities for fashion.*

main most important. *The **main** library is bigger than its branches.*

major larger, greater, or more important. *High winds caused some destruction, but flooding was the **major** cause of damage.*

principal leading all others. *Did you know that the panda's **principal** food is a kind of bamboo?*

antonyms: minor *adj.*, unimportant

create *v.* to bring into being. *Spiders **create** webs to trap insects.*

design to make a plan or drawing for something. *An art student **designed** the school's new sign.*

establish to begin or set up. *The settlers soon **established** a small town.*

invent to make something that did not exist before. *No one is sure who really **invented** the camera.*

produce to manufacture. *How many cars a year does Japan **produce**?*

antonyms: demolish, destroy, undo

D

damaged *adj.* harmed or injured. *That door will not shut because the hinge is **damaged**.*

bruised made discolored as a result of an injury that does not break the skin. *Gregory's leg was **bruised** from a bad fall.*

dented having a hollow in the surface caused by pressure or a blow. *The tin pan would not lie flat because the bottom was **dented**.*

scratched having a thin, shallow cut or mark made by or as if by a sharp tool. *We sanded and waxed the **scratched** wooden floor.*

shattered broken suddenly into many small pieces; smashed. *Pieces of the **shattered** window lay on the floor.*

tattered having torn and hanging pieces; shredded; ragged. *The **tattered** dress could no longer be mended.*

antonyms: overhauled *adj.*, patched *adj.*, repaired *adj.*

dangerous *adj.* full of danger; risky. *Riding a bicycle on a busy street is **dangerous**.*

hazardous able or likely to cause harm. *Breathing polluted air can be **hazardous** to your health.*

perilous very dangerous. *Climbing the steep, icy mountain was a **perilous** adventure.*

risky involving the possibility of suffering harm or loss. *Crossing the shaky old bridge was **risky**, but we had no choice.*

treacherous not to be trusted; dangerous. *Driving was difficult on the icy, **treacherous** roads.*

antonyms: harmless, safe *adj.*, secure *adj.*, unthreatening

decide *v.* to make up one's mind. *I **decided** to buy the red bike instead of the blue one.*

choose to pick out, especially on the basis of what one wants and thinks best. *I **chose** to spend my vacation with my grandmother.*

determine to make a firm decision. *Dr. Tsao **determined** to do all that he could to save the injured cat.*

resolve to make a firm plan. *I **resolve** to eat a good breakfast every day from now on.*

settle to arrange or decide by agreement. *They finally **settled** on a place to have the picnic.*

deserve *v.* to be worthy of or have a right to. *An animal lover like Paul **deserves** a pet of his own.*

earn to deserve as a result of effort or behavior. *The hard-working crew had **earned** a good long rest.*

merit to be worthy of; deserve. *June's courage **merits** the highest praise.*

rate to be good or valuable enough to receive. *The television show was too silly to **rate** much interest from the viewers.*

different *adj.* not identical. *David and Emily live in **different** parts of the United States.*

separate individual or independent. *Each of the cats eats from a **separate** bowl.*

unusual not usual, common, or ordinary. *Maura wears her hair in a very **unusual** style.*

Shades of Meaning

dirty *adj.*

1. full of or covered with dirt; not clean:

dingy	messy	sooty
dusty	muddy	stained
filthy	murky	tarnished
grimy	smudged	
grungy	soiled	

2. polluted:

contaminated	
impure	unsanitary
unclean	unsterile

antonyms: 1. clean *adj.*, immaculate, spotless, washed *adj.* **2.** antiseptic *adj.*, disinfected *adj.*, hygienic, pure, sanitary, sterile

display *n.* a public showing. *The science fair included a **display** of lovely seashells.*

demonstration a show and explanation of the operation of something for sale. *The salesperson gave us a **demonstration** of what the computer can do.*

exhibit something put on display, as at a museum or gallery. *At the crafts shop Mario saw an **exhibit** of Indian pottery.*

E

eager *adj.* full of strong desire; impatient. *Carly was **eager** to read the new book by her favorite author.*

enthusiastic full of or showing strong interest or eagerness. *Our performance got an **enthusiastic** response from the audience.*

keen full of enthusiasm and interest. *Alice has a **keen** interest in windsurfing.*

antonyms: bored *adj.*, indifferent, unenthusiastic, uninterested

educated *adj.* provided with formal instruction. *All college professors are highly **educated** people.*

aware having knowledge. *One purpose of a newspaper is to make the public **aware** of world events.*

informed having, displaying, or using information. ***Informed** shoppers judge a product before making a purchase.*

knowledgeable well-informed. *Since the speaker was **knowledgeable**, he was able to answer all of our questions.*

learned having or showing much knowledge or learning. *The **learned** professor had read every book ever written on Greek and Roman history.*

antonyms: ignorant, unaware, unschooled

effect *n.* something brought about by a cause. *The **effect** of too much eating can be a stomachache.*

consequence a direct outcome of something. *The musicians' fine performance was a **consequence** of their hard work.*

outcome something that happens as a result. *The **outcome** of the trial was a surprise to everyone.*

result something that happens because of something else. *The broken branches are the **result** of last night's storm.*

upshot the final result; outcome. *The **upshot** of our meeting was that we decided to have a party.*

antonyms: cause *n.*, reason *n.*, source

F

faithful *adj.* worthy of trust. *Theresa was a **faithful** friend who stood by her promises.*

constant firm in loyalty and affection; faithful. *Jonah and Dan have been **constant** friends since the day they met.*

devoted having or showing loyalty and affection. *My dog is my **devoted** companion and would follow me anywhere.*

loyal firm in supporting a person, country, or cause. *Ben was a **loyal** customer at his neighborhood market.*

true trustworthy and devoted. *Ariel was a **true** friend when I needed her.*

antonyms: changeable, disloyal, double-crossing, faithless, false

funny *adj.* causing laughter or amusement. *Sal told such a **funny** story that my sides hurt from laughing.*

amusing pleasantly entertaining. *The juggler on stilts was **amusing**.*

comical producing much laughter. *Three-legged races are always **comical** to watch.*

humorous causing a smile or a laugh. *Ron told a **humorous** story about being chased by a chicken.*

laughable causing or likely to cause laughter or amusement. *Maria did a **laughable** imitation of a cow.*

antonyms: earnest, grave *adj.*, serious

G

gather *v.* to bring or come together into one place. *They **gathered** around the campfire and sang songs.*

accumulate to gather together; pile up. *Chen has **accumulated** stacks of science fiction magazines.*

assemble to bring or come together as a group. *The band members must **assemble** in the auditorium at noon.*

bunch to gather into or form a group of things. *The puppies **bunched** together in a corner of the room.*

cluster to grow or gather in a group. *The fans **clustered** around the singer to ask for her autograph.*

collect to bring or come together in a group. *Drops of dew **collect** on our lawn each morning.*

antonyms: scatter, separate *v.*

get *v.* to receive. *Did you **get** any payment for your work in the garden?*

acquire to gain by one's own efforts. *Ed worked many hours to **acquire** his skill in typing.*

buy to gain by paying a price for. *Ana used her allowance to **buy** a gift for her mother.*

earn to gain by working or by supplying a service. *Jason **earns** money by baby-sitting for families in his neighborhood.*

obtain to gain by means of planning or effort. *Dara wants to know how she can **obtain** a driver's license in this state.*

win to receive as a prize or reward. *Did Joe **win** a prize in the school essay contest?*

antonyms: forfeit, lose

give *v.* to hand over to another. *Sara **gave** her sister a beautiful music box for her birthday.*

furnish to supply; give. *A hardware store **furnished** hoses and buckets for the fifth-grade car wash.*

offer to put forward to be accepted or refused. *Katie **offered** Ina half of a turkey sandwich.*

present to make a gift or award to. *Coach Hart **presented** a trophy to our basketball team.*

provide to give something needed or useful. *The City Hotel **provides** breakfast for its guests.*

supply to make available something that is needed. *The blood **supplies** oxygen to the brain.*

antonyms: accept, receive, take

Good can get better.

good *adj.* having positive or desirable qualities.

1. good enough:

acceptable	sufficient
adequate	suitable
satisfactory	tolerable

2. very good:

adept	desirable
admirable	fine
competent	worthy

3. extremely good:

marvelous	superb
outstanding	terrific
splendid	wonderful

antonyms: 1. inferior, second-rate, substandard **2.** bad, poor, shoddy **3.** awful, dreadful, horrible, terrible

grow *v.* to become or cause to become larger. *Lots of rain helped the plants **grow** tall.*

blossom to develop gradually. *Emily's artistic talent **blossomed** with practice.*

develop to grow or cause to grow. *Exercise **develops** strong muscles.*

flourish to grow very well; thrive. *Tomatoes **flourish** in hot, sunny weather.*

sprout to produce or appear as new growth. *New leaves **sprouted** from the dogwood tree.*

antonyms: decline *v.*, dwindle, stunt *v.*

H

happiness *n.* pleasure or joy. *Maria smiled with **happiness** as she told me the good news.*

cheer good spirits; happiness. *The holiday celebration filled us with **cheer**.*

(continued)

happiness (continued)

delight great pleasure. *The playful kittens made him laugh with **delight**.*

enjoyment a form or source of pleasure; joy. *Reading brings Kris great **enjoyment**.*

pleasure a feeling of happiness or enjoyment; delight. *Josh gazed at the lovely scene with **pleasure**.*

antonyms: depression, misery, sadness, sorrow, suffering *n.*

hide *v.* to keep or put out of sight. *The cat **hid** under the bed until the company left.*

bury to hide by placing in the ground and covering with earth. *The dog **buried** another bone under the rose bush.*

conceal to keep from being seen or known. *Allan **concealed** his sadness behind a happy face.*

cover to put something over or on. *The turtle **covered** her eggs with sand.*

mask to cover or hide. *They used vines and branches to **mask** the opening of the cave.*

antonyms: display *v.*, exhibit *v.*, expose, reveal, show *v.*

I

increase *v.* to make or become greater or larger. *The thin cattle were given extra food to **increase** their weight.*

enlarge to make or become larger. *The photographer **enlarged** the snapshot to twice its original size.*

expand to make or become larger in size, volume, or amount. *The Dashos **expanded** their house by adding a second floor.*

extend to make greater or larger. *Road workers **extended** the road another mile.*

magnify to enlarge the appearance of. *The microscope **magnified** the cells so that they could be seen by the human eye.*

antonyms: decrease *v.*, reduce, shrink

J

join *v.* to bring or come together, as by fastening. *Liz **joined** the two short poles to form one long one.*

connect to link or come together. *Electrical tape was used to **connect** the two wires.*

participate to join with others in being active; take part. *Carlos **participated** in the discussion.*

justice *n.* the quality of being just or fair. *Everyone was satisfied with the **justice** of the judge's decision.*

decency the quality of being proper or moral. *Abby found a purse and had the **decency** to call the owner.*

equality the condition of being equal, especially the condition of enjoying equal rights. *According to the Constitution of the United States, everyone has **equality** under the law.*

fairness the quality of being free of bias. *Listening to both sides of the argument was Catherine's way of showing **fairness**.*

morality the quality of being good and just. *A person of high **morality** can usually be trusted.*

antonyms: inequality, injustice, wrong *n.*

K

knowledge *n.* understanding; awareness. *Philip's **knowledge** of animal behavior comes from raising many kinds of pets over the years.*

awareness consciousness of something. *Her trip to Asia gave Ann a new **awareness** of other ways of life.*

wisdom intelligence and good judgment in knowing what to do and being able to tell the difference between good and bad and right and wrong. *People often ask my aunt for advice because she is known for her **wisdom**.*

L

lively *adj.* full of energy; active. *The **lively** baby kept climbing out of the crib.*

active busy. *No one is more **active** than my teenage sister.*

chipper full of cheer. *Ike felt **chipper** on this lovely morning.*

energetic full of energy; vigorous. *I've been watching those **energetic** children playing on the swings.*

frisky energetic, lively, and playful. *The **frisky** colt leaped and pranced around the pasture.*

spirited full of life. *Our team put on a **spirited** performance.*

antonyms: dull *adj.*, idle, inactive, lazy, lifeless, sluggish

M

mixture *n.* any combination of different ingredients, things, or kinds. *The sand was a **mixture** of crushed rocks and shells.*

blend a mixture in which the parts are combined completely. *The flavor of the sauce was a **blend** of tomatoes and spices.*

jumble a group of things mixed together without any order. *The tool box contained a **jumble** of nails, screws, nuts, and bolts.*

N

normal *adj.* of the usual or regular kind. *The guest speaker provided a break from our **normal** school schedule.*

average typical, usual, or ordinary. *The **average** person needs several hours of sleep each night.*

general widespread. *The students had a **general** feeling of excitement before the big game.*

regular usual or normal; standard. *Because our **regular** teacher is ill, we had a substitute today.*

typical showing the special traits or characteristics of a group, kind, or class; ordinary. *A **typical** circus includes clowns, acrobats, and wild animals.*

usual happening at regular intervals or all of the time; customary. *Nicole took a shortcut instead of going to school the **usual** way.*

antonyms: abnormal, extraordinary, rare, remarkable, strange, unusual

O

order *n.* a command or rule. *The patient was careful to follow the doctor's **orders**.*

arrangement a set of things that have been put in order. *The pins and earrings were displayed in an attractive **arrangement**.*

command an order or direction. *The soldiers obeyed the general's **command**.*

P

Word Bank

peaceful *adj.* marked by peace and calmness.

calm	serene
harmonious	soothing
placid	tranquil
quiet	undisturbed
relaxed	unruffled
restful	untroubled

antonyms: agitated *adj.*, anxious, distressed *adj.*, edgy, nervous, restless, tense *adj.*, troubled *adj.*, uneasy, unsettled *adj.*, upset *adj.*, worried *adj.*

perfect *adj.* having no errors, flaws, or defects. *It's a **perfect** day for sailing when the weather is sunny and slightly breezy.*

excellent of the highest quality. *The chef made our **excellent** meal from the freshest ingredients.*

ideal thought of as being the best possible. *Casey had an **ideal** vacation riding horses on a ranch.*

model worthy of imitation. *Carlos studies hard and is a **model** student.*

antonyms: faulty, flawed, poor

praise *n.* approval or admiration. *The teacher's words of **praise** made Alex beam with pride.*

admiration an expression of pleasure, wonder, and approval. *Lisa's singing won the **admiration** of her classmates.*

approval favorable judgment. *Pablo's suggestion met with everyone's **approval**.*

antonyms: criticism, disapproval, scorn *n.*

protect *v.* to keep safe from harm, attack, or injury. *Calvin wears a helmet to **protect** his head when he rides his bike.*

guard to defend or keep safe from danger. *The police **guarded** the museum against theft.*

shield to protect or cover. *Cowhands used kerchiefs to **shield** their faces from the dust.*

antonyms: endanger, menace *v.*, threaten

pull *v.* to apply force to in order to draw someone or something in the direction of the force. *I **pulled** the door toward me as hard as I could.*

drag to draw along the ground by force. *Jim **dragged** the heavy trash barrel across the lawn.*

haul to pull or carry with effort. *The horses **hauled** the wagon up the mountain.*

tow to draw along behind with a chain or rope. *Two small boats **towed** the enormous barge into the harbor.*

tug to pull at strongly. *She **tugged** at the knot until it finally came loose.*

antonyms: push *v.*, shove *v.*, thrust *v.*

put *v.* to cause to be in a particular position. ***Put** your bike in the shed.*

deposit to lay or put down. *I **deposited** a package on your front steps.*

lay to put or set down. *Be gentle when you **lay** the baby in the crib.*

locate to place or situate. *A bright, sunny spot is certainly the best place to **locate** your garden.*

place to lay something in a certain space. ***Place** your hands on your hips.*

set to cause to be in a particular location. ***Set** the books on the kitchen table before you go to your room.*

antonyms: remove, take away

Q

quick *adj.* done or happening without delay. *We took a **quick** trip to the store.*

fast moving or acting with speed. *Traveling by plane is **faster** than traveling by car.*

hasty in a hurried way. *Jim scribbled a **hasty** note and then ran out the door.*

rapid marked by speed. *The **rapid** subway train zoomed through the dark.*

speedy able to get from one place to another in a short time. *A **speedy** little rabbit outran my dog.*

swift moving or able to move very fast. *Charlie is very **swift** on his feet.*

antonyms: leisurely, slack, slow *adj.*

R

regular *adj.* appearing again and again. *Exercise should be a **regular** part of everyone's life.*

common found or occurring often. *Blizzards are **common** in this part of the country.*

routine done as part of a regular procedure. *Amanda made an appointment for a **routine** eye examination.*

S

same *adj.* being the very one. *This train is the **same** one that I rode last week.*

equal being exactly the same in amount, extent, or other measured quality. *The two questions were worth an **equal** number of points.*

identical exactly alike. *My twin brothers are **identical**; no one can tell them apart.*

uniform having the same appearance, form, or measurements as others. *Any of these screws will fit that hole because they are all perfectly **uniform**.*

antonyms: different, dissimilar, unlike

scary *adj.* causing fear. *Your story was so **scary** that I was afraid to walk home.*

alarming causing a feeling of approaching danger. *The police siren was **alarming** to the drivers on the highway.*

forbidding threatening, dangerous, or un-friendly in nature or appearance; frightening. *Brian trembled as he entered the dark, **forbidding** forest.*

frightening causing sudden, great fear. *He told us that the **frightening** crash was only thunder.*

terrifying causing overpowering fright. *The **terrifying** noise made me freeze in my tracks.*

antonyms: comforting *adj.*, reassuring *adj.*, soothing *adj.*

see *v.* to take in with the eyes. *Julie stared at the tree, but she could not **see** the bird.*

notice to take note of; pay attention to. *Ron entered quietly, but everyone **noticed** that he was late.*

observe to watch carefully. *The cat **observed** the bird in the tree.*

regard to look at. *The artist stood back from the easel to **regard** her work.*

spot to find or locate. *The sunbathers **spotted** dolphins not far from shore.*

view to look at. *We **viewed** the entire city from the top of the skyscraper.*

witness to be a witness of; see. *Several passers-by had **witnessed** the accident.*

antonyms: ignore, miss *v.*, overlook *v.*

small *adj.* little in size, amount, or extent. *A **small** dog sat on the girl's lap.*

microscopic capable of being seen only through a microscope. *The book contained an enlarged photograph of a **microscopic** plant cell.*

miniature much smaller that the usual size. *I gave my sister a **miniature** living room set for her doll house.*

minor smaller in amount, size, extent, or importance. *The hurricane that had been forecast turned out to be only a **minor** storm.*

stunted being smaller than normal due to an interference with growth. *The **stunted** growth of the trees was the result of poor soil.*

tiny extremely small. *He could hold the **tiny** baby rabbit in the palm of his hand.*

antonyms: enormous, giant *adj.*, huge, major *adj.*, tremendous

speech *n.* a public talk. *The writer gave a **speech** at the high school.*

address a formal speech. *We listened to the President's **address**.*

lecture a speech providing information on a subject, given before a class. *The class heard a **lecture** about the planets.*

T

taste *n.* a sensation produced by a substance taken into the mouth; flavor. *Coconut milk has a sweet **taste**.*

flavor the quality that causes something to have a certain taste. *The spices gave the stew a delicious **flavor**.*

preference a liking for one person or thing over another. *He likes string beans, but his **preference** is for broccoli.*

think *v.* to use one's mind to form ideas and make decisions. *You should **think** carefully before you answer the question.*

believe to expect or suppose. *I **believe** that it is going to rain.*

consider to think about before deciding. *Ellie **considered** moving to the city.*

dream to think or believe possible. *Daniel never **dreamed** that he could be so lucky.*

imagine to form a mental picture or idea of. *Try to **imagine** what life was like a hundred years ago.*

ponder to think about carefully. *Max had **pondered** the problem for hours but still had found no solution.*

Word Bank

throw *v.* to send through the air with a fast motion of the arm.

cast	*launch*
chuck	*lob*
fire	*pelt*
fling	*propel*
flip	*shoot*
heave	*sling*
hurl	*toss*

W

walk *v.* to move or cause to move on foot at an easy, steady pace. *The smooth path made it easy for us to **walk** the trail.*

limp to walk in an uneven way. *Marcia got a blister on her foot and had to **limp** home.*

march to walk with regular and measured steps, often in a group. *The baton twirlers **marched** in the parade.*

stride to walk with long steps. *Tim **strode** across the stage to receive his diploma.*

stroll to walk around in a slow, relaxed way. *At lunch hour the office workers **strolled** around the mall.*

tiptoe to walk softly, as if on the tips of one's toes. *Kevin **tiptoed** behind Julie and said, "Surprise!"*

wander to move from place to place without a special purpose or destination; roam. *Since our flight was delayed, we **wandered** around the airport to pass the time.*

warning *n.* something that urges one to watch out for danger. *The sign was a **warning** to drivers about a curve ahead.*

alarm a bell or light that alerts one to danger. *The fire **alarm** clanged as smoke filled the attic.*

alert a warning signal of attack or danger. *When a tornado is coming, the weather station sends out a special **alert**.*

caution a warning against possible trouble or danger. *The label on the can included a **caution** against improper use.*

signal a sign, gesture, or device that gives a command, a warning, or other information. *As the traffic **signal** turned from yellow to red, the cars came to a stop.*

worthy *adj.* having worth, merit, or value. *A clean-up drive for the park is a **worthy** cause.*

admirable deserving of respect. *Her hard work and devotion are most **admirable**.*

honorable deserving honor or respect. *The fire fighter was awarded for his years of **honorable** service.*

valuable of great importance, use, or service. *A hammer is a **valuable** tool to a carpenter.*

antonyms: undeserving, unimportant, useless, worthless

Spelling-Meaning Index

This Spelling-Meaning Index contains words related in spelling and meaning. The Index has three sections: Consonant Changes, Vowel Changes, and Word Parts. The first two sections contain related word pairs and other words in the same word families. The last section contains a list of Latin word roots, Greek word parts, and words that contain these word parts. The words in each section of this Index are in alphabetical order.

Consonant Changes

The letters in dark print show that the spelling stays the same even though the sound changes.

Consonant Changes: Silent to Sounded

Sometimes you can remember how to spell a word with a silent consonant by thinking of a related word in which the letter is pronounced.

bomb-bombard

bombarded, bombarder, bombardier, bombarding, bombardment, bombards, bombed, bomber, bombing, bombs

column-columnist

columnar, columned, columnists, columns

heir-inherit

disinherit, heirless, heirs, heritage, inheritance, inherited, inheriting, inherits

moist-moisten

moistened, moistening, moistens, moister, moistest, moistness

muscle-muscular

muscled, muscles, muscling, musculature

receipt-reception

receipts, receptacle, receptionist, receptions, receptive

sign-signal

signaled, signaler, signaling, signals, signature, signed, signer, signify, signing, signs

Consonant Changes: The Sound of *c*

The |k| sound spelled *c* may change to the |s| sound in some words. Thinking of a related word can help you remember that the |s| sound is spelled *c*.

critic-criticize

critical, critically, criticism, criticized, criticizer, criticizes, criticizing, critics, uncritical

practical-practice

impractical, impracticality, impractically, practicality, practically, practiced, practices, practicing, unpracticed

Consonant Changes: The Sound of *t*

The sound of a final *t* may change to the |sh| or the |ch| sound when an ending or a suffix is added. Thinking of a related word can help you remember that those sounds are spelled *t*.

affect-affection

affected, affecting, affectionate, affectionately, affective, affects, disaffected, unaffected

create-creature

created, creates, creating, creation, creative, creatively, creativity, creator, creatures, noncreative, re-create

depart-departure

departed, departing, departs, departures, undeparted

except-exception

excepted, excepting, exceptional, exceptionally, exceptions, excepts, unexceptional, unexceptionally

fact-factual

facts, factually

graduate-graduation

graduated, graduates, graduating, graduations, postgraduate, undergraduate

habit-habitual

habits, habitually

instruct-instruction

instructed, instructing, instructional, instructions, instructive, instructor, instructorship, instructs, uninstructive

invent-invention

invented, inventing, inventions, inventive, inventively, inventiveness, inventor, invents

moist-moisture

moister, moistest, moistness, moisturize, moisturizer

object-objection

objected, objecting, objectionable, objectionably, objects

part-partial

parted, partially, particle, parting, partition, partly, parts

regulate-regulation

regulated, regulates, regulating, regulations, regulator, regulatory, unregulated

suggest-suggestion

suggested, suggestible, suggesting, suggestions, suggestive, suggests

Vowel Changes

The letters in dark print show that the spelling stays the same even though the sound changes.

Vowel Changes: Long to Short Vowel Sound

Words that are related in meaning are often related in spelling, even though one word has a long vowel sound and the other word has a short vowel sound.

breathe-breath

breathable, breathed, breather, breathes, breathily, breathiness, breathing, breathless, breathlessly, breathlessness, breaths, breathtaking

Vowel Changes (continued)

cave-cavity

caved, cavern, cavernous, caves, caving, cavities

clean-cleanse

cleanable, cleaned, cleaner, cleanest, cleaning, cleanliness, cleanly, cleanness, cleans, cleansed, cleanser, cleanses, cleansing, unclean, uncleanable

cycle-bicycle

bicycled, bicycles, bicycling, bicyclist, cycled, cycler, cycles, cyclical, cycling, cyclist, recycle, tricycle, unicycle, unicyclist

deal-dealt

dealer, dealership, dealing, deals

dream-dreamt

dreamed, dreamer, dreamily, dreaminess, dreaming, dreamless, dreamlike, dreams, dreamy

heal-health

healed, healer, healing, heals, healthful, healthfully, healthfulness, healthily, healthiness, healthy, unhealthy

mean-meant

meaning, meaningful, meaningless, means, unmeant

minus-minimum

minimal, minimize, minimums, minuscule

mute-mutter

muted, mutely, muteness, mutes, muting, muttered, muttering, mutters

nation-national

denationalize, international, nationalism, nationalist, nationalistic, nationality, nationalize, nationally, nationals, nationhood, nationwide

page-paginate

paged, pages, paginated, paginates, paginating, pagination, paging

pale-pallid

paled, paleness, paler, pales, palest, paling, pallor

sole-solitary

solely, solitarily, solitariness, solitude, solo, soloist

unite-unity

reunite, unit, united, uniting

wise-wisdom

wisely, wiser, wisest

Vowel Changes: Schwa to Long Vowel Sound

You can remember how to spell the schwa sound in some words by thinking of a related word with a long vowel sound spelled the same way.

ability-able

abilities, abler, ablest, ably, disability, disable, inability, unable

equaled-equation

equal, equaling, equality, equalize, equals, equate, equations, equator, inequality, unequal

(continued)

Vowel Changes (continued)

proposition-propose

proposal, proposed, proposer, proposes, proposing, propositions

Vowel Changes: Schwa to Short Vowel Sound

You can remember how to spell the schwa sound in some words by thinking of a related word with a short vowel sound spelled the same way.

angel-angelic

angelical, angelically, angels

compete-competition

competed, competes, competing, competitions, competitive, competitively, competitiveness, competitor

democracy-democratic

democracies, democrat, democratically, democratization, democratize, undemocratic

formal-formality

form, formalism, formalist, formalities, formalize, formally, format, formula, informal, informality, informally

general-generality

generalist, generalities, generalization, generalize, generally, generalness

history-historical

historian, historic, historically, histories, prehistory

individual-individuality

individualism, individualist, individualistic, individualities, individualize, individually, individuals

legal-legality

illegal, illegality, illegally, legalese, legalism, legalities, legalize, legally

local-locality

locale, localism, localities, localize, locally

major-majority

majorities

medal-medallion

medalist, medallions, medals

mental-mentality

mentalities, mentally

metal-metallic

metallically, metallography, metallurgy, metals

method-methodical

methodic, methodically, methodicalness, methods

moral-morality

immoral, morale, moralism, moralist, moralistic, moralities, moralize, morally, morals

mortal-mortality

immortal, mortalities, mortally, mortals

normal-normality

abnormal, abnormalities, norm, normalcy, normalize, normally

personal-personality

impersonal, interpersonal, person, personalism, personalities, personalize, personally

Vowel Changes (continued)

poem-poetic

poems, poet, poetical, poetically, poetics, poetry

regular-regularity

irregular, regularities, regularize, regularly

reside-resident

resided, residence, residency, residential, residentially, resides, residing

similar-similarity

dissimilar, dissimilarity, similarities, similarly

total-totality

totaled, totaling, totalitarian, totalities, totally, totals

Word Parts

Words with the same Latin word root or the same Greek word part are related in spelling and meaning. Knowing the meaning of a word part can help you understand and spell the words in that family. The letters in dark print highlight the word part.

Latin Word Roots

aud, "to hear"

audible	**aud**it
audience	**aud**ition
audio	**aud**itorium
audio-visual	**aud**itory

dict, "to tell"

contra**dict**	**dict**ionary
dictate	pre**dict**
dictator	vale**dict**orian
diction	ver**dict**

ject, "to throw"

ad**ject**ive	pro**ject**
de**ject**	pro**ject**or
in**ject**	re**ject**
inter**ject**	sub**ject**
ob**ject**	sub**ject**ive
ob**ject**ive	

loc, "place"

allo**cate**	**loc**ate
dis**loc**ate	**loc**ation
local	**loc**omotion
locale	**loc**omotive
locality	re**loc**ate

mit, "to send"

ad**mit**	per**mit**
com**mit**	sub**mit**
com**mit**tee	trans**mit**

ped, "foot"

centi**ped**e	**ped**estrian
milli**ped**e	**ped**igree
pedal	**ped**ometer
pedestal	

port, "to carry"

de**port**	**port**er
ex**port**	re**port**
im**port**	sup**port**
im**port**ant	trans**port**
portable	

pose, "to put"

com**pose**	**pos**itive
de**pose**	**pos**ture
dis**pose**	pro**pose**
ex**pose**	re**pose**
op**pose**	sup**pose**
op**pos**ite	trans**pose**
position	

scribe or script, "to write"

de**scribe**	de**script**ion
in**scribe**	de**script**ive
pre**scribe**	in**script**ion
scribble	manu**script**
scribe	pre**script**ion

(continued)

Word Parts (continued)

subscribe   subscription
transcribe   transcription

sist, "to stand"

assist   irresistible
assistance   persist
consist   persistent
consistent   resist
insist   resistance
insistence

spect, "to look"

aspect   respect
circumspect   respectable
inspect   spectacle
inspection   spectator
inspector   specter
perspective   spectrum
prospect   suspect
prospector

tract, "to pull"

abstract   extract
attract   protract
attraction   retract
attractive   subtract
contract   tract
detract   traction
distract   tractor

vac, "to be empty"

evacuate   vacate
vacancy   vacuum
vacant

vis, "to see"

advise   visible
audio-visual   vision
improvise   visit
provision   visor
revise   vista
supervise   visual
televise   visualize
visa

Greek Word Parts

ast, "star"

aster   astronaut
asterisk   astronomer
asteroid   astronomy
astrology   disaster

phys, "nature"

physical   physics
physician   physique

poli, "city" or "government"

Acropolis   police
cosmopolitan   policy
megalopolis   politician
metropolis   politics
metropolitan

tele, "far off; distant"

telecast   telescope
telegram   telethon
telegraph   televise
telepathy   television
telephone

Spelling Dictionary

Spelling Table

This Spelling Table shows many of the letter combinations that spell the same sounds in different words. Use this table for help in looking up words that you do not know how to spell.

Sounds	Spellings	Sample Words
|ă|	a, au	bat, have, laugh
|ā|	a, ai, ay, ea	made, later, rain, play, great
|âr|	air, ar, are, eir, ere	fair, scarce, care, their, where
|ä|	a, al	father, calm
|är|	ar, ear	art, heart
|b|	b, bb	bus, rabbit
|ch|	ch, tch, tu	chin, match, culture
|d|	d, dd	dark, sudden
|ĕ|	a, ai, ay, e, ea, ie	any, said, says, went, head, friend
|ē|	e, ea, ee, ei, ey, i, ie, y	these, we, beast, fleet, receive, honey, ski, chief, bumpy, magazine
|f|	f, ff, gh	funny, off, enough
|g|	g, gg, gu	get, egg, guide
|h|	h, wh	hat, who
|hw|	wh	when
|ĭ|	a, e, ee, i, ia, u, ui, y	cottage, before, been, mix, give, carriage, busy, build, gym
|ī|	ei, i, ie, igh, y	height, time, mind, pie, fight, try, type
|îr|	ear, eer, eir, ier	near, deer, weird, pier
|j|	dge, g, ge, j	judge, gem, range, jet
|k|	c, ch, ck, k	picnic, school, tick, key
|kw|	qu	quick
|l|	l, ll	last, all
|m|	m, mb, mm, mn	mop, bomb, summer, column
|n|	gn, kn, n, nn	sign, knee, no, inn
|ng|	n, ng	think, ring
|ŏ|	a, ho, o	was, honor, pond
|ō|	o, oa, ough, ow	most, hope, float, though, row

Sounds	Spellings	Sample Words
|ô|	a, al, au, aw, o, ough	wall, talk, haunt, lawn, soft, brought
|ôr|	oar, oor, or, ore, our	roar, door, storm, store, court
|oi|	oi, oy	join, toy
|ou|	ou, ough, ow	loud, bough, now
|o͝o|	oo, ou, u	good, could, put
|o͞o|	ew, o, oe, oo, ou, u, ue, ui	flew, do, lose, shoe, spoon, you, truth, blue, juice
|p|	p, pp	paint, happen
|r|	r, rh, rr, wr	rub, rhyme, borrow, write
|s|	c, ce, ps, s, sc, ss	city, fence, psychology, same, scent, lesson
|sh|	ce, ch, ci, s, sh, ss, ti	ocean, machine, special, sure, sheep, mission, nation
|t|	ed, t, tt	stopped, talk, little
|th|	th	they, other
|th|	th	thin, teeth
|ŭ|	o, oe, oo, ou, u	front, come, does, flood, tough, sun
|yo͞o|	eau, ew, iew, u, ue	use, beauty, few, view, fuel, cue
|ûr|	ear, er, ir, or, ur	learn, herd, girl, word, turn
|v|	f, v	of, very
|w|	o, w	one, way
|y|	i, y	million, yes
|z|	s, z, zz	rise, zoo, fizz
|zh|	ge, s	garage, usual
|ə|	a, ai, e, eo, i, o, ou, u	about, captain, silent, surgeon, pencil, lemon, famous, circus

How to Use a Dictionary

Finding an Entry Word

Guide Words

The word you want to find in a dictionary is listed in alphabetical order. To find it quickly, use the guide words at the top of each page. Guide words name the first and last entries on the page.

Base Words

To find a word ending in **-ed** or **-ing,** you usually must look up its base word. To find **imitated** or **imitating,** for example, look up the base word **imitate.**

Homographs

Homographs have separate, numbered entries. For example, **sole,** meaning "the bottom of a shoe, boot, or slipper," is listed as **sole¹. Sole,** meaning "being the only one; single," is **sole².**

Reading an Entry

Read the dictionary entry below. Note the purpose of each part.

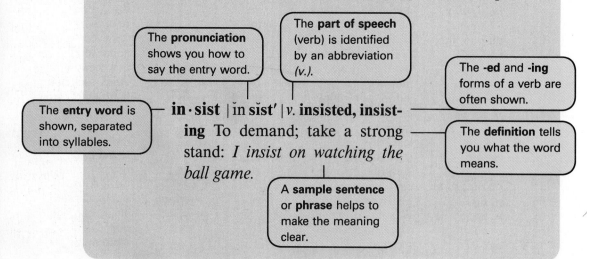

The **pronunciation** shows you how to say the entry word.

The **part of speech** (verb) is identified by an abbreviation (*v.*).

The **-ed** and **-ing** forms of a verb are often shown.

The **entry word** is shown, separated into syllables.

in·sist |ĭn sĭst′| *v.* **insisted, insist-ing** To demand; take a strong stand: *I insist on watching the ball game.*

The **definition** tells you what the word means.

A **sample sentence** or **phrase** helps to make the meaning clear.

Spelling Dictionary

A

a·bil·i·ty |ə bĭl′ ĭ tē| *n.*, *pl.* **abilities**
1. The quality of being able to do something; power: *Most people have the ability to dance.* **2.** Power to do something, especially as a result of practice; skill: *You have real ability as a dancer.*

-able A suffix that forms adjectives and means: **1.** Capable of; able to: *breakable.* **2.** Worthy of: *lovable.*

a·ble |ā′ bəl| *adj.* **abler, ablest** Having the power or ability to do something: *I will be able to see you tomorrow.*

ab·sent |ăb′ sənt| *adj.* Not present in a place or with someone: *Two students are absent today.*

ab·stain |ăb stān′| *v.* **abstained, abstaining** To keep oneself from doing by choice; hold back: *We abstained from eating too much.*

A·ca·di·a Na·tion·al Park |ə kā′ dē ə| A scenic area with rugged granite mountains along the coast of Maine.

ac·ci·dent |ăk′ sĭ dənt| *n.*, *pl.* **accidents**
1. Something that happens without being planned ahead of time: *Our meeting was a lucky accident.* **2.** An unexpected and undesirable event: *An accident held up traffic for miles.*

ac·cuse |ə kyo͞oz′| *v.* **accused, accusing** To blame for wrongdoing: *They were accused of stealing.*

act |ăkt| *v.* **acted, acting 1.** To conduct oneself; behave: *You act as if you are tired.* **2.** To perform a part, especially in a play or movie: *I want to act in the movies. n., pl.* **acts 1.** A thing done: *It was a brave act to rescue the drowning child.* **2.** One of the main divisions, especially of a play: *The first act takes place in a factory.*

ac·tion |ăk′ shən| *n.*, *pl.* **actions 1.** A thing done; act: *Take responsibility for your actions.* **2.** The activities or events of a play, story, or movie.

ac·tive |ăk′ tĭv| *adj.* Full of energy; busy.

Pronunciation Key

ă	pat	ŏ	pot	û	fur
ā	pay	ō	go	*th*	the
â	care	ô	paw, for	th	thin
ä	father	oi	oil	hw	which
ĕ	pet	o͞o	book	zh	usual
ē	be	o͞o	boot	ə	ago, item
ĭ	pit	yo͞o	cute		pencil, atom
ī	ice	ou	out		circus
î	near	ŭ	cut	ər	butter

Abbreviation Key

n.	noun	*prep.*	preposition
v.	verb	*interj.*	interjection
adj.	adjective	*sing.*	singular
adv.	adverb	*pl.*	plural
pron.	pronoun	*p.*	past
conj.	conjunction	*p. part.*	past participle

adv. **actively** *My grandfather, who is eighty-seven, still lives quite actively.*

ac·tor |ăk′ tər| *n.*, *pl.* **actors** A person who performs a part, especially in a play or motion picture.

a·dapt |ə dăpt′| *v.* **adapted, adapting** To change so as to be suitable for a different condition or purpose: *We put legs on a large tray to adapt it for use as a table.*

ad·dress |ə drĕs′| or |ăd′ rĕs′| *n.*, *pl.* **addresses 1.** The place where someone lives, works, or receives mail: *What is your home address?* **2.** A formal speech. *v.* |ə drĕs′| **addressed, addressing** To direct one's efforts or attention toward: *We addressed ourselves to our homework.*

ad·journ |ə jûrn′| *v.* **adjourned, adjourning** To bring or come to a close until later: *Our meeting was adjourned until next week.*

ad·mit |ăd mĭt′| *v.* **admitted, admitting**
1. To make known that something is true. **2.** To allow or permit to enter.

a·dore |ə dôr′| *v.* **adored, adoring 1.** To worship as a divine being. **2.** To love with deep devotion: *I adore my sisters.*

ad·ven·ture |əd **vĕn′** chər| *n., pl.* **adventures 1.** A bold, dangerous, or risky undertaking: *They set out on a daring space adventure.* **2.** An unusual or exciting experience: *The storm made our hike a real adventure.*

af·ter·noon |ăf′ tər **noon′**|*n.,pl.***afternoons** The part of the day from noon until the sun sets.

air·port |**âr′** pôrt′| *n., pl.* **airports** A place with marked, open spaces where aircraft can take off and land.

al·le·giance |ə **lē′** jəns| *n., pl.* **allegiances** Faithful devotion to one's country, a person, or a cause; loyalty: *Martin had a deep allegiance to his family and always helped them.*

al·low |ə **lou′**| *v.* **allowed, allowing 1.** To let do or happen; permit: *No ball playing allowed!* **2.** To permit to have; let have: *Please allow me to explain our project.*

all right |ôl′ **rīt′**| *adj. and adv.* Satisfactory but not excellent; good enough: *These peaches are all right, but they could be fresher.*

al·ter·a·tion |ôl′ tə **rā′** shən| *n., pl.* **alterations** A change: *We made alterations to the house by adding a den and a garage.*

al·though |ôl **thō′**| *conj.* Even though.

am·a·teur |**ăm′** ə chər| or |**ăm′** ə tər| *n., pl.* **amateurs** A person who engages in an art, science, or sport for enjoyment rather than for money. *adj.* Not professional.

a·maze |ə **māz′**| *v.* **amazed, amazing** To fill with surprise or wonder; astonish: *The idea of water carving a deep canyon out of solid rock amazes me.*

a·mend·ment |ə **mĕnd′** mənt| *n., pl.* **amendments** A change made to improve, correct, or add something: *An amendment to the United States Constitution limits the President to two full terms in office.*

a·muse |ə **myooz′**| *v.* **amused, amusing 1.** To give enjoyment to; entertain pleasantly: *Playing checkers always amuses me.* **2.** To cause to laugh or smile: *The clown's tricks amused us all.*

an·gel |**ān′** jəl| *n., pl.* **angels 1.** A spiritual being. **2.** A person who is like an angel, for example, by being kind or innocent.

an·gel·ic |ăn **jĕl′** ĭk| *adj.* Of or like angels: *She has an angelic voice.*

an·ger |**ăng′** gər| *n.* A strong feeling of not being pleased with someone or something; rage.

an·gle |**ăng′** gəl| *n., pl.* **angles 1.** The figure made by two lines that begin at the same point. **2.** A way of looking at something; point of view.

an·gry |**ăng′** grē| *adj.* **angrier, angriest** Feeling, showing, or resulting from anger: *I am angriest when you are late.*

an·i·mate |**ăn′** ə māt′| *v.* **animated, animating 1.** To give life to or make so as to seem alive. **2.** To produce as an animated cartoon: *Walt Disney animated stories such as Snow White.*

an·i·ma·tion |ăn′ ə **mā′** shən| *n.* **1.** The condition or quality of being alive; liveliness; vitality. **2.** The process or processes by which an animated cartoon is prepared. **3.** An animated cartoon.

an·kle |**ăng′** kəl| *n., pl.* **ankles** The joint between the foot and leg.

an·oth·er |ə **nŭth′** ər| *adj.* Being a second or an additional one: *I'd love another helping. pron.* An additional person or thing: *First one left and then another.*

an·swer |**ăn′** sər| *n., pl.* **answers** Something said or written in return to a question, statement, request, or letter; reply.

-ant A suffix that forms nouns and adjectives: *occupant.*

an·tic·i·pate |ăn **tĭs′** ə pāt′| *v.* **anticipated, anticipating** To look forward to; expect: *We anticipate a fine weekend.*

a·part·ment |ə **pärt′** mənt| *n., pl.* **apartments** One or more rooms usually used as a place to live.

ap·plause |ə **plôz′**| *n.* Enjoyment or approval expressed especially by the clapping of hands: *The actors loved the loud applause at the end of the play.*

ap·pre·ci·ate |ə **prē′** shē āt′| *v.* **appreciated, appreciating 1.** To enjoy and understand: *I appreciate books.* **2.** To be thankful for: *I appreciated your help.*

ap·pren·tice |ə **prĕn′** tĭs| *n., pl.* **apprentices** A person who is learning a craft or trade by working for a skilled worker.

Ar·bor Day |är′ bər| *n.* A holiday, often in the spring, observed in many areas by planting trees.

arch·er·y |är′ chə rē| *n.* The sport or skill of shooting with a bow and arrows: *He loves the sport of archery, and all of his arrows hit the target.*

ar·chi·tec·ture |är′ kĭ tĕk′ chər| *n.* **1.** The art of designing buildings. **2.** A style of building.

ar·e·a |âr′ ē ə| *n., pl.* **areas** A region, as of land: *The family moved from the city to a farming area.*

ar·my |är′ mē| *n., pl.* **armies** A large body of men and women organized and trained for land warfare.

ar·rest |ə rĕst′| *v.* **arrested, arresting** To seize and hold by authority of law; take prisoner: *The detective arrested the thief.*

ar·rive |ə rīv′| *v.* **arrived, arriving** To reach a place: *They arrived early.*

ar·row |ăr′ ō| *n., pl.* **arrows** A straight, thin shaft that is shot from a bow. An arrow has a pointed head at one end and feathers at the other.

ar·ti·fi·cial |är′ tə fĭsh′ əl| *adj.* **1.** Made by humans rather than occurring in nature: *artificial pearls.* **2.** Not genuine or natural; pretended: *an artificial smile.*

a·shamed |ə shāmd′| *adj.* Feeling shame or guilt; not proud.

as·sem·ble |ə sĕm′ bəl| *v.* **assembled, assembling** To put together the parts of; build: *The mechanic assembled the engine.*

as·sist |ə sĭst′| *v.* **assisted, assisting** To give help; aid.

as·ter |ăs′ tər| *n., pl.* **asters** A plant whose white, pink, purple, or yellow flowers have petals arranged in a starlike pattern.

ă	pat	ŏ	pot	û	fur
ā	pay	ō	go	*th*	the
â	care	ô	paw, for	th	thin
ä	father	oi	oil	hw	which
ĕ	pet	o͞o	book	zh	usual
ē	be	o͞o	boot	ə	ago, item
ĭ	pit	yo͞o	cute		pencil, atom
ī	ice	ou	out		circus
î	near	ŭ	cut	ər	butter

as·ter·isk |ăs′ tə rĭsk| *n., pl.* **asterisks** A symbol (*) used in printing to direct the reader to another part of the page.

as·ter·oid |ăs′ tə roid′| *n., pl.* **asteroids** One of the thousands of small planets that orbit the sun.

as·ton·ish |ə stŏn′ ĭsh| *v.* **astonished, astonishing** To surprise greatly; amaze: *The brilliant sunrise astonished us.*

a·stound |ə stound′| *v.* **astounded, astounding** To astonish: *Her brilliant performance astounded the audience.*

as·tro·naut |ăs′ trə nôt′| *n., pl.* **astronauts** A person trained to travel in a spacecraft.

as·tron·o·mer |ə strŏn′ ə mər| *n., pl.* **astronomers** An expert in astronomy.

as·tron·o·my |ə strŏn′ ə mē| *n.* The scientific study and observation of the part of the universe beyond the earth, including stars, planets, comets, and galaxies.

At·lan·tic O·cean |ăt lăn′ tĭk ō′ shən| The second largest of the oceans, extending from the Arctic to the Antarctic between the Americas on the west and Europe and Africa on the east.

at·tend |ə tĕnd′| *v.* **attended, attending** To be present at: *I will attend Teri's party.*

at·ten·tion |ə tĕn′ shən| *n., pl.* **attentions** **1.** The ability to concentrate: *The story held our attention for more than an hour.* **2.** The act of noticing or giving careful thought: *Your letter has come to our attention.*

au·di·tion |ô dĭsh′ ən| *n., pl.* **auditions** A short performance to test the ability of a musician, singer, dancer, or actor. *v.* **auditioned, auditioning** To test or perform in an audition: *Have you auditioned for the lead in the school play?*

av·e·nue |ăv′ ə nōō′| or |ăv′ ə nyōō′| *n.*, *pl.* **avenues** A usually wide street.

av·er·age |ăv′ ər ĭj| *adj.* Typical, usual, or ordinary: *The average two-year-old loves teddy bears.*

a·wait |ə wāt′| *v.* **awaited, awaiting** To wait for; expect: *We are awaiting our test scores.*

a·ware |ə wâr′| *adj.* Conscious of something: *We are aware of the time.*

awe·struck |ô′ strŭk′| *adj.* Full of or exhibiting awe or wonder.

aw·ful |ô′ fəl| *adj.* Very bad; horrible.

awk·ward |ôk′ wərd| *adj.* Not graceful; clumsy: *Seals are awkward when out of water.*

B

ba·by-sit |bā′ bē sĭt′| *v.* **baby-sat, baby-sitting** To take care of a child or children when the parents are not at home.

bac·te·ri·a |băk tîr′ ē ə| *pl. n.* Tiny one-celled organisms. Some bacteria help digest food; other bacteria cause diseases.

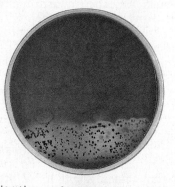

badge |băj| *n., pl.* **badges** Something worn to show that a person belongs to a certain group, such as a police force: *Every police officer carries a badge.*

Bad·lands Na·tion·al Park |băd′ lăndz′| *pl. n.* A scenic area in South Dakota characterized by eroded ridges, peaks, and mesas. The area contains fossil remains.

baf·fle |băf′ əl| *v.* **baffled, baffling** To be too difficult or confusing to understand or solve: *These strange events baffle me.*

bag·gage |băg′ ĭj| *n.* The suitcases and other containers that a person carries when traveling.

bald |bôld| *adj.* **balder, baldest 1.** Lacking hair on the top of the head. **2.** Lacking natural or usual covering; bare: *The fire left a bald spot in the lawn.*

bal·lad |băl′ əd| *n., pl.* **ballads** A poem or song that has a plot and characters and tells a story, usually about love.

ball bear·ing |bôl′ bâr′ ĭng| *n., pl.* **ball bearings** A bearing in which the moving part slides on a number of loose steel balls in a groove. Ball bearings reduce friction between machine parts.

ball game |bôl′ gām| A game, especially baseball, that is played with a ball.

ball·room |bôl′ rōōm′| or |bôl′ rŏŏm′| *n., pl.* **ballrooms** A large room for dancing.

bal·lot |băl′ ət| *n., pl.* **ballots** A piece of paper on which a voter marks a choice or choices: *She went into the voting booth and marked her ballot.*

band·age |băn′ dĭj| *n., pl.* **bandages** A strip of cloth or other material used to bind, cover, or protect a wound or other injury.

ban·ner |băn′ ər| *n., pl.* **banners** A flag or similar piece of material with words or a special design on it.

barge |bärj| *n., pl.* **barges** A large boat with a flat bottom, used to carry freight on rivers and canals.

bar·rel |băr′ əl| *n., pl.* **barrels** A large container with bulging sides and round, flat ends. Barrels are usually made of narrow strips of wood held together by hoops.

base·ment |bās′ mənt| *n., pl.* **basements** The lowest floor of a building, usually below ground level; cellar.

ba·sic |bā′ sĭk| *adj.* Main, essential, primary: *Her basic chores were mopping and emptying the trash.*

bas·ket·ball |băs′ kĭt bôl′| *n., pl.* **basketballs 1.** A game played by two teams of five players each on a court with a raised basket at each end. Players score by throwing the ball through the basket defended by the other team. **2.** The large, round ball used in this game.

bas·ket weave |băs′ kĭt wēv′| *n., pl.* **basket weaves** A pattern of weaving in which double threads are woven together to produce a plain, regular effect.

bat·tle·ground |băt′ l ground′| *n., pl.* **battlegrounds** A place of fighting or conflict; battlefield.

beast |bēst| *n., pl.* **beasts** An animal other than a human, especially a large, four-footed animal.

beau·ti·ful |byoo′ tə fəl| *adj.* Being very pleasing to the senses or mind: *Beautiful music filled the air.*

beg |bĕg| *v.* **begged, begging** To ask earnestly as a favor; plead.

be·have |bĭ hāv′| *v.* **behaved, behaving 1.** To function in a certain way: *The car behaves well in snow.* **2.** To act in a given way: *You behaved badly.*

ber·ry |bĕr′ ē| *n., pl.* **berries** A usually small, juicy fruit that has many seeds.
♦ *These sound alike* **berry, bury.**

berth |bûrth| *n., pl.* **berths** A bunk, as on a ship or railroad sleeping car: *She slept on the top berth as the train sped along.*

be·ware |bĭ wâr′| *v.* To be careful; look out: *Beware of the dog.*

bill |bĭl| *n., pl.* **bills** A draft of a law presented for approval to a legislature: *The bill passed by only three votes.*

bis·cuit |bĭs′ kĭt| *n., pl.* **biscuits** A small cake of baked bread dough: *We ate the biscuits while they were still hot.*

blew |bloo| *v.* Past tense of **blow**: *The wind blew John's hat off.*

blos·som |blŏs′ əm| *n., pl.* **blossoms** A flower, especially of a fruit-bearing plant. *v.* **blossomed, blossoming** To come into flower; bloom.

blur |blûr| *n., pl.* **blurs** Something that is dim or hard to see.

board |bôrd| *v.* **boarded, boarding** To go aboard: *We boarded the plane.*

boast |bōst| *v.* **boasted, boasting** To praise oneself, one's belongings, or one's actions; brag.

bore |bôr| *v.* **bored, boring** To cause to feel that one has had enough, as by seeming dull or uninteresting.
♦ *These sound alike* **bore, boar.**

ă	pat	ŏ	pot	û	fur
ā	pay	ō	go	*th*	the
â	care	ô	paw, for	th	thin
ä	father	oi	oil	hw	which
ĕ	pet	oo	book	zh	usual
ē	be	oo	boot	ə	ago, item
ĭ	pit	yoo	cute		pencil, atom
ī	ice	ou	out		circus
î	near	ŭ	cut	ər	butter

bor·row |bŏr′ ō| *v.* **borrowed, borrowing** To get from someone else with the understanding that what is gotten will be returned or replaced; to take on loan: *The book I borrowed from the library is due today.*

bot·tom |bŏt′ əm| *n., pl.* **bottoms 1.** The lowest part of something. **2.** The land under a body of water: *At the bottom of the lake I found buried treasure.*

bou·tique |boo tēk′| *n., pl.* **boutiques** A shop or store that sells such things as gifts or clothes: *She bought a very stylish dress at the boutique.*

boy·cott |boi′ kŏt′| *v.* **boycotted, boycotting** To refuse as part of an organized group to use, buy from, or deal with a store, company, person, or nation. Boycotting may be an act of protest or punishment: *boycott a store; boycott an airline.*

brag |brăg| *v.* **bragged, bragging** To speak with too much pride about oneself in an attempt to show off; boast.

brain |brān| *n., pl.* **brains** The main organ of the nervous system in humans and other animals with backbones. The brain controls voluntary actions such as speaking and many involuntary actions such as breathing. In humans the brain is the center of memory, learning, and emotion.

break·fast |brĕk′ fəst| *n., pl.* **breakfasts** The first meal of the day.

breath |brĕth| *n., pl.* **breaths** The air taken into the lungs and forced out when a person breathes.

breathe |brēth| *v.* **breathed, breathing** To take air into the lungs and force it out; inhale and exhale: *All mammals breathe air.*

breath·less |brĕth′ lĭs| *adj.* **1.** Out of breath; panting: *We were breathless after running up the stairs.* **2.** Holding the breath from excitement or suspense.

bridge |brĭj| *n., pl.* **bridges** A structure built over a river, railroad, or other obstacle so that people or vehicles can cross from one side to the other.

broad·cast |brôd′ kăst′| *v.* **broadcast** *or* **broadcasted, broadcasting** To send out over a wide area by radio or television: *All the networks will broadcast the governor's speech.*

broke |brōk| *v.* Past tense of **break**: *He ran faster than anyone else ever had, and he broke the record for the fifty-meter dash.*

broth·er-in-law |brŭth′ ər ĭn lô′| *n., pl.* **brothers-in-law** **1.** The brother of one's husband or wife. **2.** The husband of one's sister.

bruise |brōōz| *n., pl.* **bruises** An injury that leaves a mark on the skin but does not break it.

bub·bler |bŭb′ lər| *n., pl.* **bubblers** A drinking fountain in which the water flows upward through a small nozzle.

bunch |bŭnch| *n., pl.* **bunches** A group of things of the same kind that are growing, fastened, or placed together: *I put the bunch of keys in my pocket.*

bunk |bŭngk| *n., pl.* **bunks** **1.** A narrow bed built like a shelf against a wall. **2.** A double-decker bed.

bur·glar |bûr′ glər| *n., pl.* **burglars** A person who breaks into a building in order to steal; a thief.

burnt |bûrnt| *v.* A past tense and past participle of **burn**. Damaged by heat; scorched: *We burnt the roast by leaving it in the oven too long.*

bur·y |bĕr′ ē| *v.* **buried, burying** To hide by placing in the ground and covering with earth: *The dog buried the bone in the garden.*

♦ *These sound alike* **bury, berry**.

bush·el |bŏŏsh′ əl| *n, pl.* **bushels** A unit of measure for dry things, such as fruit or grain, equal to 4 pecks or 32 quarts.

bus·y |bĭz′ ē| *adj.* **busier, busiest** **1.** Engaged in work or other activity: *I am busy studying for an important exam.* **2.** Crowded with activity: *Today I had a busy morning.*

C

Cab·ot |kăb′ ət|, **John** 1450–1498. Italian explorer in the service of England; discovered the mainland of North America in 1497.

cam·el |kăm′ əl| *n., pl.* **camels** A large animal with a long neck and one or two humps. Camels are found in northern Africa and western Asia.

cam·er·a |kăm′ ər ə| *n., pl.* **cameras** **1.** A device for taking photographs or motion pictures. **2.** A device that receives an image and changes it into electrical signals for television.

cam·paign |kăm pān′| *n., pl.* **campaigns** Organized activity to gain a goal, as electing a candidate to office.

camp·fire |kămp′ fīr′| *n., pl.* **campfires** An outdoor fire used for warmth or cooking: *The children sat around the campfire and roasted potatoes.*

camp·site |kămp′ sīt′| *n., pl.* **campsites** An area used for camping.

ca·nar·y |kə nâr′ ē| *n., pl.* **canaries** A songbird, often yellow in color, that can be kept as a pet.

can·di·date |kăn′ dĭ dāt′| *n., pl.* **candidates** A person who seeks or is put forward by others for an office or honor.

ca·noe |kə nōō′| *n., pl.* **canoes** A light, slender boat with pointed ends that is propelled by paddles: *The campers paddled their canoes across the lake.*

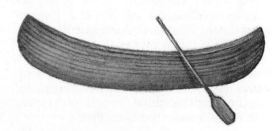

can·vas |kăn′ vəs| *n., pl.* **canvases** A heavy coarse cloth of cotton, hemp, or flax that is used for making tents and sails and is the material on which artists make paintings.
♦ *These sound alike* **canvas, canvass.**

can·vass |kăn′ vəs| *v.* **canvassed, canvassing** To visit (a person or region) to get votes, hear opinions, or make sales; to poll or survey.
♦ *These sound alike* **canvass, canvas.**

Cap·i·tol |kăp′ ĭ tl| *n.* The domed building in Washington, D.C., in which the Congress of the United States meets.

cap·tain |kăp′ tən| *n., pl.* **captains** 1. The leader of a group; chief. 2. The person in command of a ship. 3. An Army, Air Force, or Marine Corps officer ranking above a lieutenant.

cap·tive |kăp′ tĭv| *adj.* Held prisoner or kept under the control of another. *n., pl.* **captives** A person or animal held captive.

cap·ture |kăp′ chər| *v.* **captured, capturing** 1. To seize and hold, as by force or skill: *The team captured the trophy.* 2. To hold or preserve in permanent form: *capture the excitement.*

car·di·nal |kär′ dn əl| *n., pl.* **cardinals** A North American songbird with a crest on its head and bright red feathers.

ca·reer |kə rîr′| *n., pl.* **careers** A profession that a person chooses as a life's work; occupation: *My cousin has a career as a scientist.*

care·less |kâr′ lĭs| *adj.* Not taking the necessary care: *a careless mistake.*

car·rot |kăr′ ət| *n., pl.* **carrots** The long, tapering, yellow-orange edible root of a garden plant.

carve |kärv| *v.* **carved, carving** To make by cutting: *I carved a clown from a bar of soap.*

cas·se·role |kăs′ ə rōl′| *n., pl.* **casseroles** Food baked and served in a dish made of pottery or glass: *a shrimp casserole.*

ca·ter |kā′ tər| *v.* **catered, catering** To provide food, supplies, and sometimes service and entertainment, as for a party.

cause |kôz| *n., pl.* **causes** Someone or something that makes something happen: *What was the cause of the fire?*

ă	pat	ŏ	pot	û	fur
ā	pay	ō	go	*th*	the
â	care	ô	paw, for	th	thin
ä	father	oi	oil	hw	which
ĕ	pet	o͞o	book	zh	usual
ē	be	o͞o	boot	ə	ago, item
ĭ	pit	yo͞o	cute		pencil, atom
ī	ice	ou	out		circus
î	near	ŭ	cut	ər	butter

cau·tion |kô′ shən| *n., pl.* **cautions** Great care so as to avoid possible danger or trouble: *Use caution when you climb the rocky cliff.*

cave |kāv| *n., pl.* **caves** A hollow area in the earth, usually on the side of a hill or mountain, with an opening to the outside.

cav·i·ty |kăv′ ĭ tē| *n., pl.* **cavities** A hollow place or area; hole: *The dentist filled two cavities in my teeth.*

cease |sēs| *v.* **ceased, ceasing** To come or bring to an end; stop: *The storm ceased at daybreak.*

cell |sĕl| *n., pl.* **cells** The smallest and most basic part of a plant or animal. Most cells consist of protoplasm, have a small mass called a nucleus near the center, and are enclosed by a thin membrane.

cen·ti·pede |sĕn′ tə pēd′| *n., pl.* **centipedes** A wormlike animal that has many pairs of legs.

chalk·board |chôk′ bôrd′| *n., pl.* **chalkboards** A panel, usually green or black, for writing on with chalk; a blackboard.

cham·ber |chām′ bər| *n., pl.* **chambers** A room in a house, especially a bedroom.

cham·pi·on |chăm′ pē ən| *n., pl.* **champions** The winner of a game or contest, accepted as the best of all.

chan·nel |chăn′ əl| *n., pl.* **channels** A band of radio waves used for broadcasting, as on television: *Change the channel so I can watch my favorite TV show.*

char·ac·ter |kăr′ ĭk tər| *n., pl.* **characters** A person in a book, play, or movie.

char·ter |chär′ tər| *n., pl.* **charters** A formal written document from an authority, as a ruler or government, granting rights or privileges.

check |chĕk| *v.* **checked, checking** To test or examine to find out if something is correct or in good condition: *Check your answers after doing the math problems.*

cheer·ful |chîr′ fəl| *adj.* Showing or full of cheer; happy; not gloomy.

cheer·lead·er |chîr′ lē′ dər| *n., pl.* **cheerleaders** A person who starts and leads the cheering of spectators at a game.

chem·i·cal |kĕm′ ĭ kəl| *n., pl.* **chemicals** Any of the substances classed as elements or the compounds formed from them: *Oxygen and hydrogen are chemicals.*

choose |chōōz| *v.* **chose, chosen, choosing** To pick out, especially on the basis of what one wants and thinks best: *I chose four games to take on my trip.*

cin·e·ma |sĭn′ ə mə| *n., pl.* **cinemas** A motion-picture theater: *We saw a movie at the cinema.*

cin·na·mon |sĭn′ ə mən| *n.* A spice made from the dried or ground bark of a tropical tree: *She sprinkled cinnamon on her toast.*

cir·cuit |sûr′ kĭt| *n., pl.* **circuits** A device that can store information and through which electricity can flow.

cit·y |sĭt′ ē| *n., pl.* **cities** A place where many people live close to one another. Cities are larger than towns and are usually centers of business activity.

cit·y hall |sĭt′ ē hôl′| *n., pl.* **city halls** The building in which the offices of a city or local government are located.

claim |klām| *n., pl.* **claims** A right to something. *v.* **claimed, claiming** To state to be true; assert: *I claim that I can run faster than you.*

clam·or |klăm′ ər| *n., pl.* **clamors** A loud noise, as of a crowd shouting; a great uproar: *Instead of silence a great clamor filled the kitchen.*

class·mate |klăs′ māt′| *n., pl.* **classmates** A member of the same class in school.

claw |klô| *n., pl.* **claws** A sharp, often curved nail on the toe of an animal or bird. *v.* **clawed, clawing** To dig, scratch, or scrape with or as if with claws: *The kitten clawed the couch.*

cleanse |klĕnz| *v.* **cleansed, cleansing** To make clean.

climb |klīm| *v.* **climbed, climbing** To go in various directions, such as up, down, or over, often by use of the hands and feet.

close |klōs| *adj.* **closer, closest 1.** Near in space or time: *The airport is close to town.* **2.** Near in relationship; intimate: *She is my close friend. n.* **closeness** *There was a fond closeness between Cheryl and her grandfather.*

clos·et |klŏz′ ĭt| *n., pl.* **closets** A small room in which clothes or household supplies can be kept.

clo·ver |klō′ vər| *n., pl.* **clovers** Any of several plants with leaves divided into three leaflets and rounded heads of small flowers.

clue |klōō| *n., pl.* **clues** Something that helps to solve a problem or mystery: *I'll give you one more clue to the riddle.*

History • clue

Clue comes from an Old English word *clewe,* meaning a "ball of thread."

code |kōd| *n. pl.* **codes** A system of signals, symbols, or letters given special meanings and used in sending messages and especially in keeping them secret.

col·lapse |kə lăps′| *v.* **collapsed, collapsing** To fall down suddenly; cave in; topple: *Part of the roof collapsed under the weight of the snow.*

col·lar |kŏl′ ər| *n., pl.* **collars** The part of a garment that fits around the neck.

col·lect |kə lĕkt′| *v.* **collected, collecting 1.** To bring or come together in a group; accumulate: *We collected wood to build a campfire.* **2.** To gather as a hobby or for study: *I collect stamps.*

col·lide |kə līd′| *v.* **collided, colliding** To strike together with force; crash: *The kites collided high in the air.*

col·o·ny |kŏl′ ə nē| *n., pl.* **colonies 1.** A group of people who settle in a distant land but remain citizens of their native country; settlement. **2. Colonies** The 13 British colonies that became the United States.

Co·lum·bus |kə lŭm′ bəs|, **Christopher** 1451–1506. Italian navigator and explorer; opened the New World to exploration. He sailed for the Indies, but instead reached America in 1492.

col·umn |kŏl′ əm| *n., pl.* **columns** An article that appears regularly in a newspaper or magazine: *the sports column.*

col·um·nist |kŏl′ əm nĭst| or |kŏl′ ə mĭst| *n., pl.* **columnists** One who writes a column for a newspaper or magazine.

com- See **con-**.

com·fort·a·ble |kŭm′ fər tə bəl| *adj.* **1.** Giving comfort: *Every living room needs a comfortable couch.* **2.** In a state of comfort; at ease: *We tried to make our guests comfortable.*

com·mand |kə mănd′| *n., pl.* **commands** A signal that tells a computer to start, stop, or continue a specific operation: *Type your command on the computer keyboard.*

com·mer·cial |kə mûr′ shəl| *n., pl.* **commercials** An advertisement on television or radio: *Who is the actor in that toothpaste commercial?*

com·mit·tee |kə mĭt′ ē| *n., pl.* **committees** A group of people chosen to do a particular job: *Please join the committee to raise money for a new hospital.*

com·mon |kŏm′ ən| *adj.* **commoner, commonest 1.** Belonging to or shared equally by everybody: *The swamp was drained for common use.* **2.** Found or occurring often; widespread: *Cats are common pets.*

com·pan·ion |kəm păn′ yən| *n., pl.* **companions** A person who often accompanies or associates with another person; friend.

com·pare |kəm pâr′| *v.* **compared, comparing 1.** To represent as similar; liken: *We can compare the wings of a bird to those of an airplane.* **2.** To study in order to note similarities and differences: *We compared the habits of bees and spiders.*

com·plain |kəm plān′| *v.* **complained, complaining** To express unhappiness or discontent: *Don't complain about the food.*

com·plex |kəm plĕks′| or |kŏm′ plĕks′| *adj.* Difficult to understand; not simple: *Computers are used to help solve complex mathematical problems.*

ă	pat	ŏ	pot	û	fur
ā	pay	ō	go	*th*	the
â	care	ô	paw, for	th	thin
ä	father	oi	oil	hw	which
ĕ	pet	ōō	book	zh	usual
ē	be	ōō	boot	ə	ago, item
ĭ	pit	yōō	cute		pencil, atom
ī	ice	ou	out		circus
î	near	ŭ	cut	ər	butter

com·pose |kəm pōz′| *v.* **composed, composing** To make or create by putting parts or elements together: *An artist composes a picture by arranging forms and colors.*

com·pound |kŏm′ pound′| *n., pl.* **compounds** A word made by combining two or more other words. *Basketball, up-to-date,* and *test tube* are compounds.

com·pro·mise |kŏm′ prə mīz′| *n., pl.* **compromises** A settlement of an argument or dispute reached by each side giving up some of its claims or demands: *The children compromised by taking turns.*

com·put·er |kəm pyōō′ tər| *n., pl.* **computers** A complex electronic machine that can accept information, work on the information to solve a problem, and produce an answer or result.

con- A prefix that means "together"; "with": *contain.*

con·cern |kən sûrn′| *v.* **concerned, concerning** To worry or trouble: *The hikers were concerned about the rain clouds.*

con·cise |kən sīs′| *adj.* Saying much in a few words; brief and to the point: *Write a concise book report.*

con·di·tion |kən dĭsh′ ən| *n., pl.* **conditions 1.** The way someone or something is: *The house was in poor condition after the flood.* **2.** Working order: *Our car is in good condition.*

con·dor |kŏn′ dər| *n., pl.* **condors** A large bird, a vulture, that lives in the mountains of California and South America.

con·duct |kən dŭkt′| *v.* **conducted, conducting 1.** To lead, guide, or direct: *The guide conducts daily tours.* **2.** To behave in a certain way. *n.* |kŏn′ dŭkt′| The way a person acts; behavior.

con·fess |kən fĕs'| *v.* **confessed, confessing** To admit that one has done something bad or illegal: *I confess that I broke the window.*

con·fes·sion |kən fĕsh' ən| *n., pl.* **confessions** The act of confessing or admitting guilt.

Con·gress |kŏng' grĭs| *n.* The United States Senate and House of Representatives, the assemblies that make laws.

con·science |kŏn' shəns| *n., pl.* **consciences** Inner feelings and ideas that tell a person what is right and what is wrong: *My conscience tells me to be honest.*

con·sent |kən sĕnt'| *v.* **consented, consenting** To give permission: *My parents consented to my plans. n., pl.* **consents** Permission; approval: *I have my teacher's consent to go to the library.*

con·sid·er |kən sĭd' ər| *v.* **considered, considering 1.** To think about before deciding: *Chen is considering a new job in Ohio.* **2.** To think of as; believe to be: *I consider you the best player on the team.*

con·sist |kən sĭst'| *v.* **consisted, consisting** To be made up: *A week consists of seven days.*

con·stant |kŏn' stənt| *adj.* Always remaining the same; not changing: *We kept a constant speed of 55mph.*

Con·sti·tu·tion |kŏn stĭ tōo' shən| or |kŏn stĭ tyōo' shən| *n.* The written laws and principles by which the United States is governed, adopted in 1787 and put into effect in 1789.

con·tain |kən tān'| *v.* **contained, containing 1.** To have within itself; hold: *Orange juice contains vitamins.* **2.** To consist of or include: *A gallon contains four quarts.*

con·tam·i·nate |kən tăm' ə nāt'| *v.* **contaminated, contaminating** To make impure or unfit for use by mixture or contact; pollute.

con·tam·i·na·tion |kən tăm' ə nā' shən| *n.* **1.** The act or process of contaminating, or the condition of being contaminated. **2.** An impurity: *Fumes from cars contaminate the air.*

con·tent·ment |kən tĕnt' mənt| *n.* Happiness and satisfaction; peace of mind.

con·tin·ue |kən tĭn' yōo| *v.* **continued, continuing 1.** To keep on or persist in: *The rain continued for days.* **2.** To begin again after stopping; resume: *Our program will continue after a word from our sponsor.*

con·vene |kən vēn'| *v.* **convened, convening** To assemble or cause to assemble; come together: *Congress will convene next month.*

con·ven·tion |kən vĕn' shən| *n., pl.* **conventions** A formal assembly or meeting: *A convention was held to select a presidential candidate.*

con·vict |kən vĭkt'| *v.* **convicted, convicting** To find or prove guilty. *n.* |kŏn' vĭkt'|, *pl.* **convicts** A person serving a prison sentence; criminal.

con·vic·tion |kən vĭk' shən| *n., pl.* **convictions** The act or process of finding or proving guilty.

con·vince |kən vĭns'| *v.* **convinced, convincing** To persuade to do or believe: *Can you convince your parents to let you go on the trip?*

co·op·er·a·tive |kō ŏp' ər ə tĭv| or |kō ŏp' ə rā' tĭv| *adj.* **1.** Done in cooperation or by working together with others: *The team made a cooperative effort.* **2.** Willing to help or cooperate: *The nurse said you are a cooperative patient.*

cork |kôrk| *n., pl.* **corks** A cork, rubber, or plastic stopper for a bottle or jug.

cor·ner |kôr' nər| *n., pl.* **corners 1.** The point or place at which two lines or surfaces meet: *a corner of the room.* **2.** The place where two roads or streets meet.

cor·rect |kə rĕkt'| *adj.* Free from error; accurate: *Your addition is correct.*

cor·rec·tion |kə rĕk' shən| *n., pl.* **corrections 1.** The act or process of removing errors or mistakes. **2.** Something that replaces a mistake.

cot·tage |kŏt' ĭj| *n., pl.* **cottages** A small house in the country.

coun·sel·or |koun' sə lər| *n., pl.* **counselors** A person who supervises children at a summer camp: *The counselor told the campers to get ready for swimming.*

count·less |kount' lĭs| *adj.* Too many to count: *The stars are not few, but countless.*

coun·try |kŭn′ trē| *n., pl.* **countries** A land in which people live under a single government; nation: *We studied several foreign countries.*

court |kôrt| *n., pl.* **courts** A level area marked for playing a game, as tennis or basketball: *Jill is the best player on the court.*

cov·er |kŭv′ ər| *v.* **covered, covering** To put something over or on: *I covered my ears with my hands.*

cow·ard |kou′ ərd| *n., pl.* **cowards** A person who has no courage.

craft |krăft| *n., pl.* **crafts** An occupation, trade, or hobby that requires special skill, especially with the hands: *We learned the craft of pottery at camp.*

cre·ate |krē āt′| *v.* **created, creating** To bring into being; invent: *Thomas Edison created hundreds of useful devices.*

cre·a·tive |krē ā′ tĭv| *adj.* Having the ability to create things; having original ideas; inventive.

crea·ture |krē′ chər| *n., pl.* **creatures** A living being, especially an animal.

cred·it |krĕd′ ĭt| *n., pl.* **credits** 1. Belief or confidence in the truth of something; trust: *I gave full credit to what you told me.* 2. A system of buying things and paying for them later.

crim·i·nal |krĭm′ ə nəl| *n., pl.* **criminals** A person who has committed a crime or been convicted of one; a convict: *The criminal was sentenced to two years in prison.*

cross·walk |krôs′ wôk′| *n., pl.* **crosswalks** A specially marked path for people walking across a street: *Cross the street only at a crosswalk.*

ă	pat	ŏ	pot	û	fur
ā	pay	ō	go	*th*	the
â	care	ô	paw, for	th	thin
ä	father	oi	oil	hw	which
ĕ	pet	o͞o	book	zh	usual
ē	be	o͞o	boot	ə	ago, item
ĭ	pit	yo͞o	cute		pencil, atom
ī	ice	ou	out		circus
î	near	ŭ	cut	ər	butter

cru·el |kro͞o′ əl| *adj.* **crueler, cruelest** Liking to cause pain or suffering; unkind.

cruise |kro͞oz| *n., pl.* **cruises** A sea voyage for pleasure. *v.* **cruised, cruising** To drive about in an area without having a definite destination.

crush |krŭsh| *v.* **crushed, crushing** To press, squeeze, or bear down on with enough force to break or injure; crumple: *The tree fell on the car and crushed it.*

crys·tal |krĭs′ təl| *n., pl.* **crystals** 1. A solid piece of matter that has a regular pattern of flat surfaces and angles between the surfaces. Water vapor forms ice crystals, or snow. 2. Glass that is clear, colorless, and of high quality.

cue |kyo͞o| *n., pl.* **cues** A word or signal given to remind a performer to begin a speech or movement: *The actor waited for a cue before going on-stage.*

cul·ture |kŭl′ chər| *n., pl.* **cultures** The customs, beliefs, laws, ways of living, and all other results of human work and thought that belong to a people: *ancient Egyptian culture.*

cun·ning |kŭn′ ĭng| *n.* The quality or condition of being sly: *His cunning helped him find a way to get what he wanted.*

cur·rent |kûr′ ənt| *adj.* Belonging to the present time: *Newspapers and weekly magazines report on current events.*

cur·tain |kûr′ tn| *n., pl.* **curtains** A piece of material hanging in a window or other opening.

curve |kûrv| *n., pl.* **curves** A line or surface that keeps bending smoothly without sharp angles.

cus·toms |kŭs′ təmz| *n. (used with a singular verb)* **1.** A tax that must be paid on goods brought in from another country: *We had to pay customs on the jewelry we bought in Italy.* **2.** The inspection of goods and baggage entering a country, as for a tax.

D

dam·age |dăm′ ĭj| *v.* **damaged, damaging** To harm or injure: *The plants were damaged by insects.*

dance |dăns| *v.* **danced, dancing** To move with rhythmic steps and motions, usually in time to music.

dan·ger·ous |dān′ jər əs| *adj.* Full of danger; risky.

dare |dâr| *v.* **dared, daring** **1.** To be brave or bold enough: *The explorer dared to sail alone across the ocean.* **2.** To challenge: *My friend dared me to climb over the fence.*

da·ta |dā′ tə| or |dăt′ ə| *pl. n.* Facts and figures, especially for use in making decisions: *The scientists examined the data on measles and recommended immunization for every child.*

dawn |dôn| *n., pl.* **dawns** The time each morning when the sun comes up.

day·time |dā′ tīm′| *n.* The time between dawn and dark.

deaf |děf| *adj.* **deafer, deafest** Unable to hear or to hear well.

deal |dēl| *v.* **dealt, dealing** **1.** To hand out (cards) to players in a card game. **2.** To act toward; treat: *Deal fairly with your friends. n., pl.* **deals** **1.** A bargain: *I got a deal on some used books.* **2.** A business agreement.

dealt |dělt| *v.* Past tense and past participle of **deal:** *Lisa dealt with her money wisely.*

de·cath·lon |dĭ kăth′ lən| or |dĭ kăth′ lŏn′| *n., pl.* **decathlons** An athletic contest in which each contestant participates in ten different track and field events.

de·cide |dĭ sīd′| *v.* **decided, deciding** To make up one's mind: *I decided to become a mechanic.*

dec·o·rate |děk′ ə rāt′| *v.* **decorated, decorating** To furnish with something attractive or beautiful; beautify; adorn: *We decorated the room with flowers.*

dec·o·ra·tion |děk′ ə rā′ shən| *n., pl.* **decorations** **1.** The act or process of decorating. **2.** Something that decorates; ornament.

de·fense |dĭ fěns′| *n., pl.* **defenses** Something that protects: *Storm windows are a good defense against winter winds. adj.* **defenseless** *Newly hatched turtles are quite defenseless.*

de·light·ful |dĭ līt′ fəl| *adj.* Very pleasing: *I had a delightful visit with you.*

de·liv·er |dĭ lĭv′ ər| *v.* **delivered, delivering** To take and turn over to the proper person or at the proper destination; bring to: *The mail carrier delivered a package today.*

Dem·o·crat |děm′ ə krăt′| *n., pl.* **Democrats** A member of the Democratic Party: *The Democrats held their convention in Atlanta, Georgia.*

de·part |dĭ pärt′| *v.* **departed, departing** To go away or away from: *We departed for our vacation.*

de·par·ture |dĭ pär′ chər| *n., pl.* **departures** The act of going away: *The train's departure will be at 1 P.M. Its arrival in New York will be at 5:30 P.M.*

de·pend·a·ble |dĭ pěn′ də bəl| *adj.* Capable of being depended on; reliable.

de·pos·it |dĭ pŏz′ ĭt| *n., pl.* **deposits** **1.** An amount of money deposited in a bank account. **2.** A mass of material, as a mineral, that builds up by a natural process: *Prospectors looked for gold deposits.*

depth |děpth| *n., pl.* **depths** Distance from top to bottom or front to back.

dep·u·ty |děp′ yə tē| *n., pl.* **deputies** A person appointed to act for or as an assistant to another: *The sheriff asked his deputy to help with the investigation.*

de·serve |dĭ zûrv′| *v.* **deserved, deserving** To be worthy of or have a right to: *You deserved the reward.*

de·sign·er |dĭ zī′ nər| *n., pl.* **designers** A person who creates ideas for clothing and stage settings.

de·stroy |dǐ stroi'| *v.* **destroyed, destroying** To completely ruin: *The explosion destroyed several homes.*

de·tail |dǐ tāl'| or |dē' tāl'| *n., pl.* **details** A small part of a whole; item: *Give me all the details of your plan.*

de·tec·tive |dǐ těk' tǐv| *n., pl.* **detectives** A person whose work is to get information about crimes and try to solve them.

de·vice |dǐ vīs'| *n., pl.* **devices** A piece of equipment that is made for a particular purpose: *A broom is a device for sweeping.*

dev·il |děv' əl| *n., pl.* **devils** A wicked, evil, or mischievous person.

dew |doo| or |dyoo| *n.* Moisture that condenses and collects on cool surfaces, usually at night.

di·al |dī' əl| *n., pl.* **dials** 1. A control that chooses the setting on a radio or television set. 2. The face of a clock.

di·a·logue |dī' ə lôg'| *n., pl.* **dialogues** The words spoken in conversation by the characters of a written work, as a play: *Susan had to learn her lines for a ten-minute dialogue in the third act.*

di·a·mond |dī' ə mənd| *n., pl.* **diamonds** An extremely hard, usually colorless, mineral that is a crystal form of carbon. Diamonds are used for cutting and grinding, and as jewelry.

di·a·ry |dī' ə rē| *n., pl.* **diaries** A daily written record of a person's thoughts, activities, opinions, and experiences; a journal: *I write my private thoughts in my diary.*

di·et |dī' ĭt| *n., pl.* **diets** 1. The usual food and drink taken in by a person or an animal: *a balanced diet.* 2. Special foods eaten especially to cause one to lose weight or to improve the health.

ă	pat	ŏ	pot	û	fur
ā	pay	ō	go	*th*	the
â	care	ô	paw, for	th	thin
ä	father	oi	oil	hw	which
ĕ	pet	oo	book	zh	usual
ē	be	oo	boot	ə	ago, item
ĭ	pit	yoo	cute		pencil, atom
ī	ice	ou	out		circus
î	near	ŭ	cut	ər	butter

dif·fer·ent |dĭf' ər ənt| *adj.* 1. Partly or completely unlike another: *The sea horse is different from any other fish.* 2. Not identical; separate: *I visited you on two different days.*

dim |dĭm| *adj.* **dimmer, dimmest** 1. Somewhat dark: *The cat lay in a dim corner of the hall.* 2. Giving off little light: *Don't try to read by a dim lamp. v.* **dimmed, dimming** To make or become dim.

di·rect |dǐ rěkt'| *v.* **directed, directing** 1. To aim, point, or guide to or toward: *Please direct me to the post office.* 2. To be in charge of; manage: *My sister is directing her class play.*

dirt·y |dûr' tē| *adj.* **dirtier, dirtiest** Full of or covered with dirt; not clean.

dis- A prefix that means: 1. Not; opposite: *dishonest.* 2. Not having; lack of: *discomfort; disagreement.*

dis·a·gree |dĭs' ə grē'| *v.* **disagreed, disagreeing** To fail to agree; be different: *Your answer disagrees with mine.*

dis·as·ter |dǐ zǎs' tər| *n., pl.* **disasters** Something, such as a flood, that causes great destruction.

dis·cov·er |dǐ skŭv' ər| *v.* **discovered, discovering** To find out; learn: *I looked down and discovered that my shoelace was untied and ripped.*

dis·cus |dĭs' kəs| *n., pl.* **discuses** A disk of wood and metal that is hurled for distance in athletic contests.

dis·like |dĭs līk'| *v.* **disliked, disliking** To have a feeling of not liking: *I dislike having to get up early.*

dis·lo·cate |dĭs′ lō kāt′| *v.* **dislocated, dislocating** To put or force out of a normal position: *The football player dislocated his shoulder when he fell.*

dis·miss |dĭs mĭs′| *v.* **dismissed, dismissing** **1.** To allow or ask to leave; send away: *At two o'clock our teacher dismissed the class.* **2.** To put out of one's mind; ignore.

dis·or·der |dĭs ôr′ dər| *n., pl.* **disorders** Lack of order; confusion: *The kitchen is in disorder.*

dis·play |dĭ splā′| *v.* **displayed, displaying** To put on view; exhibit; show: *The store displayed suits in the window.* *n., pl.* **displays** An advertisement designed to catch the eye: *The store made a display for all the items on sale.*

dis·pute |dĭ spyo͞ot′| *v.* **disputed, disputing** To argue about; debate: *In the debate the students disputed the question of a dress code.*

dis·tance |dĭs′ təns| *n., pl.* **distances** The amount of space between two places, things, or points.

dis·trict |dĭs′ trĭkt| *n., pl.* **districts** **1.** A part, as of a city, that is set aside for a particular purpose: *Our town is divided into three school districts.* **2.** An area or region that has a certain use or character: *The city has several shopping districts.*

dis·trust |dĭs trŭst′| *n.* Lack of trust; suspicion. *v.* **distrusted, distrusting** To doubt.

ditch |dĭch| *n., pl.* **ditches** A long, narrow trench; hole; pit.

di·vi·sion |dĭ vĭzh′ ən| *n., pl.* **divisions** **1.** The mathematical process of dividing. **2.** The act of dividing or the condition of being divided; separation.

diz·zy |dĭz′ ē| *adj.* **dizzier, dizziest** Having a sensation of whirling or feeling a tendency to fall. *n.* **dizziness** *Spinning around causes dizziness.*

dock |dŏk| *n., pl.* **docks** **1.** A group of piers that serves as a landing area for ships and boats; a wharf. **2.** A platform for loading or unloading.

doc·tor |dŏk′ tər| *n., pl.* **doctors** A physician, dentist, or veterinarian who is trained in and licensed to practice a healing art.

doc·u·men·ta·ry |dŏk′ yə měn′ tə rē| *n., pl.* **documentaries** A motion picture giving a factual account of some subject and often showing actual events: *We saw a documentary about the heart.*

dol·phin |dŏl′ fĭn| *n., pl.* **dolphins** A sea animal that is related to the whales but is smaller and has a snout that looks like a beak.

dou·ble |dŭb′ əl| *adj.* **1.** Twice as much in size, strength, number, or amount. **2.** Made up of two parts: *double doors.*

dough |dō| *n., pl.* **doughs** A soft, thick mixture of flour or meal and liquids that is used to make bread and baked goods.

doz·en |dŭz′ ən| *n., pl.* **dozens** *or* **dozen** A set of twelve.

Drake |drāk|, **Sir Francis** 1540?–1596. English naval hero and explorer. He led the British navy under Queen Elizabeth I, and was the first Englishman to sail around the world.

dram·a·tize |drăm′ ə tīz′| *or* |dräm′ ə tīz′| *v.* **dramatized, dramatizing 1.** To make a play of; act out. **2.** To present or portray in a serious way.

dread·ful |drĕd′ fəl| *adj.* **1.** Causing great fear; terrible. **2.** Very unpleasant, bad or shocking: *The snowstorm turned a wonderful day into a dreadful one.*

dream |drēm| *v.* **dreamed** *or* **dreamt, dreaming** To have a series of pictures, thoughts, or emotions occurring during sleep.

dreamt |drĕmt| *v.* Past tense and past participle of **dream**: *Last night I dreamt of a flying horse.*

drear·y |drîr′ ē| *adj.* **drearier, dreariest** Gloomy; dismal; not cheerful.

drib·ble |drĭb′ əl| *v.* **dribbled, dribbling** To move a ball along by bouncing or kicking, as in basketball: *She dribbled the basketball down the court.*

drip |drĭp| *v.* **dripped, dripping** To fall or let fall in drops.

drought |drout| *n., pl.* **droughts** A period of little or no rain.

drown |droun| *v.* **drowned, drowning** To be loud enough to overpower: *The lawnmower drowned out my voice.*

duke |dook| or |dyook| *n., pl.* **dukes** A member of the highest level of the British nobility.

du·ra·ble |door′ ə bəl| or |dyoor′ ə bəl| *adj.* Capable of withstanding hard wear or long use; sturdy.

du·ty |doo′ tē| or |dyoo′ tē| *n., pl.* **duties** **1.** Something that a person ought to do; responsibility: *It is my duty to clean my room.* **2.** Action that a person's occupation or job requires; task: *The duties of a police officer are to enforce the laws.*

dwell |dwĕl| *v.* **dwelt** or **dwelled, dwelling** To live as a resident; reside: *A monarch often dwells in a palace.*

E

ear·ly |ûr′ lē| *adj.* **earlier, earliest 1.** Of or happening near the beginning: *We ate breakfast in the early morning.* **2.** Coming or happening before the usual or expected time: *We ate an early dinner.* *adv.* **earlier, earliest** At or near the beginning: *We always get up early in the morning.*

eas·y |ē′ zē| *adj.* **easier, easiest** Needing very little effort; not hard.

ed·u·cate |ĕj′ ə kāt′| *v.* **educated, educating** To provide with formal instruction; teach.

ef·fort |ĕf′ ərt| *n., pl.* **efforts** An earnest attempt; try: *Please make an effort to arrive on time.*

e·lect |ĭ lĕkt′| *v.* **elected, electing** To choose by vote: *We elected a class president in September.*

ă	pat	ŏ	pot	û	fur
ā	pay	ō	go	*th*	the
â	care	ô	paw, for	th	thin
ä	father	oi	oil	hw	which
ĕ	pet	oo	book	zh	usual
ē	be	oo	boot	ə	ago, item
ĭ	pit	yoo	cute		pencil, atom
ī	ice	ou	out		circus
î	near	ŭ	cut	ər	butter

e·lec·tion |ĭ lĕk′ shən| *n., pl.* **elections** The act or process of electing, or the condition of being elected: *Did you vote in the presidential election?*

el·e·gant |ĕl′ ĭ gənt| *adj.* Marked by good taste and refinement: *We had dinner last night in an elegant restaurant.*

em·er·ald |ĕm′ ər əld| *n., pl.* **emeralds** A bright-green stone, often found in granite, that is used as a gem. An emerald is six-sided.

e·merge |ĭ mûrj′| *v.* **emerged, emerging** To come into view; appear: *The butterfly emerged from the cocoon.*

e·mer·gen·cy |ĭ mûr′ jən sē| *n., pl.* **emergencies** A situation that develops suddenly and unexpectedly and calls for immediate action.

e·mo·tion |ĭ mō′ shən| *n., pl.* **emotions** A strong feeling, as love, sorrow, hate, or joy.

em·pire |ĕm′ pīr′| *n., pl.* **empires** A group of territories or nations headed by a single ruler; a kingdom.

em·ploy |ĕm ploi′| *v.* **employed, employing** To engage the services of; hire: *The construction company employed many workers to build the skyscraper.*

emp·ty |ĕmp′ tē| *adj.* **emptier, emptiest 1.** Containing nothing: *The gas tank is empty, so the car will not start.* **2.** Vacant; unoccupied. *n.* **emptiness** *Astronauts have experienced emptiness in outer space.*

en- A prefix that means "to put or go in, into, or on": *endanger.*

en·act |ĕn ăkt′| *v.* **enacted, enacting** To establish by passing a law; decree: *The Senate enacted legislation to stop pollution. n.* **enactment** *The enactment of a bill depends on the President.*

en•close |ĕn klōz′| *v.* **enclosed, enclosing** To close in on all sides; surround: *A high fence encloses the garden.*

en•e•my |ĕn′ ə mē| *n., pl.* **enemies** A person, animal, or group that hates or wishes harm to another; foe.

en•er•gy |ĕn′ ər jē| *n., pl.* **energies** Heat or electric power usable for doing physical work, such as moving or lifting objects.

en•force |ĕn fôrs′| *v.* **enforced, enforcing** To force others to obey: *Police officers have the power to enforce the laws.*

en•gage |ĕn gāj′| *v.* **engaged, engaging** To draw into; involve: *engage someone in debate.*

en•joy•ment |ĕn joi′ mənt| *n., pl.* **enjoyments** A form or source of pleasure: *We work in the garden for enjoyment.*

-ent A suffix that forms adjectives and nouns: *different, resident.*

en•ter |ĕn′ tər| *v.* **entered, entering 1.** To come or go in or into: *The ship entered the harbor.* **2.** To become a member of; join: *to enter the army.*

en•ter•tain |ĕn′ tər tān′| *v.* **entertained, entertaining** To hold the attention of in an agreeable way; amuse: *We entertained them with stories about our trip to Hawaii.*

en•thu•si•as•tic |ĕn thoo′ zē ăs′ tĭk| *adj.* Full of or showing strong interest or eagerness; eager: *My parents are enthusiastic skiers.*

en•trance |ĕn′ trəns| *n., pl.* **entrances 1.** The act or example of entering: *The audience applauded the singer's entrance.* **2.** A door or passageway; entry.

en•try |ĕn′ trē| *n., pl.* **entries 1.** The act or right of entering: *You need a passport for entry into the country.* **2.** A place, as a passage or door, through which to enter.

en•vi•ron•ment |ĕn vī′ rən mənt| *n., pl.* **environments** Surroundings and conditions that affect natural processes and the growth and development of living things: *Protecting Earth's environment from pollution is a major challenge for everyone.*

ep•i•sode |ĕp′ ĭ sōd′| *n., pl.* **episodes** A distinct part of a story or a separate part of a continuing story: *We saw the first episode of a ten-part mystery series.*

e•qual |ē′ kwəl| *adj.* Being exactly the same in amount, extent, or other measured quality: *Three feet are equal to one yard.* *v.* **equaled, equaling** To be the same as: *Two pints equal one quart.*

Er•ic•son |ĕr′ ĭk sən|, **Leif** Norwegian navigator, believed to have landed in North America in about the year A.D. 1000.

es•say |ĕs′ ā′| *n., pl.* **essays** A short piece of writing that gives the author's opinions on a certain subject; composition.

e•vac•u•ate |ĭ văk′ yoo āt′| *v.* **evacuated, evacuating** To leave or send away from a dangerous place: *The residents quickly evacuated the burning building.*

e•ven•tu•al |ĭ věn′ choo əl| *adj.* Occurring in the near or far future; to happen sooner or later: *He never lost hope of eventual victory.* *adv.* **eventually** *We will arrive at the park eventually.*

Ev•er•glades Na•tion•al Park |ĕv′ ər glādz′| Area enclosing a swampy region in southern Florida, abundant in wildlife and tropical plants.

eve•ry•bod•y |ĕv′ rē bŏd′ ē| *pron.* Every person; everyone: *Everybody makes a mistake sometimes.*

eve•ry•where |ĕv′ rē hwâr′| *adv.* In every place; in all places: *I looked everywhere for my lost keys.*

ev•i•dence |ĕv′ ĭ dəns| *n.* Facts or signs that help one find out the truth or come to a conclusion: *The broken window was evidence that a burglary had taken place.*

e•vil |ē′ vəl| *adj.* **eviler, evilest** Bad, wrong, or wicked.

ex- A prefix that means: **1.** Out; out of: *exchange.* **2.** Former: *ex-president.*

ex•act |ĭg zăkt'| *adj.* Accurate in every detail: *The exact amount was $5.03.*

ex•ceed |ĭk sēd'| *v.* **exceeded, exceeding** To go beyond: *Be careful not to exceed the speed limit.*

ex•change |ĭks chānj'| *v.* **exchanged, exchanging** To give one thing for another; trade: *The traders exchanged cheap trinkets for valuable furs.*

ex•cite |ĭk sīt'| *v.* **excited, exciting** **1.** To stir up; arouse: *News of the party excited the children.* **2.** To make more active; stimulate: *Do not excite the bees.*

ex•cuse |ĭk skyōōz'| *v.* **excused, excusing** **1.** To forgive: *Please excuse me for what I did.* **2.** To release from a duty or promise. |ĭk skyōōs'| *n., pl.* **excuses** Something given as a reason for excusing: *a written excuse for an absence.*

ex•ert |ĭg zûrt'| *v.* **exerted, exerting** To put into use; apply effort: *I exerted all my strength to move the stone.*

ex•haust |ĭg zôst'| *v.* **exhausted, exhausting** To wear out completely; tire: *The long swim exhausted me.*

ex•it |ĕg' zĭt| or |ĕk' sĭt| *n., pl.* **exits** **1.** A way out. **2.** The act of going away or out: *We made a hasty exit from the room.*

ex•per•i•ment |ĭk spĕr' ə mĕnt'| *n., pl.* **experiments** A test used to find out or prove something: *The scientists did an experiment to learn more about blood cells.*

ex•pert |ĕk' spûrt'| *n., pl.* **experts** A person who has great knowledge or skill in a special area: *My teacher is an expert on American history.*

ex•plain |ĭk splān'| *v.* **explained, explaining** To make clear or understandable; clarify: *The science teacher explained atoms for us.*

ex•pose |ĭk spōz'| *v.* **exposed, exposing** To leave without cover or protection; put out in the open.

ex•press |ĭk sprĕs'| *v.* **expressed, expressing** **1.** To make known; reveal: *This story expresses the writer's love of animals.* **2.** To put into words; state: *I must express my opinion to the teacher.*

ă	pat	ŏ	pot	û	fur
ā	pay	ō	go	*th*	the
â	care	ô	paw, for	th	thin
ä	father	oi	oil	hw	which
ĕ	pet	ōō	book	zh	usual
ē	be	ōō	boot	ə	ago, item
ĭ	pit	yōō	cute		pencil, atom
ī	ice	ou	out		circus
î	near	ŭ	cut	ər	butter

ex•pres•sion |ĭk sprĕsh' ən| *n., pl.* **expressions** **1.** The act of expressing: *We believe in the free expression of ideas.* **2.** A lively manner of speaking: *The lecturer spoke with great expression.*

ex•tend |ĭk stĕnd'| *v.* **extended, extending** To make greater or larger; expand: *The empire sought to extend its boundaries.*

ex•traor•di•nar•y |ĭk strôr' dn ĕr' ē| or |ĕk' strə ôr' dn ĕr' ē| *adj.* Very unusual; remarkable: *Landing on the moon was an extraordinary accomplishment.*

ex•trav•a•gant |ĭk străv' ə gənt| *adj.* **1.** Costing or spending too much; expensive; wasteful. **2.** Going beyond the limits of reason; excessive.

ex•treme |ĭk strēm'| *adj.* **1.** Very great or intense: *The Arctic explorers suffered from the extreme cold.* **2.** The farthest possible: *the extreme end of the island.*

eye•ball |ī' bôl| *n., pl.* **eyeballs** The ball-shaped part of the eye, enclosed by the sockets and eyelids.

F

fab•ric |făb' rĭk| *n., pl.* **fabrics** A material that is produced by joining fibers together, as by weaving; cloth.

fact |făkt| *n., pl.* **facts** Something that has really happened or really exists: *It is a fact that the sun is a star.*

fac•tu•al |făk' chōō əl| *adj.* Of or based on facts: *Just give a factual account of what happened.*

fad |făd| *n., pl.* **fads** Something that is very popular for a short time; craze: *Silly shoelaces were a fad last month.*

fal·con |făl′ kən| *or* |fôl′ kən| *n., pl.* **falcons** A hawk with long wings and hooked claws, especially one that is trained to hunt small animals and birds.

false |fôls| *adj.* **falser, falsest** Not true, real, honest, or correct: *Is that conclusion false?*

fam·i·ly |făm′ ə lē| *n., pl.* **families 1.** A group consisting of parents and their children. **2.** A group of persons related by blood; relatives.

fa·mous |fā′ məs| *adj.* Very well known.

fare |fâr| *n., pl.* **fares** The money a person pays to travel, as on a plane, train, or bus.
♦ *These sound alike* **fare, fair.**

far·ther |fär′ thər| *adv.* To or at a greater distance: *The drive to the beach was farther than we thought. adj.* More distant: *We docked the boat on the farther shore.*

fas·ci·nate |făs′ ə nāt′| *v.* **fascinated, fascinating** To attract and hold the interest and attention of.

fas·ci·na·tion |făs′ ə nā′ shən| *n.* **1.** The condition of being fascinated: *Everyone watched in fascination.* **2.** The power of fascinating; a strong attraction: *The sea has always held fascination for me.*

fash·ion·a·ble |făsh′ ə nə bəl| *adj.* Following the current style or latest fashion; stylish.

fau·cet |fô′ sĭt| *n., pl.* **faucets** A device for controlling the flow of liquid, as from a pipe; tap.

fault |fôlt| *n., pl.* **faults 1.** Responsibility for a mistake or offense: *Failing the test was my own fault.* **2.** A mistake; error: *I found many faults in spelling and grammar in my report.*

fa·vor·ite |fā′ vər ĭt| *n., pl.* **favorites** Someone or something that is preferred above all others. *adj.* Preferred above all others; liked.

fawn |fôn| *n., pl.* **fawns** A young deer, especially one that is less than a year old.

fear·ful |fîr′ fəl| *adj.* Feeling fear; afraid: *I was fearful of losing my way in the forest.*

feat |fēt| *n., pl.* **feats** An act or accomplishment that shows skill, strength, or bravery: *The gymnasts performed remarkable feats.*

fea·ture |fē′ chər| *n., pl.* **features 1.** One of the distinct parts, as the chin or nose, of the face. **2.** A full-length movie.

fenc·ing |fĕn′ sĭng| *n.* The sport of fighting with long, slender swords: *Helmets and padded jackets are worn for fencing.*

fes·ti·val |fĕs′ tə vəl| *n., pl.* **festivals 1.** A day or period of celebrating; holiday. **2.** A series of special cultural events, such as parades, films, concerts, or exhibitions.

fil·i·bus·ter |fĭl′ ə bŭs′ tər| *n., pl.* **filibusters** An example of the tactic, used especially in the United States Senate, of delaying or trying to prevent the passage of legislation by making extremely long speeches: *The senator's filibuster against the bill failed in every respect.*

fin·ger |fĭng′ gər| *n., pl.* **fingers** One of the five extensions of the hand.

fin·ish |fĭn′ ĭsh| *v.* **finished, finishing 1.** To bring or come to an end; get done: *I have finished my lunch.* **2.** To use all of.

fire·crack·er |fīr′ krăk′ ər| *n., pl.* **firecrackers** A small explosive charge in a paper tube. Firecrackers are set off to make loud noise during celebrations.

firm |fûrm| *adj.* **firmer, firmest** Not giving way when pressed or pushed; solid: *The firm ground of the track was ideal for running.*

first aid |fûrst′ ād′| *n.* Emergency care given to an injured or sick person before a doctor comes.

fix·ture |fĭks′ chər| *n., pl.* **fixtures** Something fixed or attached permanently in a place: *There are two light fixtures on the ceiling.*

flair |flâr| *n., pl.* **flairs** A natural talent or aptitude.
♦ *These sound alike* **flair, flare.**

fla·min·go |flə mǐng′ gō| *n., pl.* **flamingos** *or* **flamingoes** A tropical wading bird that has long legs, a long neck, and reddish or pinkish feathers.

flare |flâr| *v.* **flared, flaring** To burn with a sudden or unsteady flame: *The candle flared just before going out.*
♦ *These sound alike* **flare, flair.**

flash·light |flǎsh′ līt′| *n., pl.* **flashlights** A lamp or lantern powered by batteries that is small enough to be carried around.

fla·vor |flā′ vər| *n., pl.* **flavors** **1.** The quality that causes something to have a certain taste: *The sauce had a burnt flavor.* **2.** A quality felt to be characteristic of a thing: *the mysterious flavor of the Orient.*

flea |flē| *n., pl.* **fleas** A small, wingless insect that sucks blood from animals and humans.
♦ *These sound alike* **flea, flee.**

flee |flē| *v.* **fled, fleeing** To run away.
♦ *These sound alike* **flee, flea.**

fleet |flēt| *n., pl.* **fleets** A number of boats, ships, or vehicles that form a group: *The company owns a fleet of cars.*

flip |flǐp| *v.* **flipped, flipping** **1.** To move or turn by tossing in the air: *Let's flip a coin to decide who goes first.* **2.** *Slang.* To be overwhelmed: *I flipped when I saw the high grade on my test.*

floor |flôr| *n., pl.* **floors** **1.** The bottom surface of a room, on which one stands. **2.** The ground or lowest surface, as of a forest or ocean.
◇ *Idioms* **get in on the ground floor** Be part of something from the beginning. **take the floor** Rise to give a formal speech.

flow |flō| *v.* **flowed, flowing** To move or run freely in or as if in a stream: *Air flowed in through the window.*

flute |floōt| *n., pl.* **flutes** A pipe-shaped musical instrument played by blowing across or into a hole near one end.

fo·cus |fō′ kəs| *n., pl.* **focuses** The adjustment of a lens, an eye, or a camera that gives the best image: *The camera was out of focus, so the picture was blurred.*

ă	pat	ŏ	pot	û	fur
ā	pay	ō	go	*th*	the
â	care	ô	paw, for	th	thin
ä	father	oi	oil	hw	which
ĕ	pet	oō	book	zh	usual
ē	be	ōō	boot	ə	ago, item
ǐ	pit	yōō	cute		pencil, atom
ī	ice	ou	out		circus
î	near	ŭ	cut	ər	butter

folk·lore |fōk′ lôr′| *n.* The beliefs, legends, fables, myths, customs, and other traditions handed down by a people from generation to generation.

fond |fŏnd| *adj.* **fonder, fondest** **1.** Loving or affectionate. **2.** Having a liking for: *My cousin is very fond of skiing.*

foot·ball |foōt′ bôl′| *n.* A team game played with an inflated oval ball on a long field with goals at either end.

for·bid |fər bǐd′| *v.* **forbade** *or* **forbad, forbidden, forbidding** **1.** To order against with authority; not allow: *The rules forbid running in the hallways.* **2.** To order not to do something: *I forbid you to go.*

for·get·ful |fər gĕt′ fəl| *adj.* Apt to forget; likely not to remember: *I am so forgetful I often leave my keys at home.*

for·ward |fôr′ wərd| *n., pl.* **forwards** A player in certain games, as basketball, who is part of the front line: *The forward scored ten baskets in the first half of the game.*

fos·sil |fŏs′ əl| *n., pl.* **fossils** The remains or traces of a plant or animal of an earlier age. Fossils are embedded in rock or in the earth's crust.

foul |foul| *n., pl.* **fouls** A violation of a rule of play in a game or sport: *The game stops when a foul is called.*

foun·tain |foun′ tən| *n., pl.* **fountains** A stream or jet of water, as for drinking or for decoration.

free |frē| *adj.* **freer, freest** Given or provided at no cost: *We won a free meal at a fancy restaurant.*

free·dom |frē′ dəm| *n., pl.* **freedoms** The right to use or enjoy something freely: *Freedom of speech and religion are guaranteed by the Constitution.*

freeze |frēz| *v.* **froze, frozen, freezing 1.** To change from a liquid to a solid by loss of heat: *The pond froze over during the cold night.* **2.** To be uncomfortably cold: *I forgot my gloves, and my hands are freezing.*

fresh |frĕsh| *adj.* **fresher, freshest** Just made, grown, or gathered: *We ate warm, fresh bread with our salad.*

fruit |frōōt| *n., pl.* **fruit** or **fruits** A seed-bearing plant part that is fleshy or juicy, eaten as food. Apples, oranges, grapes, strawberries, and bananas are fruits.

fu·el |fyōō′ əl| *n., pl.* **fuels** A substance that is burned to give off heat or produce energy. Coal, wood, oil, gas, and gasoline are fuels.

-ful A suffix that forms adjectives and means: **1.** Full of: *beautiful.* **2.** Able or apt to: *forgetful.* **3.** An amount that fills: *cupful; handful.*

fume |fyōōm| *n., pl.* **fumes** An irritating or strong-smelling smoke, vapor, or gas: *The fumes from the car were making me sick.*

func·tion |fŭngk′ shən| *n., pl.* **functions** The proper activity; purpose or use: *The function of a knife is to cut.*

fund |fŭnd| *n., pl.* **funds 1.** A sum of money raised or kept for a certain purpose: *The family has a vacation fund.* **2.** A source of supply; stock: *A library is a fund of information.*

fur·nish |fûr′ nĭsh| *v.* **furnished, furnishing 1.** To equip with furniture: *We are furnishing a new home.* **2.** To supply; give: *The company furnishes the bats and balls for our baseball league.*

fur·ni·ture |fûr′ nə chər| *n.* The movable objects that are needed to make a room or office fit for living or working. Chairs, tables, and beds are pieces of furniture.

fur·ther·more |fûr′ thər môr′| *adv.* In addition; moreover: *Fresh vegetables are nutritious; furthermore, they are cheaper than frozen ones.*

fu·ry |fyŏŏr′ ē| *n., pl.* **furies** Violent anger; rage.

fu·ture |fyōō′ chər| *n., pl.* **futures** The time that is to come: *We must plan now for the future. adj.* Occurring in time that is to come: *We will meet at some future date.*

G

gain |gān| *v.* **gained, gaining** To get, achieve, or obtain by effort: *We gained experience by working in a number of jobs.*

gar·bage |gär′ bĭj| *n.* Food and trash to be thrown away, as from a kitchen.

gar·lic |gär′ lĭk| *n.* A plant that is related to the onion. Cloves of the strong-tasting bulb of garlic are used to flavor food.

gar·ment |gär′ mənt| *n., pl.* **garments** An article of clothing: *That shop makes shirts, pants, and other garments.*

gar·ret |găr′ ĭt| *n., pl.* **garrets** A room or space in a house, directly under a sloping roof; attic.

gath·er |găth′ ər| *v.* **gathered, gathering 1.** To bring or come together into one place; collect: *I gathered the papers together.* **2.** To pick up from many sources: *Squirrels gather nuts.*

gen·er·al |jĕn′ ər əl| *adj.* Of or involving all: *a general election. n., pl.* **generals** An Army, Air Force, or Marine Corps officer ranking above a colonel.

gen·tle |jĕn′ tl| *adj.* **gentler, gentlest 1.** Mild and soft; not harsh: *a gentle breeze.* **2.** Thoughtful: *a gentle nature.*

germ |jûrm| *n., pl.* **germs** A very tiny organism that can cause disease.

gi·ant |jī′ ənt| *n., pl.* **giants** A huge, very strong, imaginary creature resembling a human. *adj.* Extremely large; huge.

gla·cier |glā′ shər| *n., pl.* **glaciers** A large mass of ice that moves very slowly down a mountain or through a valley. Glaciers are formed from snow on the tops of huge mountains.

Gla·cier Na·tion·al Park |glā′ shər| A scenic area in Montana, containing many small glaciers. The park borders Canada.

goal |gōl| *n., pl.* **goals** Something wanted or worked for; purpose: *My goal in life is to help other people.*

good·ness |gŏŏd′ nĭs| *n.* The quality or condition of being good.

gov·ern |gŭv′ ərn| *v.* **governed, governing** To direct the public affairs of a country or state: *Congress and the President govern the United States.*

gov·ern·ment |gŭv′ ərn mənt| *n., pl.* **governments 1.** The act or process of governing, especially the direction of the public affairs of a country, state, or city. **2.** A form or system by which a political unit, as a country, is governed: *In a democratic government elected representatives make the laws.*

gov·er·nor |gŭv′ ər nər| *n., pl.* **governors 1.** A person who is appointed to govern a colony or territory. **2.** The person elected as head of state in the United States.

Grand Can·yon |grănd′ kăn′ yən| A huge gorge, 4 to 18 miles wide and 1 mile deep, formed by the Colorado River in northern Arizona.

grand·par·ent |grănd′ păr′ ənt| *n., pl.* **grandparents** A parent of one's father or mother.

grape·fruit |grāp′ frōot′| *n., pl.* **grapefruit** *or* **grapefruits** A large, round fruit that has yellow skin, is related to the orange, and has a somewhat sour taste.

graph |grăf| *n., pl.* **graphs** A drawing or diagram that shows the relationships between things: *This graph shows how prices have risen over the past ten years.*

grasp |grăsp| *v.* **grasped, grasping** To grab and hold firmly with or as if with the hand: *Grasp the railing so you won't fall.*

gray |grā| *n., pl.* **grays** A color made by mixing black and white.

great-grand·child |grāt′ grănd′ chīld′| *n., pl.* **great-grandchildren** A child of one's grandchild.

greet |grēt| *v.* **greeted, greeting** To welcome or speak to in a friendly or polite way: *We greeted our guests at the door.*

gro·cer·y |grō′ sə rē| *n., pl.* **groceries** A store selling food and household supplies.

group |grōop| *n., pl.* **groups** A number of persons or things gathered or located together; a bunch: *A group of people are waiting for the bus.*

grouse |grous| *n., pl.* **grouse** *or* **grouses** A game bird, similar to a turkey or a quail, that has a plump body and brownish or grayish feathers.

growth |grōth| *n., pl.* **growths** The process of becoming larger in size or becoming

ă	pat	ŏ	pot	û	fur
ā	pay	ō	go	*th*	the
â	care	ô	paw, for	th	thin
ä	father	oi	oil	hw	which
ĕ	pet	ōō	book	zh	usual
ē	be	ōō	boot	ə	ago, item
ĭ	pit	yōō	cute		pencil, atom
ī	ice	ou	out		circus
î	near	ŭ	cut	ər	butter

capable of doing well, especially in a particular climate or environment: *We saw the growth of some species of fish and the decline of others.*

guilt·y |gĭl′ tē| *adj.* **guiltier, guiltiest** Having committed a crime or bad deed: *The jury found them guilty of stealing.*

gym·na·si·um |jĭm nā′ zē əm| *n., pl.* **gymnasiums** A room or building with equipment for physical exercises and training and for indoor sports.

gym·nas·tics |jĭm năs′ tĭks| *pl. n. (used with a singular or plural verb)* Physical exercises done with the use of floor mats, stationary bars, and other equipment in a gymnasium.

H

hab·it |hăb′ ĭt| *n., pl.* **habits** An activity or action done so often that one does it without thinking: *I have the habit of getting up early every morning.*

ha·bit·u·al |hə bĭch′ ōō əl| *adj.* Done again and again: *Leah's pencil chewing became habitual.*

hai·ku |hī′ kōō| *n., pl.* **haiku** A Japanese lyric poem of a fixed 17-syllable form, usually on a subject that is drawn from nature.

half·heart·ed |hăf′ här′ tĭd| *adj.* Showing little eagerness or interest.

hall |hôl| *n., pl.* **halls** A passageway in a house or building; corridor.
♦ *These sound alike* **hall, haul.**

hand·some |hăn′ səm| *adj.* **handsomer, handsomest** Pleasing in appearance; good-looking.

hap·py |hăp′ ē| *adj.* **happier, happiest** Having, showing, or marked by a feeling of joy or pleasure: *This is the happiest day of my life.* *n.* **happiness** *Toby found happiness in her work.*

hard·ship |härd′ shĭp′| *n., pl.* **hardships** Something that causes suffering or difficulty: *The early pioneers suffered great hardships on the frontier.*

hare |hâr| *n., pl.* **hares** An animal that is related to and looks like a rabbit. A hare has longer ears and larger hind feet than a rabbit.
♦ *These sound alike* **hare, hair.**

har·mo·ny |här′ mə nē| *n., pl.* **harmonies 1.** The sounding together of musical notes in a chord. **2.** A pleasing combination of the parts that make up a whole.

harsh |härsh| *adj.* **harsher, harshest 1.** Unpleasant to hear or taste. **2.** Very severe or demanding; cruel.

har·vest |här′ vĭst| *n., pl.* **harvests 1.** The act or process of gathering a crop: *The farmer hired extra workers for the harvest.* **2.** The crop that is gathered or is ready for gathering: *Everyone helped to bring in the corn harvest.*

haul |hôl| *v.* **hauled, hauling** To pull or carry with effort; drag: *We hauled the sled up the hill.*
♦ *These sound alike* **haul, hall.**

haunt |hônt| *v.* **haunted, haunting 1.** To come to the mind of again and again: *A certain melody haunted Alex throughout the day.* **2.** To visit, live in, or appear to in the form of a ghost.

hawk |hôk| *n., pl.* **hawks** A large bird with a short, hooked bill, strong claws, and keen eyesight. Hawks catch small birds and animals for food.

head·quar·ters |hĕd′ kwôr′ tərz| *pl. n.* A center of operations: *police headquarters.*

heal |hēl| *v.* **healed, healing** To make or become healthy again; mend: *The wound healed quickly.*
♦ *These sound alike* **heal, heel.**

health |hĕlth| *n.* **1.** The condition of the body or mind: *Bad eating habits can put you in poor health.* **2.** Freedom from disease or injury: *We wish you a speedy return to health.*

heel |hēl| *n., pl.* **heels** The rounded back part of the human foot.
♦ *These sound alike* **heel, heal.**

height |hīt| *n., pl.* **heights 1.** The distance from bottom to top: *The height of the flagpole is twenty feet.* **2.** The distance from foot to head: *My height increased two inches this year.* **3.** The highest point; peak: *the height of the storm.*

heir |âr| *n., pl.* **heirs** A person who receives or has the right to receive the property of another person when the other person dies.

herb |ûrb| *or* |hûrb| *n., pl.* **herbs** A plant whose leaves, roots, or other parts are used to flavor food or are used as medicine. Parsley and basil are herbs.

her·i·tage |hĕr′ ĭ tĭj| *n., pl.* **heritages** Something handed down to later generations from earlier generations: *Freedom of speech is part of our national heritage.*

hide |hīd| *v.* **hid, hidden** *or* **hid, hiding** To keep or put out of sight: *The presents were hidden in the closet.*

hid·den |hĭd′ n| *v.* A past participle of **hide.** *adj.* Not visible; not exposed.

high-rise |hī′ rīz| *n., pl.* **high-rises** A tall building with many stories; skyscraper.

high spir·it·ed |hī′ spĭr′ ĭ tĭd| *adj.* **1.** Having a proud or unbroken spirit; brave. **2.** Lively.

high·way |hī′ wā′| *n., pl.* **highways** A main public road.

his·tor·i·cal |hĭ stôr′ ĭ kəl| **1.** Of or relating to history. **2.** Based on or concerned with events in history.

his·to·ry |hĭs′ tə rē| *n., pl.* **histories** **1.** The continuing events of the past leading up to the present: *The invention of the printing press was one of the most important in history.* **2.** The study of past events as a special field of knowledge.

hit |hĭt| *v.* **hit, hitting** To propel by striking with a bat or racket.

hoard |hôrd| *n., pl.* **hoards** A supply that is stored away, often secretly. *v.* **hoarded, hoarding** To save and store away.
♦ *These sound alike* **hoard, horde.**

hol·i·day |hŏl′ ĭ dā′| *n., pl.* **holidays** A day or period of time set aside to honor someone or to celebrate a special event.

home·made |hōm′ mād′| *adj.* Made at home.

home·sick |hōm′ sĭk′| *adj.* Unhappy because one is away from one's home and family; longing for home.

hon·est |ŏn′ ĭst| *adj.* Not lying, stealing, or cheating.

hon·or |ŏn′ ər| *n., pl.* **honors** **1.** Special respect or high regard: *We display the flag to show honor to the United States.* **2.** A special privilege or mark of excellence: *Election as class president is an honor.*

hon·or·a·ble |ŏn′ ər ə bəl| *adj.* Having or showing a strong sense of what is right or just: *an honorable person.*

horde |hôrd| *n., pl.* **hordes** A large crowd or swarm.
♦ *These sound alike* **horde, hoard.**

hor·ri·ble |hôr′ ə bəl| *adj.* **1.** Causing horror; dreadful. **2.** Very unpleasant.

horse |hôrs| *n., pl.* **horses** A large hoofed animal that has a long mane and tail.

hose |hōz| *n., pl.* **hose** *or* **hoses** **1.** A long flexible tube used for carrying fluid or air. **2.** Stockings or socks.

ă	pat	ŏ	pot	û	fur
ā	pay	ō	go	*th*	the
â	care	ô	paw, for	th	thin
ä	father	oi	oil	hw	which
ĕ	pet	o͞o	book	zh	usual
ē	be	o͞o	boot	ə	ago, item
ĭ	pit	yo͞o	cute		pencil, atom
ī	ice	ou	out		circus
î	near	ŭ	cut	ər	butter

hos·pi·tal |hŏs′ pĭ təl| *n., pl.* **hospitals** A medical institution that treats sick and injured people.

house·hold |hous′ hōld′| *n., pl.* **households** A home and its activities.

how·ev·er |hou ĕv′ ər| *adv.* By whatever way or means: *However you get there, be there on time.*

howl |houl| *n., pl.* **howls** **1.** A long, wailing cry, such as the one made by a dog, wolf, or coyote. **2.** A loud cry, scream, or hoot.

hu·man |hyo͞o′ mən| *adj.* Of or characteristic of people: *the human body. n., pl.* **humans** A person.

hu·mor |hyo͞o′ mər| *n., pl.* **humors** The quality of being comical or funny: *I could find no humor in the dull jokes.*

hun·dred |hŭn′ drĭd| *n., pl.* **hundreds** The number, written 100, that is equal to the product of 10 X 10.

hun·gry |hŭng′ grē| *adj.* **hungrier, hungriest** Wanting food.

hurl |hûrl| *v.* **hurled, hurling** To throw with a great force; fling.

I

-ible A form of the suffix **-able.**

ice·berg |īs′ bûrg′| *n., pl.* **icebergs** A very large mass of ice floating in the ocean. Icebergs are pieces of a glacier that have broken off.

i·de·a |ī dē′ ə| *n., pl.* **ideas** A thought or plan carefully formed in the mind: *I have some idea as to how I want to redecorate my bedroom.*

ill·ness |ĭl′ nĭs| *n., pl.* **illnesses** A sickness or disease: *Polio is a serious illness.*

im·age |ĭm′ ĭj| *n., pl.* **images** A picture in the mind: *Images of food came into the hungry child's head.*

i·mag·ine |ĭ măj′ ĭn| *v.* **imagined, imagining 1.** To form a mental picture or idea of: *Can you imagine a blue horse with a yellow mane?* **2.** To use the imagination; pretend.

im·i·tate |ĭm′ ĭ tāt′| *v.* **imitated, imitating** To copy the actions, looks, or sounds of: *Little children imitate their parents.*

im·i·ta·tion |ĭm′ ĭ tā′ shən| *n., pl.* **imitations 1.** The act or process of imitating or copying: *I learned the song through imitation.* **2.** Something made to look or seem just like something else; copy: *This vase is an imitation of one in the museum.*

im·por·tant |ĭm pôr′ tnt| *adj.* Strongly affecting the course of events or the nature of things; significant: *This is an important message.*

im·press |ĭm prĕs′| *v.* **impressed, impressing** To have a strong, often favorable effect on the mind or feelings of: *The size of the tall building impressed me.*

im·pres·sion |ĭm prĕsh′ ən| *n., pl.* **impressions** An effect, image, or feeling that stays in the mind: *My new friend made a good impression on my parents.*

im·prove |ĭm prōōv′| *v.* **improved, improving** To make or become better: *I improved my tennis serve by practicing.*

in-¹ A prefix that means "without, not": *inaccurate.*

in-² A prefix that means "in, within, or into": *inbound.*

in·crease |ĭn krēs′| *v.* **increased, increasing** To make or become greater or larger: *I increased my spending money by taking a job after school. n.* |ĭn′ krēs′|, *pl.* **increases** The act of increasing; growth: *When you get to high school, you will find an increase in homework.*

in·de·pend·ence |ĭn dĭ pĕn′ dəns| *n.* The quality or condition of being independent or not governed by a foreign country: *The American Colonies won independence from Britain in the American Revolution.*

in·dus·try |ĭn′ də strē| *n., pl.* **industries** A large-scale enterprise that provides a product or service: *Hollywood is the capital of the motion picture industry.*

in·flate |ĭn flāt′| *v.* **inflated, inflating** To fill with gas and expand: *Did you inflate the tires on the bicycle?*

in·form |ĭn fôrm′| *v.* **informed, informing** To tell about something; notify: *Please inform me as to the time of your arrival.*

in·her·it |ĭn hĕr′ ĭt| *v.* **inherited, inheriting** To receive money or property after someone's death.

in·ning |ĭn′ ĭng| *n., pl.* **innings** One of the divisions of a baseball game when each team comes to bat.

in·quir·y |ĭn kwîr′ ē| or |ĭn′ kwə rē| *n., pl.* **inquiries 1.** The act or process of asking in order to find out. **2.** A detailed examination of a matter; an investigation.

in·sist |ĭn sĭst′| *v.* **insisted, insisting** To demand; take a strong stand: *I insist on watching the ball game.*

in·spect |ĭn spĕkt′| *v.* **inspected, inspecting 1.** To look over carefully. **2.** To examine in an official or formal way.

in·spec·tion |ĭn spĕk′ shən| *n., pl.* **inspections 1.** The act of inspecting. **2.** An official examination or review: *Elevators must undergo an annual safety inspection.*

in·spec·tor |ĭn spĕk′ tər| *n., pl.* **inspectors** A person who examines or reviews things.

in·stall |ĭn stôl′| *v.* **installed, installing** To put in position for use or service: *They installed the telephone today.*

in·sult |ĭn sŭlt′| *v.* **insulted, insulting** To speak to or treat impolitely and disrespectfully: *Don't insult me by calling me dishonest.*

in·ter·na·tion·al |ĭn′ tər **năsh′** ə nəl| *adj.* Of, relating to, or carried on between two or more nations.

in·ter·pret |ĭn **tûr′** prĭt| *v.* **interpreted, interpreting** To tell the meaning or importance of; explain: *Can you interpret this graph?*

in·ter·sec·tion |ĭn′ tər **sĕk′** shən| *n., pl.* **intersections** The point where two or more things cross: *There is a traffic light at the intersection of the two streets.*

in·trude |ĭn **trood′**| *v.* **intruded, intruding.** To break, come, or force in without being wanted or asked; trespass; invade: *Don't intrude on my privacy.*

-ion A suffix that forms nouns and means "an act or process" or "the outcome of an act": *election.*

ir·ri·tate |ĭr′ ĭ **tāt′**| *v.* **irritated, irritating** To make angry or impatient; annoy: *Your endless questions irritate me.*

ir·ri·ta·tion |ĭr ĭ **tā′** shən| *n., pl.* **irritations 1.** The act or process of irritating. **2.** The condition of being irritated. **3.** Something that irritates; an annoyance.

J

jade |jād| *n., pl.* **jades** A hard, pale green or white stone. Jade is used for jewelry, ornaments, and statues.

jave·lin |jăv′ lĭn| *n., pl.* **javelins** A light spear that is thrown for distance in an athletic contest.

jew·el |joo′ əl| *n., pl.* **jewels 1.** A precious stone; gem. **2.** A valuable ornament, as a ring or necklace, especially one made of precious metal and set with gems.

joint |joint| *n., pl.* **joints 1.** A place where two or more bones come together. **2.** A place where two or more things, such as pipes, come together.

jun·ior high school |joon′ yər hī′ skool′| *n., pl.* **junior high schools** A secondary school including the seventh, the eighth, and sometimes the ninth grades.

jus·tice |jŭs′ tĭs| *n., pl.* **justices 1.** The quality of being just or fair. **2.** The carrying out of the law or the way in which the law is carried out: *The courts make sure that justice is achieved.*

ă	pat	ŏ	pot	û	fur
ā	pay	ō	go	*th*	the
â	care	ô	paw, for	th	thin
ä	father	oi	oil	hw	which
ĕ	pet	oo	book	zh	usual
ē	be	oo	boot	ə	ago, item
ĭ	pit	yoo	cute		pencil, atom
ī	ice	ou	out		circus
î	near	ŭ	cut	ər	butter

K

kay·ak |kī′ ăk′| *n., pl.* **kayaks** A canoe made of skins or canvas stretched over a light wooden frame. The top of a kayak is closed except for an opening in the middle in which the paddler sits.

ker·nel |kûr′ nəl| *n., pl.* **kernels 1.** A grain or seed, especially of corn, wheat, or a similar cereal plant: *The kernels of corn were ground to make corn meal.* **2.** The part found inside the shell of a nut: *If you crack the walnut shell, you will find the kernel.*

knap·sack |năp′ săk′| *n., pl.* **knapsacks** A canvas or leather bag that is designed to be carried on the back. A knapsack is used to hold supplies, as on a hike or march.

knowl·edge |nŏl′ ĭj| *n.* **1.** Facts and ideas; information: *Books are a great source of knowledge.* **2.** Understanding; awareness: *It may take a few years to gain solid knowledge of a new language.*

L

la·bel |lā′ bəl| *n., pl.* **labels** A tag or sticker that is attached to something to tell what it is or what it contains: *The label lists the contents of the can.*

lab·o·ra·to·ry |lăb′ rə tôr′ ē| *n., pl.* **laboratories** A room or building with special equipment for doing scientific tests and experiments.

La·bor Day |lā′ bər| *n.* A legal holiday in honor of workers that comes on the first Monday in September.

la·dy |lā′ dē| *n., pl.* **ladies** A woman: *A lady on the bus gave us directions.*

laid |lād| *v.* Past tense and past participle of **lay**: *He laid the books on his desk.*

lair |lâr| *n., pl.* **lairs** The den or home of a wild animal.

land |lănd| *v.* **landed, landing 1.** To come or bring to shore: *The boat landed at the dock.* **2.** To come down or bring to rest on a surface: *The pilot landed the plane.*

lan·guage |lăng′ gwĭj| *n., pl.* **languages 1.** Spoken or written human speech. People use language to communicate thoughts and feelings. **2.** A system of words and expressions shared by a people: *What is your native language?*

la·ser |lā′ zər| *n., pl.* **lasers** A device that sends out a very narrow and extremely powerful beam of light. Laser beams are used to cut through steel and perform delicate surgery.

late·ly |lāt′ lē| *adv.* In the near past; recently; not long ago.

laugh·a·ble |lăf′ ə bəl| *adj.* Causing or likely to cause laughter or amusement.

laugh·ter |lăf′ tər| *n.* **1.** The act or sound of laughing. **2.** Happiness or amusement expressed by laughing.

launch¹ |lônch| *v.* **launched, launching 1.** To set afloat: *The new ship was launched today.* **2.** To begin or start: *We launched a new project.*

launch² |lônch| *n., pl.* **launches** A large motorboat.

lay·er |lā′ ər| *v.* **layered, layering** To put several thicknesses or sheets on top of each other.

leaf |lēf| *n., pl.* **leaves** A usually thin, flat, green plant part attached to a stem or stalk.

league |lēg| *n., pl.* **leagues** An association of sports teams that compete mainly among themselves: *Ten high schools formed a football league.*

learn |lûrn| *v.* **learned** *or* **learnt, learning 1.** To get knowledge of or skill in through study or instruction: *The third-graders are learning Spanish.* **2.** To find out: *I just learned about your accident.*

lease |lēs| *n., pl.* **leases** A written agreement by which an owner of property allows someone else to rent it for a certain period of time. *v.* **leased, leasing** To rent.

least |lēst| *adj.* Smallest in degree or size: *Making friends was Jacki's least worry.*

lec·ture |lĕk′ chər| *n., pl.* **lectures 1.** A speech providing information on a subject, given before a class. **2.** A serious scolding.

le·gal |lē′ gəl| *adj.* Based on or authorized by law; lawful: *Our parents are the legal owners of the house.*

le·gal·i·ty |lĭ găl′ ĭ tē| *n., pl.* **legalities** The fact of being legal; lawfulness.

leg·is·la·tion |lĕj′ ĭs lā′ shən| *n.* A law or group of laws that have been proposed or made: *The Senate passed legislation to raise the minimum wage.*

lei·sure |lē′ zhər| *or* |lĕzh′ ər| *n.* Free time in which to relax and do as one pleases.

-less A suffix that forms adjectives and means "not having" or "without": *harmless; shoeless.*

lev·el |lĕv′ əl| *n., pl.* **levels** A particular height: *I waded in until the water was at chest level. adj.* Having a flat, even surface; not tilted: *We found a level piece of ground for our picnic.*

lev·y |lĕv′ ē| *v.* **levied, levying** To order to be paid; to impose a tax or other fee: *The town levied a tax on new cars.*

Lew·is |lōō′ ĭs|, **Meriwether** 1774–1809. American Pacific Northwest explorer.

li·ar |lī′ ər| *n., pl.* **liars** A person who says things that are not true.

lib·er·ty |lĭb′ ər tē| *n., pl.* **liberties** Freedom from the control of others; independence: *Freedom of speech is a basic liberty.*

li·brar·y |lī′ brĕr′ ē| *n., pl.* **libraries** A place where books, magazines, records, and reference materials are kept for reading or borrowing.

life·boat |līf′ bōt′| *n., pl.* **lifeboats** A strong boat used for saving lives at sea or from a shore: *Everyone got into lifeboats as the ship sank.*

light·house |līt′ hous′| *n., pl.* **lighthouses** A tower with a powerful light at the top that is used to guide ships.

ă	pat	ŏ	pot	û	fur
ā	pay	ō	go	*th*	the
â	care	ô	paw, for	th	thin
ä	father	oi	oil	hw	which
ĕ	pet	ōō	book	zh	usual
ē	be	ōō	boot	ə	ago, item
ĭ	pit	yōō	cute		pencil, atom
ī	ice	ou	out		circus
î	near	ŭ	cut	ər	butter

light·ning bug |līt′ nĭng bŭg| *n., pl.* **lightning bugs** A firefly.

lil·y |lĭl′ ē| *n., pl.* **lilies** Any of several related plants that grow from bulbs and have tall, leafy stems and white or brightly colored flowers shaped like trumpets.

lime·light |līm′ līt′| *n.* The center of public attention: *The President is always in the limelight.*

lim·er·ick |lĭm′ ər ĭk| *n., pl.* **limericks** An amusing poem of five lines.

li·on |lī′ ən| *n., pl.* **lions** A very large light-brown wild cat of Africa and India.

lis·ten |lĭs′ ən| *v.* **listened, listening 1.** To try to hear something: *If you listen, you can hear the ocean.* **2.** To pay attention.

lit·ter |lĭt′ ər| *n.* Pieces of paper, empty cans and bottles, and other waste material left lying around. *v.* **littered, littering** To make messy by leaving trash around: *Don't litter the picnic area.*

loaf |lōf| *v.* **loafed, loafing** To spend time lazily or not working; idle: *Don't loaf; please get the job done.*

loan |lōn| *v.* **loaned, loaning** To lend: *Please loan me your sleeping bag.*
♦ *These sound alike* **loan, lone.**

lob·by·ist |lŏb′ ē ĭst| *n., pl.* **lobbyists** A person who lobbies or tries to influence law makers: *Lobbyists discussed the issue with the Senator.*

lo·cal |lō′ kəl| *adj.* Of a certain limited area or place: *The town has its own local government.*

lo·cal·i·ty |lō kăl′ ĭ tē| *n., pl.* **localities** A particular place, region, or neighborhood.

lo·cate |lō′ kāt′| *v.* **located, locating** To find and show the position of.

lo·ca·tion |lō kā′ shən| *n., pl.* **locations** **1.** A position. **2.** A place away from a movie or television studio at which a scene is filmed.

lo·co·mo·tion |lō′ kə mō′ shən| *n., pl.* **locomotions** The act of moving or the ability to move from one place to another.

log·ic |lŏj′ ĭk| *n.* Rational thought; sound reasoning.

loi·ter |loi′ tər| *v.* **loitered, loitering** To stand around doing nothing; to linger; to not hurry.

lone |lōn| *adj.* **1.** Without others: *A lone sailor stood watch.* **2.** By itself: *A lone tree stood in the meadow.*
♦ *These sound alike* **lone, loan.**

lone·ly |lōn′ lē| *adj.* **lonelier, loneliest** Sad at being alone.

loop |lōōp| *n., pl.* **loops** A circular path or pattern.

loose |lōōs| *adj.* **looser, loosest 1.** Not fastened tightly: *Your shoelaces are loose.* **2.** Not confined or tied up; free: *Chickens were loose in the yard.* **3.** Not bound, bundled, or joined together: *Some loose pages fell out of the book.*

lord |lôrd| *n., pl.* **lords** A man of noble rank in Great Britain.

lose |lōōz| *v.* **lost, losing 1.** To miss from one's possession; misplace; fail to find: *I lost my spelling book.* **2.** To be unable to keep: *I lost my balance and fell.* **3.** To give up in a natural process; shed: *Many trees lose their leaves in the fall.* **4.** To fail to win: *We lost both games.*

loy·al |loi′ əl| *adj.* Firm in supporting a person, country, or cause; faithful; true.

lug·gage |lŭg′ ĭj| *n.* Bags and suitcases that a person takes on a trip; baggage.

lu·nar |loo′ nər| *adj.* Of, on, or having to do with the moon: *The spacecraft made a perfect lunar landing.*

lunch·eon |lŭn′ chən| *n., pl.* **luncheons** A midday meal; lunch.

lux·u·ry |lŭg′ zhə rē| or |lŭk′ shə rē| *n., pl.* **luxuries** Something that is not really needed but that gives great pleasure, enjoyment, or comfort: *A luxury is often expensive or hard to get.*

-ly A suffix that forms adverbs and means "in a certain way": *accidentally, happily.*

M

mag·a·zine |măg′ ə zēn′| or |măg′ ə zēn′| *n., pl.* **magazines** A publication that is issued regularly, as every week or month.

Ma·gel·lan |mə jĕl′ ən|, **Ferdinand** 1480?– 1521. Portuguese navigator in the service of Spain; he died while commanding the first expedition that sailed around the world.

mag·ni·fy |măg′ nə fī′| *v.* **magnified, magnifying** To enlarge the appearance of: *A microscope magnifies bacteria.*

main |mān| *adj.* Most important; chief: *Look for the main idea in each paragraph.*
♦ *These sound alike* **main, mane.**

ma·jes·tic |mə jĕs′ tĭk| *adj.* Stately and dignified; regal: *The monarch gave a majestic wave.*

ma·jor |mā′ jər| *adj.* Larger, greater, or more important: *Students spend the major part of the day in school.*

ma·jor·i·ty |mə jôr′ ĭ tē| *n., pl.* **majorities** The greater number or part; more than half: *Girls make up the majority of the class.*

make-be·lieve |māk′ bĭ lēv′| *adj.* Pretended; imaginary.

male |māl| *n., pl.* **males** A man or boy.

mal·lard |măl′ ərd| *n., pl.* **mallards** A wild green-headed duck of North America, Europe, and northern Asia.

man·age |măn′ ĭj| *v.* **managed, managing** **1.** To have control over; direct: *Who will manage the business while your parents are away?* **2.** To succeed in doing something: *I managed to finish my work.*

mane |mān| *n., pl.* **manes** The long, heavy hair growing from the neck and head of an animal such as a horse or a male lion.
♦ *These sound alike* **mane, main.**

mar·a·thon |măr′ ə thŏn′| *n., pl.* **marathons** A race for runners over a distance of 26 miles, 385 yards.

mar·riage |măr′ ĭj| *n., pl.* **marriages** **1.** The condition of living together as husband and wife. **2.** Wedding: *The marriage will take place in September.*

Mar·tin Lu·ther King Day *n.* A holiday celebrating the birthday of Martin Luther King, Jr., a civil rights leader. This holiday falls on the third Monday in January.

mar·vel·ous |mär′ və ləs| *adj.* **1.** Causing surprise, astonishment, or wonder: *You have a marvelous gift for science.* **2.** Of the highest or best kind or quality: *I just read a marvelous biography.*

mas·cot |măs′ kŏt′| *n., pl.* **mascots** Someone or something believed to bring good luck, often to a team: *The mascot of the football team is a donkey.*

mas·ter·piece |măs′ tər pēs′| *n., pl.* **masterpieces** An outstanding piece of work, especially an artist's or composer's greatest work.

mat·i·nee |măt′ n ā′| *n., pl.* **matinees** A theatrical performance or movie that is given or shown in the afternoon: *The matinee begins at 2 P.M.*

mat·ter |măt′ ər| *n., pl.* **matters** Substance or content; material: *The flood was the subject matter of the newscast.* *v.* **mattered, mattering** To be important: *We tried to pretend that it didn't matter.*

May·flow·er |mā′ flou′ ər| *n.* The ship on which the Pilgrims sailed to America from England in 1620.

may·or |mā′ ər| *n., pl.* **mayors** The chief government official of a city or town.

meas·ure |mĕzh′ ər| *v.* **measured, measuring** To find the size, amount, capacity, or degree of: *We measured the room twice.*

meat |mēt| *n., pl.* **meats** The flesh of an animal eaten as food.

♦ *These sound alike* **meat, meet.**

me·chan·i·cal |mə kăn′ ĭ kəl| *adj.* Operated or performed by a machine: *The garage has a mechanical door that opens when you press a button.*

meet |mēt| *v.* **met, meeting** To come together; connect or touch: *The two rivers meet near the capital. n., pl.* **meets** A gathering for a sports competition: *The school held a track meet.*

♦ *These sound alike* **meet, meat.**

Me·mo·ri·al Day |mə môr′ ē əl| *n.* A holiday in honor of members of the United States armed forces who have died in wars. In most states Memorial Day is celebrated on the last Monday in May.

mem·o·ry |mĕm′ ə rē| *n., pl.* **memories** 1. The power or ability to remember. 2. Something that is remembered: *My earliest memory is of my third birthday.*

-ment A suffix that forms nouns and means: 1. Action or process: *government.* 2. The result of an action or process: *measurement.* 3. Condition: *amazement; retirement.*

mer·chant |mûr′ chənt| *n., pl.* **merchants** A person who buys and sells goods, especially a person who runs a store.

mes·sage |mĕs′ ĭj| *n., pl.* **messages** 1. Words that are sent from one person or group to another. 2. A speech or other formal communication: *the President's message to Congress.*

met·al |mĕt′ l| *n., pl.* **metals** A substance, such as copper, iron, silver, or gold, that is usually shiny and hard, conducts heat and electricity, and can be hammered or cast into a desired shape.

mi·cro·scope |mī′ krə skōp′| *n., pl.* **microscopes** An instrument with a special lens for making a very small object appear larger, especially objects too small to be seen by the naked eye: *We examined the cell under the microscope.*

mid·dle |mĭd′ l| *n., pl.* **middles** A point or part that is the same distance from each side or end: *A deer stood in the middle of the road.*

ă	pat	ŏ	pot	û	fur
ā	pay	ō	go	*th*	the
â	care	ô	paw, for	th	thin
ä	father	oi	oil	hw	which
ĕ	pet	ōo	book	zh	usual
ē	be	ōō	boot	ə	ago, item
ĭ	pit	yōō	cute		pencil, atom
ī	ice	ou	out		circus
î	near	ŭ	cut	ər	butter

mi·grate |mī′ grāt′| *v.* **migrated, migrating** 1. To move from one country or region and settle in another. 2. To move regularly from one region or climate to another: *Many birds migrate in the fall.*

mi·gra·tion |mī grā′ shən| *n., pl.* **migrations** 1. The act or an example of migrating. 2. A group migrating together.

mild |mīld| *adj.* **milder, mildest** 1. Gentle in manner. 2. Moderate in action or effect; not stormy: *We had a mild winter.*

mil·lion |mĭl′ yən| *n., pl.* **million** *or* **millions** One thousand thousands; 1,000,000.

min·er |mī′ nər| *n., pl.* **miners** A person who works in a mine.

♦ *These sound alike* **miner, minor.**

min·er·al |mĭn′ ər əl| *n., pl.* **minerals** 1. A natural substance, such as a diamond or salt, that is not of plant or animal origin: *Many valuable gems are minerals.* 2. A natural substance, such as ore, coal, or petroleum, that is mined for human use: *He sold the rights to the minerals on his land.*

mi·nor |mī′ nər| *adj.* Smaller in amount, size, extent, or importance.

♦ *These sound alike* **minor, miner.**

History • miner, minor

Miner may come from the Common Celtic *meini*, meaning "ore." **Minor** comes from the Latin word *minor*, meaning "less."

min·ute |mĭn′ ĭt| *n., pl.* **minutes** A unit of time equal to 60 seconds.

mir·ror |mĭr′ ər| *n., pl.* **mirrors** A surface, as of glass, that reflects the image of an object placed in front of it.

mis·chief |mĭs′ chĭf| *n.* **1.** Naughty or bad behavior. **2.** Harm or damage caused by someone or something.

mist |mĭst| *n., pl.* **mists 1.** A mass of tiny drops of water in the air. **2.** A mass of tiny drops of any liquid, as perfume, sprayed into the air.

mis·take |mĭ stāk′| *n., pl.* **mistakes** Something that is thought up, done, or figured out in an incorrect way.

mix |mĭks| *v.* **mixed, mixing** To blend or combine into a single mass or substance: *Mix the flour, water, and eggs to form dough.*

mix·ture |mĭks′ chər| *n., pl.* **mixtures** Any combination of different ingredients, things, or kinds; blend: *mixture of flour and water.*

mod·el |mŏd′ l| *n., pl.* **models 1.** A small copy: *I built a model of a sailboat.* **2.** A person hired to display merchandise, such as clothing, that is for sale. *v.* **modeled, modeling** To display by wearing.

mod·ule |mŏj′ o͞ol| or |mŏd′ yo͞ol| *n.* **1.** A standard or unit of measurement. **2.** Any of the self-contained parts of a spacecraft, each of which is used for a particular job or set of jobs within the mission: *The captain operated the spacecraft from the command module.*

moist |moist| *adj.* **moister, moistest** Slightly wet; damp: *a moist towel.*

moist·en |moi′ sən| *v.* **moistened, moistening** To make moist; to dampen.

mois·ture |mois′ chər| *n.* Liquid, as water, that is present in the air or in the ground or that forms tiny drops on a surface; dampness.

mo·ment |mō′ mənt| *n., pl.* **moments** A very short period of time; instant: *Wait a moment while I wash my hands.*

mon·ster |mŏn′ stər| *n., pl.* **monsters** An imaginary creature that is huge and very frightening.

mon·u·ment |mŏn′ yə mənt| *n., pl.* **monuments 1.** Something, as a statue or building, put up to help people continue to remember a person, group, or thing. **2.** A place, area, or region preserved by a government for its beauty or significance.

mood |mo͞od| *n., pl.* **moods** A person's state of mind; a feeling: *Playing with my friends puts me in a happy mood.*

mor·tal |môr′ tl| *adj.* **1.** Certain to die. **2.** Causing death; fatal: *a mortal wound.*

mor·tal·i·ty |môr tăl′ ĭ tē| *n., pl.* **mortalities 1.** The condition of being subject to death: *The dying man thought about his own mortality.* **2.** Death, especially of large numbers of beings.

mo·sa·ic |mō zā′ ĭk| *n., pl.* **mosaics** A picture or design made on a surface by fitting and cementing together small pieces of colored tile, glass, or stone.

mos·qui·to |mə skē′ tō| *n., pl.* **mosquitoes** *or* **mosquitos** A small flying insect. The female mosquito bites and sucks blood from animals and human beings.

mo·tive |mō′ tĭv| *n., pl.* **motives** A reason that causes a person to act: *Curiosity was Jamey's motive for reading books.*

mound |mound| *n., pl.* **mounds** The pitcher's area in the middle of a baseball diamond raised about ten inches above the ground.

moun·tain |moun′ tən| *n., pl.* **mountains** An area of land that rises to a great height.

move·ment |mo͞ov′ mənt| *n., pl.* **movements** The act or process of changing position: *the slow movement of the hands on the clock.*

mov·ie |mo͞o′ vē| *n., pl.* **movies** A motion picture.

mule |myo͞ol| *n., pl.* **mules** An animal that is the offspring of a male donkey and a female horse, generally thought of as being stubborn.

mus•cle |mŭs′ əl| *n., pl.* **muscles** A type of body tissue that can be contracted and relaxed to cause movement or exert force.

mus•cu•lar |mŭs′ kyə lər| *adj.* Having strong muscles: *I have muscular legs from riding my bicycle every single day.*

mu•sic |myōō′ zĭk| *n.* **1.** The art of combining tones or sounds in a pleasing or meaningful way. **2.** Vocal or instrumental sounds that have a tune and a beat.

mys•te•ry |mĭs′ tə rē| *n., pl.* **mysteries** **1.** Something that is not fully understood or is kept secret: *That person's identity remains a mystery.* **2.** A piece of fiction dealing with a puzzling crime: *The mystery about the jewel theft had a surprise ending.*

ă	pat	ŏ	pot	û	fur
ā	pay	ō	go	*th*	the
â	care	ô	paw, for	th	thin
ä	father	oi	oil	hw	which
ĕ	pet	ōō	book	zh	usual
ē	be	ōō	boot	ə	ago, item
ĭ	pit	yōō	cute		pencil, atom
ī	ice	ou	out		circus
î	near	ŭ	cut	ər	butter

N

na•tion |nā′ shən| *n., pl.* **nations** A group of people who share the same territory and are organized under a single government; country: *The United States is a nation.*

na•tion•al |năsh′ ə nəl| *adj.* Of, having to do with, or belonging to a nation.

na•tion•al•i•ty |năsh′ ə năl′ ĭ tē| *n., pl.* **nationalities** The condition of belonging to a particluar nation. *Children born in the United States are of American nationality.*

na•tive |nā′ tĭv| *adj.* Belonging to a person because of the person's place of birth: *native language. n., pl.* **natives** A person born in a certain place or country: *I am a native of New England.*

na•ture |nā′ chər| *n., pl.* **natures** The world of living things and the outdoors; wildlife and natural scenery: *We slept outdoors to enjoy the beauties of nature.*

nee•dle |nēd′ l| *n., pl.* **needles** A small, slender tool for sewing, usually made of polished steel. It has a sharp point at one end and an eye at the other end through which thread is passed.

ne•glect |nĭ glĕkt′| *v.* **neglected, neglecting** To fail to give proper care and attention to: *A good student doesn't neglect homework or class assignments.*

nerve |nûrv| *n., pl.* **nerves** **1.** Any of the bundles of fibers that carry messages between the brain or spinal cord and other parts of the body. **2.** Courage or daring: *It took all my nerve to jump that high fence.*

-ness A suffix that forms nouns and means "condition" or "quality." *Kindness* is the condition or quality of being kind.

net•work |nĕt′ wûrk′| *n., pl.* **networks** A group of related radio or television stations that share programs.

neu•tral |nōō′ trəl| or |nyōō′ trəl| *adj.* **1.** Not taking sides in a war, quarrel, or contest: *The teacher was a neutral listener as the students debated the issue.* **2.** Having little color: *Gray is a neutral shade.*

news•cast |nōōz′ kăst′| or |nyōōz′ kăst′| *n., pl.* **newscasts** A broadcast of news on radio or television.

New Year's Day |nōō′ yîrz| or |nyōō′ yîrz| *n.* January 1, the first day of the year, a holiday in many parts of the world.

nick•el |nĭk′ əl| *n., pl.* **nickels** A United States or Canadian coin worth five cents.

niece |nēs| *n., pl.* **nieces** The daughter of one's brother or sister.

nine•ty-nine |nīn′ tē nīn′| *n.* The number written 99.

nom•i•nate |nŏm′ ə nāt′| *v.* **nominated, nominating** To propose or select as a candidate for election, appointment to office, or an honor.

nor•mal |nôr′ məl| *adj.* **1.** Of the usual or regular kind: *My weight is normal for my height.* **2.** Happening in a natural, healthy way: *The baby has a normal heartbeat.*

nor•mal•i•ty |nôr măl′ ĭ tē| *n.* The condition of being normal: *After the flood the town quickly returned to normality.*

no•tice |nō′ tĭs| *v.* **noticed, noticing** To take note of; pay attention to: *I sat in the last row and hoped nobody would notice me.*

nov•el[1] |nŏv′ əl| *adj.* Very new, unusual, or different.

nov•el[2] |nŏv′ əl| *n., pl.* **novels** A made-up story that is long enough to fill a book.

nui•sance |noō′ səns| or |nyoō′ səns| *n., pl.* **nuisances** Someone or something that is annoying; a pest.

O

ob•ject[1] |ŏb′ jĭkt| *n., pl.* **objects** Something that has shape and can be felt or seen: *There were several objects on the table.*

ob•ject[2] |əb jĕkt′| *v.* **objected, objecting** To express an opposing view or argument; to be against; disapprove of: *I object to long drives.*

ob•jec•tion |əb jĕk′ shən| *n., pl.* **objections** The expression of an opposing point of view or argument: *You should have made an objection if you didn't like the idea.*

ob•vi•ous |ŏb′ vē əs| *adj.* Easily seen or understood; clear: *The student made an obvious mistake in subtraction.*

o•cean |ō′ shən| *n., pl.* **oceans** 1. The great mass of salt water that covers about 72 percent of the earth's surface. 2. One of the four main divisions of this mass of salt water: *The Arctic Ocean surrounds the North Pole.*

odd |ŏd| *adj.* **odder, oddest** Not ordinary or usual; peculiar: *The car is making an odd noise.*

of•fer |ô′ fər| *v.* **offered, offering** 1. To present for consideration; propose: *The editor offered some suggestions for improving the story.* 2. To show readiness to do; volunteer. 3. To put forward to be accepted or refused: *Julia offered me soup.*

of•fice |ô′ fĭs| *n., pl.* **offices** A place, as a room or series of rooms, in which the work of a business or profession is carried on.

of•fi•cer |ô′ fĭ sər| *n., pl.* **officers** A member of the police force.

of•fi•cial |ə fĭsh′ əl| *n., pl.* **officials** A person in a position of authority.

O•lym•pics |ō lĭm′ pĭks| *pl. n.* An international athletic competition held every four years in a different part of the world. The modern Olympics are a revival of a festival of contests held in Olympia in ancient Greece.

on•ion |ŭn′ yən| *n., pl.* **onions** A plant with an edible round yellow bulb that is widely grown as a vegetable. The bulb has a strong smell and a sharp taste.

on•yx |ŏn′ ĭks| *n.* A type of quartz that occurs in bands of different colors, often black and white. Onyx may be dyed and carved.

o•pal |ō′ pəl| *n., pl.* **opals** A mineral having many rainbowlike colors, often used as a gem. It can be found in rock cavities.

op•er•ate |ŏp′ ə rāt′| *v.* **operated, operating** 1. To work or run: *This machine operates well.* 2. To perform surgery.

op•po•nent |ə pō′ nənt| *n., pl.* **opponents** A person who is against another in a fight, contest, or debate; rival; not a friend.

op•pose |ə pōz′| *v.* **opposed, opposing** To be or fight against; resist: *Senator Huertas will oppose the plan for new taxes.*

op•tion |ŏp′ shən| *n., pl.* **options** The act of choosing; choice: *Luis has the option of going to summer camp or staying home.*

or•chard |ôr′ chərd| *n., pl.* **orchards** A piece of land where fruit trees are grown.

or•deal |ôr dēl′| *n., pl.* **ordeals** A very difficult or painful experience; hardship.

or·der |ôr′ dər| *v.* **ordered, ordering 1.** To give a command to: *The teacher ordered the class to open their books.* **2.** To arrange things in a sequence one after another: *The books are ordered alphabetically.*

or·phan |ôr′ fən| *n., pl.* **orphans** A child whose parents are dead.

os·trich |ôs′ trĭch| *n., pl.* **ostriches** A large African bird that cannot fly but can run very fast. Ostriches have fluffy plumes.

ounce |ouns| *n., pl.* **ounces** A unit of weight and mass equal to 1/16 pound.

-ous A suffix that forms adjectives and means "full of" or "having the qualities of": *joyous.*

out·field |out′ fēld′| *n., pl.* **outfields** The playing area that extends outward from a baseball diamond and is divided into right, center, and left fields.

out·spo·ken |out spō′ kən| *adj.* Not speaking or spoken with reserve; frank and honest; bold: *You are too outspoken about your political views.*

o·va·tion |ō vā′ shən| *n., pl.* **ovations** A loud and enthusiastic display of approval, usually in the form of shouting or hearty applause.

owe |ō| *v.* **owed, owing 1.** To have to pay or repay: *We owe the store $20.* **2.** To be obliged for: *We owe the discovery of polio vaccine to a famous scientist.*

P

pack·age |păk′ ĭj| *n., pl.* **packages** A bundle of things packed together.

pale |pāl| *adj.* **paler, palest** Having skin that is lighter than usual, often because of illness; lacking color. *n.* **paleness** *My paleness left when I recovered from the flu.*

par·ent |pâr′ ənt| *n., pl.* **parents** A father or mother.

part·ner |pärt′ nər| *n., pl.* **partners 1.** One of two or more persons associated in a business. **2.** Either of a pair of persons dancing together.

part of speech |pärt′ ŭv spēch′| or |pärt′ ŏv spēch′| *n., pl.* **parts of speech** A grammatical class, such as a noun, pronoun, verb, adjective, adverb, preposition, conjunction, or interjection, into which a word can be placed according to the way it is used in a phrase or sentence.

ă	pat	ŏ	pot	û	fur
ā	pay	ō	go	*th*	the
â	care	ô	paw, for	th	thin
ä	father	oi	oil	hw	which
ĕ	pet	ōō	book	zh	usual
ē	be	ōō	boot	ə	ago, item
ĭ	pit	yōō	cute		pencil, atom
ī	ice	ou	out		circus
î	near	ŭ	cut	ər	butter

par·ty |pär′ tē| *n., pl.* **parties** A group of people who are organized for political activity: *Which party do your parents belong to?*

pas·sage |păs′ ĭj| *n., pl.* **passages 1.** The act or process of passing: *The river is deep enough for safe passage.* **2.** A journey. **3.** A narrow path or channel. **4.** Approval of law by a legislative body. **5.** A part of a written work or piece of music.

pas·sen·ger |păs′ ən jər| *n., pl.* **passengers** A person riding in or on a vehicle or vessel: *There were twenty passengers on the bus.*

pass·port |păs′ pôrt| *n., pl.* **passports** A government document that gives a citizen permission to travel in foreign countries.

pas·ture |păs′ chər| *n., pl.* **pastures** Ground where animals graze.

pa·tri·ot |pā′ trē ət| *n., pl.* **patriots** A person who loves, supports, and defends his or her country.

pat·tern |păt′ ərn| *n., pl.* **patterns** An artistic design used for decoration: *The wallpaper has a pattern of flowers.*

pause |pôz| *n., pl.* **pauses** A brief stop. *v.* **paused, pausing** To stop briefly.

peace |pēs| *n.* **1.** The absence of war or fighting. **2.** Freedom from mental or emotional upset: *I need peace and quiet.*
♦ *These sound alike* **peace, piece.**

pea·nut |pē′ nŭt| *n., pl.* **peanuts** A vine similar to the pea that bears oily, edible, light-brown seeds that ripen underground; goober.

pearl |pûrl| *n., pl.* **pearls** A smooth, rounded, white or grayish growth formed inside the shells of oysters and used as a gem.

Pea·ry |pîr′ ē|, **Robert Edwin** 1856–1920. American naval officer and Arctic explorer; discovered North Pole in 1909.

ped·al |pĕd′ l| *n., pl.* **pedals** A lever, as on a piano, that is worked by the foot. *v.* **pedaled, pedaling** To ride a bicycle or tricycle: *It is hard to pedal up a steep hill.*

ped·es·tal |pĕd′ ĭ stəl| *n., pl.* **pedestals** A base or support, as for a column or a statue.

pe·des·tri·an |pə dĕs′ trē ən| *n., pl.* **pedestrians** A person traveling on foot: *The pedestrians crossed the street when the cars stopped for a red light.*

peer |pîr| *v.* **peered, peering** To look intently, closely, or with difficulty: *peer through a microscope.*
  ◆ *These sound alike* **peer, pier.**

pen·al·ty |pĕn′ əl tē| *n., pl.* **penalties** Something that must be given up for breaking a rule in a game or sport: *That foul cost our football team a ten-yard penalty, and we lost the game.*

pen·guin |pĕn′ gwĭn| or |pĕng′ gwĭn| *n., pl.* **penguins** A sea bird that lives near the South Pole, has webbed feet, and cannot fly. A penguin has black and white feathers and flipperlike wings.

per·cent·age |pər sĕn′ tĭj| *n., pl.* **percentages** A fraction with 100 as its denominator: *What percentage of your time do you spend asleep?*

per·haps |pər hăps′| *adv.* Maybe but not definitely; possibly: *Perhaps you'll come with us.*

pe·ri·od |pîr′ ē əd| *n., pl.* **periods 1.** An interval or portion of time: *A year is a period of twelve months.* **2.** A punctuation mark (.) used to indicate the end of a sentence or an abbreviation. **3.** A time in history.

per·mit |pər mĭt′| *v.* **permitted, permitting** To give permission to; allow: *Standing is not permitted in the back of the theater.* *n.* |pûr′ mĭt′| or |pər mĭt′|, *pl.* **permits** A written certificate of permission, such as a license.

per·son |pûr′ sən| *n., pl.* **persons** A human; individual: *Any person who wants to can come to the game.*

per·son·al |pûr′ sə nəl| *adj.* Of, relating to, or belonging to a person; private: *My clothes are my personal property.*

pic·ture |pĭk′ chər| *n., pl.* **pictures** A painting, drawing, or photograph of a person or thing.

piece |pēs| *n., pl.* **pieces 1.** A portion of something larger: *We bought a piece of land in the country.* **2.** An object that is a member of a group or class: *a piece of furniture.*
  ◆ *These sound alike* **piece, peace.**

pier |pîr| *n., pl.* **piers** A platform that extends into water. A pier can be used to protect a harbor or serve as a landing place for ships and boats; a dock; wharf.
  ◆ *These sound alike* **pier, peer.**

pil·grim |pĭl′ grĭm| *n., pl.* **pilgrims 1.** A person who travels to a sacred place. **2. Pilgrim** One of the English settlers who founded Plymouth Colony in New England in 1620.

pil·lar |pĭl′ ər| *n., pl.* **pillars** An upright structure that serves as a support, as for a bridge or a building, or stands alone as a monument; column.

pin |pĭn| *n., pl.* **pins** A short, straight, stiff piece of wire with a head at one end and a sharp point at the other.
  ◇ *Idiom* **on pins and needles** In a state of anxiety; nervous.

pitch·er |pĭch′ ər| *n., pl.* **pitchers** The baseball player who pitches the ball to the batter.

pit·y |pĭt′ ē| *n., pl.* **pities** A feeling of sorrow or sympathy for the suffering of another. *v.* **pitied, pitying** To feel sorry for.

plan |plăn| *v.* **planned, planning** To have in mind; intend.

plat·form |plăt′ fôrm′| *n., pl.* **platforms** A formal statement of principles or policy, as of a political party: *The party debated its platform during the convention.*

play·wright |plā′ rīt′| *n., pl.* **playwrights** A person who writes plays.

pleas·ure |plĕzh′ ər| *n., pl.* **pleasures** A feeling of happiness or enjoyment; delight: *She smiled with pleasure.*

plight |plīt| *n., pl.* **plights** A serious condition or a situation of difficulty or danger: *The plight of the families living in the drought-stricken area has not improved.*

Plym·outh |plĭm′ əth| *n.* A town in Massachusetts where the Pilgrims landed in 1620. The colony was founded later that year.

po·em |pō′ əm| *n., pl.* **poems** A piece of writing, often in rhyme, in which words are chosen for their sound and beauty as well as meaning.

po·et |pō′ ĭt| *n., pl.* **poets** One who writes poems.

po·et·ic |pō ĕt′ ĭk| *adj.* Of, relating to, or like poetry: *Poetic language is beautiful.*

poise |poiz| *v.* **poised, poising** To balance or be balanced: *The horse poised for the jump. n.* Sureness and confidence of manner: *The child recited the poem with poise.*

poi·son i·vy |poi′ zən ī′ vē| *n.* A plant with leaflets in groups of three that can cause an itching skin rash if touched.

po·lar |pō′ lər| *adj.* Of, relating to, or near the North Pole or the South Pole.

pole |pōl| *n., pl.* **poles 1.** A long slender rod: *We used a branch as a fishing pole.* **2.** An upright post: *a telephone pole.*
♦ *These sound alike* **pole, poll.**

Po·lo |pō′ lō|, **Marco** 1254?–1324? Venetian traveler and merchant who visited China.

poll |pōl| *n., pl.* **polls** A survey made to find out what people think.
♦ *These sound alike* **poll, pole.**

ă	pat	ŏ	pot	û	fur
ā	pay	ō	go	*th*	the
â	care	ô	paw, for	th	thin
ä	father	oi	oil	hw	which
ĕ	pet	ŏŏ	book	zh	usual
ē	be	ōō	boot	ə	ago, item
ĭ	pit	yōō	cute		pencil, atom
ī	ice	ou	out		circus
î	near	ŭ	cut	ər	butter

pol·lute |pə lōōt′| *v.* **polluted, polluting** To make dirty or impure; contaminate: *Gasoline exhaust pollutes the air.*

pol·lu·tion |pə lōō′ shən| *n.* The act of polluting or condition of being polluted.

pop·u·lar |pŏp′ yə lər| *adj.* Enjoyed or liked by many or most people: *Running is a popular sport.*

pop·u·late |pŏp′ yə lāt′| *v.* **populated, populating 1.** To supply with residents. **2.** To live in; reside.

pop·u·la·tion |pŏp′ yə lā′ shən| *n., pl.* **populations** The total number of people living in a certain place.

pore¹ |pôr| *n., pl.* **pores** A tiny opening, as in the skin or on the surface of a plant.
♦ *These sound alike* **pore, pour.**

pore² |pôr| *v.* **pored, poring** To examine with great care and attention: *I pored over the magazine.*
♦ *These sound alike* **pore, pour.**

port·a·ble |pôr′ tə bəl| *adj.* Capable of being carried or moved: *We bought a portable radio to take to the beach.*

por·ter |pôr′ tər| *n., pl.* **porters** A person hired to carry baggage, as at a railroad station: *The porter helped us get the suitcases onto the train.*

por·tray |pôr trā′| *v.* **portrayed, portraying** To play the part of: *A young actor is portraying a construction worker in the new movie.*

pos·si·ble |pŏs′ ə bəl| *adj.* **1.** Capable of happening or being done: *It is possible to get to the airport by bus.* **2.** Capable of being used for a certain purpose: *That field is a possible site for the new school.*

post·age |pō′ stĭj| *n.* The charge for mailing something.

post of·fice |pōst′ ô′ fĭs| *n., pl.* **post offices 1.** A government department or agency responsible for sending and delivering mail. **2.** A local office where mail is received, sorted, and sent out.

po·ta·to |pə tā′ tō| *n., pl.* **potatoes** A vegetable that has firm white flesh. Potatoes grow underground and are the thick, rounded stems of a leafy plant.

pour |pôr| *v.* **poured, pouring** To flow or cause to flow in a steady stream: *When you pour the milk, pour slowly.*
  ◆ *These sound alike* **pour, pore.**

pow·der |pou′ dər| *n., pl.* **powders 1.** A dry substance consisting of many very small particles. **2.** Something, such as a cosmetic, in the form of a powder.

pow·er·ful |pou′ ər fəl| *adj.* Having power, authority, or influence: *The United States of America is a powerful nation.*

prac·ti·cal |prăk′ tĭ′ kəl| *adj.* Having or serving a useful purpose: *It's not easy to turn an idea into a practical invention.*

prac·tice |prăk′ tĭs| *v.* **practiced, practicing 1.** To do or work over and over in order to acquire skill: *I practice playing the piano every day.* **2.** To make a habit of: *Learn to practice self-control.*

praise |prāz| *n., pl.* **praises** Approval or admiration: *Praise from the coach meant a lot to me.*

prank |prăngk| *n., pl.* **pranks** A playful trick or joke: *He liked to play funny pranks on his friends.*

pre- A prefix that means "earlier," "before," or "in advance": *preview.*

pre·am·ble |prē′ ăm′ bəl| *n., pl.* **preambles** An introduction to a formal document explaining its purpose or the reasons behind it.

pre·dict |prĭ dĭkt′| *v.* **predicted, predicting** To tell about in advance: *The weather report predicts showers.*

pre·fer |prĭ fûr′| *v.* **preferred, preferring** To like better: *I prefer books to television.*

pre·fix |prē′ fĭks′| *n., pl.* **prefixes** A word part added to the beginning of a base word or word root. A prefix changes the meaning. The word *discomfort* is made up of the prefix *dis-* and the base word *comfort.*

pre·serve |prĭ zûrv′| *v.* **preserved, preserving 1.** To protect, as from injury or destruction: *We want to preserve our forests.* **2.** To protect food from spoiling, as by freezing, canning, or pickling.

pres·i·dent |prĕz′ ĭ dənt| *n., pl.* **presidents 1.** The chief executive of a republic, such as the United States. **2.** The chief officer of a company, organization, or institution.

pre·sume |prĭ zoōm′| *v.* **presumed, presuming** To suppose to be true; take for granted: *A good detective will not presume anything.*

pre·view |prē′ vyoō′| *n., pl.* **previews** A showing of something, as a movie, to an invited audience before presenting it to the public.

prim·i·tive |prĭm′ ĭ tĭv| *adj.* **1.** Of or in an early stage in the development of human culture: *Some of the primitive cave people were skillful artists.* **2.** Simple or crude: *The primitive table we built out of old wood collapsed.*

pro-¹ A prefix that means: **1.** Favor or support: *propose.* **2.** Acting as; substituting for: *pronoun.*

pro-² A prefix that means "before; in front of": *proceed.*

pro·ce·dure |prə sē′ jər| *n., pl.* **procedures** A way of doing something or getting something done, especially by a series of steps.

prof·it·a·ble |prŏf′ ĭ tə bəl| *adj.* Yielding a profit; money-making: *The computer industry is very profitable.*

pro·gram |prō′ grăm′| *n., pl.* **programs 1.** A list of information, as the order of events and the names of those taking part in a public performance or presentation. **2.** A performance, especially before an audience: *Which television programs do you like?*

proj·ect |prŏj′ ĕkt′| *n., pl.* **projects 1.** A plan for doing something: *The mayor approved the building project.* **2.** A special study carried on by students: *a science project.* *v.* **pro·ject** |prə jĕkt′| **projected, projecting 1.** To stick out. **2.** To cause an image to appear on a surface: *We projected the slides on the wall.*

pro·jec·tor |prə jĕk′ tər| *n., pl.* **projectors**
A machine that projects an image onto a
screen: *The teacher set up the movie projector and the class watched the film.*

ă	pat	ŏ	pot	û	fur
ā	pay	ō	go	*th*	the
â	care	ô	paw, for	th	thin
ä	father	oi	oil	hw	which
ĕ	pet	o͞o	book	zh	usual
ē	be	o͞o	boot	ə	ago, item
ĭ	pit	yo͞o	cute		pencil, atom
ī	ice	ou	out		circus
î	near	ŭ	cut	ər	butter

prom·i·nent |prŏm′ ə nənt| *adj.* **1.** Very
easy to see: *The new courthouse is quite
prominent.* **2.** Widely known: *Our neigh-
bor is a prominent scientist.*

pro·mote |prə mōt′| *v.* **promoted, promot-
ing 1.** To help the progress, development,
or growth of; further: *Regular exercise
promotes physical fitness.* **2.** To raise to a
higher rank, position, or class: *She was
promoted to the sixth grade.*

pro·mo·tion |prə mō′ shən| *n., pl.* **promo-
tions 1.** The act of promoting; encourage-
ment. **2.** Advancement in rank, position,
or class: *a job promotion.*

pro·noun |prō′ noun′| *n., pl.* **pronouns** A
word that can take the place of a noun. In
the sentence *John takes the train when he
travels,*the word *he* is a pronoun that takes
the place of *John.*

proof |pro͞of| *n., pl.* **proofs** Evidence of
truth or accuracy: *We have no proof that
the money was stolen.*

prop·er·ty |prŏp′ ər tē| *n., pl.* **properties**
Something, as money or land, that is
owned; possession.

pro·pose |prə pōz′| *v.* **proposed, propos-
ing** To put forward for consideration; suggest: *I propose a trip to the museum.*

prop·o·si·tion |prŏp′ ə zĭsh′ ən| *n., pl.*
propositions Something proposed; offer.

pros·per |prŏs′ pər| *v.* **prospered, prosper-
ing** To be fortunate or successful; thrive:
She works hard, and her business prospers.

pro·tect |prə tĕkt′| *v.* **protected, protect-
ing** To keep safe from harm, attack, or
injury; guard: *Anti-pollution laws help protect our wildlife.*

pro·tec·tion |prə tĕk′ shən| *n., pl.* **protec-
tions 1.** The condition of being protect-
ed. **2.** The act of protecting. **3.** Someone
or something that protects.

prov·erb |prŏv′ ûrb′| *n., pl.* **proverbs** A
short, common saying that tells a truth.
"A rolling stone gathers no moss" and
"Better late than never" are proverbs.

pro·vide |prə vīd′| *v.* **provided, providing**
To give something needed or useful; supply: *My father is providing me with help on
my homework.*

pro·voke |prə vōk′| *v.* **provoked, provoking**
To make angry; annoy: *The man's rude-
ness provoked me.*

prowl |proul| *v.* **prowled, prowling** To
move about secretly and quietly as if looking for prey: *City cats prowl through alleys.*

pub·lish |pŭb′ lĭsh| *v.* **published, publish-
ing** To print and offer for public sale or
distribution: *The newspaper published my
letter.*

Pu·ri·tan |pyo͝or′ ĭ tn| *n., pl.* **Puritans** In
the sixteenth and seventeenth centuries, a
member of a religious group in England or
the American Colonies that wanted simple forms of worship.

pur·suit |pər so͞ot′| *n., pl.* **pursuits** The act
of chasing in order to catch: *The detective
went in pursuit of the criminals.*

puz·zle |pŭz′ əl| *n., pl.* **puzzles 1.** Some-
thing that is hard to understand; mystery:
*It's a puzzle to me how you can finish your
work so fast.* **2.** A problem, toy, or game
that makes one think and tests one's skill.

Q

quail |kwāl| *n., pl.* **quail** *or* **quails** A small, rather plump bird that has a short tail and brownish feathers.

quar·ter |kwôr′ tər| *n., pl.* **quarters** **1.** Any of four equal parts into which something can be divided: *I cut the apple into quarters.* **2.** A coin used in the United States or Canada that is worth 25 cents. **3.** One of four time periods that make up a game. **4.** A district or section of a city. **5.** One fourth of the time it takes for the moon to revolve around the earth.

ques·tion |kwĕs′ chən| *n., pl.* **questions** Something that is asked: *I don't understand your question.* *v.* **questioned, questioning** To ask questions of: *My parents questioned me about my new job.*

ques·tion·naire |kwĕs′ chə **nâr′**| *n., pl.* **questionnaires** A printed form with a series of questions, often used to sample public opinion on a certain subject.

quick-wit·ted |kwĭk′ wĭt′ ĭd| *adj.* Mentally alert; clever.

qui·et |kwī′ ĭt| *adj.* **quieter, quietest** **1.** Marked by little or no noise; silent or nearly silent: *A library is a quiet place to study.* **2.** Free or nearly free from activity or motion; calm.

R

ra·di·o |rā′ dē ō| *n., pl.* **radios** **1.** A way of using energy waves to carry signals between points without using wires.

2. The sending forth of programs of entertainment, news, and information in this way.

raise |rāz| *v.* **raised, raising** To move or lift to a higher position; boost: *I raised my arm and waved at my friend.* *n., pl.* **raises** An increase in amount, as in wages.

ran·dom |răn′ dəm| *adj.* Lacking a definite plan, pattern, or purpose: *I made a few random marks on the canvas.*
◇ *Idiom* **at random** Without a definite purpose or method; by chance.

rap·id |răp′ ĭd| *adj.* Marked by speed; fast.

rare |râr| *adj.* **rarer, rarest** **1.** Not often found, seen, or happening: *Our cat is a rare breed.* **2.** Unusually good; excellent: *a rare friendship.*

re- A prefix that means: **1.** Again: *refill.* **2.** Back; backward: *recalled.*

re·act |rē ăkt′| *v.* **reacted, reacting** To act in response, as to an experience or the behavior of another: *The audience reacted with pleasure to the play.*

re·ac·tion |rē ăk′ shən| *n., pl.* **reactions** A response to something: *I developed a rash as a reaction to the medicine.*

rear |rîr| *n., pl.* **rears** The area or direction closest to or at the back.

rea·son·a·ble |rē′ zə nə bəl| *adj.* Showing good judgment; sensible or logical: *We came up with a reasonable solution.*

re·bel |rĭ bĕl′| *v.* **rebelled, rebelling** To resist or fight against a government or an authority.

re·build |rē bĭld′| *v.* **rebuilt, rebuilding** To build again; reconstruct: *rebuild a house.*

rec·ord |rĕk′ ərd| *n., pl.* **records** A disk that can be played on a phonograph. **re·cord** *v.* |rĭ kôrd′| **recorded, recording** To set down in writing: *Record the time you spent on each test question.*

re·cy·cle |rē sī′ kəl| *v.* **recycled, recycling** To treat materials that have been thrown away in order to use them again: *The city recycles glass, cans, and paper.*

reel |rēl| *n., pl.* **reels** A spoollike device that is used for winding something flexible, such as fishing line or film: *Put the first reel of film in the projector.*

ref•e•ree |rĕf′ ə rē′| *n., pl.* **referees** An official who enforces the rules in a sports contest: *The referee called a foul on one of the basketball players.*

ref•uge |rĕf′ yōōj| *n., pl.* **refuges** Protection or shelter from danger or trouble.

re•gard |rĭ gärd′| *v.* **regarded, regarding** To hold in affection or esteem; think highly of. *n., pl.* **regards** Consideration: *Have you no regard for Tammy's feelings?*

re•gion |rē′ jən| *n., pl.* **regions** An area without distinct boundaries: *In this region of the country there are few tall trees.*

reg•is•ter |rĕj′ ĭ stər| *v.* **registered, registering** To record or have one's name recorded on an official written list: *You must register to be able to vote.*

reg•u•lar |rĕg′ yə lər| *adj.* **1.** Usual or normal; standard: *Those shirts are $5.00 below the regular price.* **2.** Appearing again and again: *a regular customer.*

reg•u•lar•i•ty |rĕg′ yə lăr′ ĭ tē| *n., pl.* **regularities 1.** Something that is usual or standard. **2.** Something that happens again and again.

reg•u•late |rĕg′ yə lāt′| *v.* **regulated, regulations** To control or direct according to rules: *The government regulates the printing of money.*

reg•u•la•tion |rĕg′ yə lā′ shən| *n., pl.* **regulations 1.** The act of regulating. **2.** A rule of law: *a traffic regulation.*

re•hearse |rĭ hûrs′| *v.* **rehearsed, rehearsing** To practice in preparation for a public performance: *rehearsing our lines.*

re•ject |rĭ jĕkt′| *v.* **rejected, rejecting** To refuse to accept or consider.

rel•a•tive |rĕl′ ə tĭv| *n., pl.* **relatives** A person related to another by family: *None of Katie's relatives live near her.*

re•lax |rĭ lăks′| *v.* **relaxed, relaxing** To make or become less tight or tense: *Try to relax your muscles.*

re•mark•a•ble |rĭ mär′ kə bəl| *adj.* That which is worthy of notice; extraordinary: *The landing on the moon was a remarkable achievement.*

re•mem•ber |rĭ mĕm′ bər| *v.* **remembered, remembering 1.** To bring back to the mind; think of again: *I could not*

ă	pat	ŏ	pot	û	fur
ā	pay	ō	go	*th*	the
â	care	ô	paw, for	th	thin
ä	father	oi	oil	hw	which
ĕ	pet	ōō	book	zh	usual
ē	be	ōō	boot	ə	ago, item
ĭ	pit	yōō	cute		pencil, atom
ī	ice	ou	out		circus
î	near	ŭ	cut	ər	butter

remember how to stop the machine. **2.** To keep carefully in one's memory: *Remember that we have to leave early tonight.*

re•mind |rĭ mīnd′| *v.* **reminded, reminding** To cause someone to remember or think of something.

re•mote con•trol |rĭ mōt′ kən trōl′| *n., pl.* **remote controls** The control of an activity, process, or machine from a distance, especially by a radio or electricity: *You can operate this robot by remote control.*

re•pair |rĭ pâr′| *v.* **repaired, repairing** To put back into proper or useful condition; fix; mend.

re•peat |rĭ pēt′| *v.* **repeated, repeating** To say, do, or go through again.

re•ply |rĭ plī′| *v.* **replied, replying** To say or give an answer: *I replied that I would go. n., pl.* **replies** An answer or response: *I didn't hear your reply to my question.*

re•port |rĭ pôrt′| *n., pl.* **reports 1.** A spoken or written description: *weather report.* **2.** A formal account of the activities of a group. *v.* **reported, reporting 1.** To provide an account for publication. **2.** To present oneself.

rep•re•sent |rĕp′ rĭ zĕnt′| *v.* **represented, representing** To act for: *Two Senators are elected to represent each state in Congress.*

re•proach |rĭ prōch′| *v.* **reproached, reproaching** To criticize severely; blame. *n., pl.* **reproaches** Blame; disapproval.

Re•pub•li•can |rĭ pŭb′ lĭ kən| *n., pl.* **Republicans** A member of the Republican Party: *The Republicans introduced a bill into Congress.*

re•side |rĭ zīd′| *v.* **resided, residing** To make one's home; live: *The Smiths resided in Los Angeles for a year.*

resident | rub

res·i·dent |rĕz′ ĭ dənt| *n., pl.* **residents** A person who lives in a particular place.

re·sist |rĭ zĭst′| *v.* **resisted, resisting** To work against; oppose: *The lock resisted our efforts to open it.*

re·spond |rĭ spŏnd′| *v.* **responded, responding** To make a reply; answer: *I'll respond to your question in a minute.*

re·spon·si·ble |rĭ spŏn′ sə bəl| *adj.* **1.** Having a certain duty or obligation: *We are responsible for cleaning our rooms.* **2.** Being the cause or source of something: *Viruses are responsible for many diseases.*

re·sult |rĭ zŭlt′| *n., pl.* **results** Something that happens because of something else. *v.* **resulted, resulting 1.** To come about as a result of something: *Floods resulted from the hurricane.* **2.** To lead to a certain result: *Hard work results in success.*

re·tire |rĭ tīr′| *v.* **retired, retiring** To give up one's work, business, or career, usually because of advancing age: *He will retire from baseball. n.* **retirement** *Nancy's father took an early retirement.*

re·venge |rĭ vĕnj′| *v.* **revenged, revenging** To injure or harm in return for an earlier injury or harm; to get even.

rev·er·ence |rĕv′ ər əns| *n.* A feeling of awe and deep respect mixed with love; adoration: *Janet looked at the beautiful painting with reverence.*

re·vers·i·ble |rĭ vûr′ sə bəl| *adj.* Capable of being worn or used with either side out, often having a different color, pattern, or fabric on the opposite side.

re·view |rĭ vyoo′| *n., pl.* **reviews** The act or process of studying again.

rev·o·lu·tion |rĕv′ ə loo′ shən| *n., pl.* **revolutions** A complete change in government or rule: *In the American Revolution British rule was overthrown.*

rhyme |rīm| *v.* **rhymed, rhyming** To correspond in sound: *"Hour" rhymes with "sour."*

rhythm |rĭth′ əm| *n., pl.* **rhythms** A sound pattern with a series of regularly accented beats: *We clapped our hands to the rhythm of the song.*

right of way |rīt′ əv wā′| *n., pl.* **rights of way** *or* **right of ways** The right of one person, vessel, or vehicle to pass in front of another: *Police and emergency vehicles always have the right of way.*

ri·ot |rī′ ət| *n., pl.* **riots** Disturbance created by a large number of people.

rise |rīz| *v.* **rose, risen, rising 1.** To go up; ascend: *The kite is rising in the air.* **2.** To improve in rank or condition: *Education will help you rise in the world.*

ri·val·ry |rī′ vəl rē| *n., pl.* **rivalries** The effort of striving to equal or outdo another; competition.

ro·bot |rō′ bət| *or* |rō′ bŏt′| *n., pl.* **robots** A machine that can perform human tasks or imitate human actions. A robot has a computer that processes information, such as commands.

History · robot

Robot comes from the Czech word *robota,* meaning "forced labor; hard, boring work."

ro·de·o |rō′ dē ō′| *or* |rō dā′ ō| *n., pl.* **rodeos** A show in which cowhands display their skill in riding horses and steers and compete in events such as roping cattle.

role |rōl| *n., pl.* **roles** A part played by an actor: *I tried out for the role of the hero in the class play.*

ro·man·tic |rō măn′ tĭk| *adj.* Of, relating to, or marked by love or romance: *I read a romantic novel.*

rook·ie |rook′ ē| *n., pl.* **rookies** A person who lacks training: *The rookies on the police force were carefully supervised.*

rough |rŭf| *adj.* **rougher, roughest 1.** Bumpy or uneven; not smooth: *Hickory trees have rough bark.* **2.** Not calm.

route |root| *or* |rout| *n., pl.* **routes** A road, path, or lane of travel between two places.

roy·al |roi′ əl| *adj.* Of or having to do with a queen or king: *The royal family led the procession.*

rub |rŭb| *v.* **rubbed, rubbing** To press something against a surface and move it back and forth: *We rubbed the table with a clean cloth.*

ru·by |roo′ bē| *n., pl.* **rubies** A deep-red precious stone found in riverbeds.

rude |rood| *adj.* **ruder, rudest** Not considerate of others; impolite.

rug·ged |rŭg′ ĭd| *adj.* Having a rough surface or jagged outline: *rugged mountains.*

ru·in |roo′ ĭn| *v.* **ruined, ruining** To damage beyond repair; wreck.

rule |rool| *n., pl.* **rules** A statement or principle that controls behavior or action: *a rule against running in the school halls.* *v.* **ruled, ruling** To have power or authority over; to govern: *The king and queen ruled the land for many years.*

rus·tic |rŭs′ tĭk| *adj.* Of or typical of the country; rural: *Smithtown is a rustic community in the mountains.*

S

sac·ri·fice |săk′ rə fīs′| *n., pl.* **sacrifices** An offering: *a sacrifice of grain and meat.* *v.* **sacrificed, sacrificing** To give up something valuable for the sake of someone or something else.

safe |sāf| *adj.* **safer, safest** Free from danger, risk, or threat of harm. *adv.* **safely** *We got home safely before the storm began.*

sales·per·son |sālz′ pûr′ sən| *n., pl.* **salespersons** A person who sells goods or services.

sa·lute |sə loot′| *v.* **saluted, saluting** 1. To show respect by raising the right hand stiffly to the forehead or by firing guns. 2. To greet with a polite gesture. *n., pl.* **salutes** An act of saluting.

sam·ple |săm′ pəl| *n., pl.* **samples** A part of a larger group, used for estimating what the larger group is like: *A sample of 500 people were questioned for a survey.*

sand·wich |sănd′ wĭch| *n., pl.* **sandwiches** Two or more slices of bread with a filling between them.

sap·phire |săf′ īr′| *n., pl.* **sapphires** A hard, deep-blue precious stone that is valued as a gem.

scal·lop |skŏl′ əp| or |skăl′ əp| *v.* **scalloped, scalloping** To bake in a casserole with a sauce and often with bread crumbs.

ă	pat	ŏ	pot	û	fur
ā	pay	ō	go	*th*	the
â	care	ô	paw, for	th	thin
ä	father	oi	oil	hw	which
ĕ	pet	oo	book	zh	usual
ē	be	oo	boot	ə	ago, item
ĭ	pit	yoo	cute		pencil, atom
ī	ice	ou	out		circus
î	near	ŭ	cut	ər	butter

scar |skär| *n., pl.* **scars** A mark left on the skin by a healed wound. *v.* **scarred, scarring** To mark with or form a scar: *The deep wound scarred Nina's knee.*

scare |skâr| *v.* **scared, scaring** To frighten or become frightened.

scar·y |skâr′ ē| *adj.* **scarier, scariest** Easily frightened; timid.

scene |sēn| *n., pl.* **scenes** 1. The place where an action or event takes place: *The tow truck finally arrived at the scene of the wreck.* 2. A short section of a play or movie.
♦ *These sound alike* **scene, seen.**

sce·nic |sē′ nĭk| *adj.* Of attractive natural scenery: *We drove along a scenic route in the mountains.*

sched·ule |skĕj′ ool| or |skĕj′ əl| *n., pl.* **schedules** A list of the times for departures and arrivals: *According to the schedule, the plane will take off at four o'clock.*

schol·ar |skŏl′ ər| *n., pl.* **scholars** A person who has a great deal of knowledge.

sci·ence |sī′ əns| *n., pl.* **sciences** 1. The study and explanation of things that happen in nature and the universe. 2. An area of knowledge in which observation, experiments, and study are used.

scoop |skoop| *n., pl.* **scoops** 1. A utensil that is like a small shovel, used to take up or dish out foods. 2. The amount a scoop holds: *Add another scoop of flour to the dough.* *v.* **scooped, scooping** To lift out with or as if with a scoop; to dish out.

scowl |skoul| *v.* **scowled, scowling** To lower the eyebrows in anger or disapproval; frown.

screen·play |skrēn′ plā′| *n., pl.* **screenplays** The script for a motion picture.

script |skrĭpt| *n., pl.* **scripts** The written text of a play or movie or of a radio or television show, often divided into acts and scenes.

seal |sēl| *n., pl.* **seals** A design used as an official mark of authority. *v.* **sealed, sealing** To close or fasten tightly.

seat belt |sēt′ bĕlt′| *n., pl.* **seat belts** A safety strap or harness that is designed to hold a person securely in a seat, as in a car or airplane.

seek |sēk| *v.* **sought, seeking** To try to find or get: *We are seeking a new place to live.*

seen |sēn| Past participle of **see**: *I have seen that movie.*
 ♦ *These sound alike* **seen, scene.**

self-as·sured |sĕlf′ ə shŏŏrd′| *adj.* Having or showing confidence in oneself.

Sen·ate |sĕn′ ĭt| *n., pl.* **senates** The upper house of the United States Congress. Its members are elected every six years.

sen·si·tive |sĕn′ sĭ tĭv| *adj* **1.** Sore: *My bruise is still sensitive.* **2.** Easily affected, influenced, or hurt: *Don't be so sensitive to criticism.*

sen·sor |sĕn′ sər| or |sĕn′ sôr′| *n., pl.* **sensors** A device, such as a thermostat, that reacts in a predictable way to a particular type of change, such as a change in light or temperature.

se·ries |sîr′ ēz| *n., pl.* **series** A television or radio show that is presented at regular intervals: *a comedy series.*

se·ri·ous |sîr′ ē əs| *adj.* **1.** Grave; not humorous: *Mike wondered what was wrong when he saw the serious look on his father's face.* **2.** Important: *Getting married is a serious step. n.* **seriousness** *Alex did not understand the seriousness of the problem.*

serv·ant |sûr′ vənt| *n., pl.* **servants** **1.** A person who works for wages in someone else's household. **2.** A person who is hired to perform services for another: *Police officers are public servants.*

serv·ice |sûr′ vĭs| *n., pl.* **services** **1.** The act or work of helping others; aid: *They spend their lives in service to the poor.* **2.** The act or manner of satisfying customers' requests: *The service at that restaurant is very slow.*

ses·sion |sĕsh′ ən| *n., pl.* **sessions** A meeting or series of meetings of a court or legislature.

set |sĕt| *n., pl.* **sets** The scenery, furniture, and other objects on the stage of a play or movie.

set·tle·ment |sĕt′ l mənt| *n., pl.* **settlements** A small community; village: *a fishing settlement.*

shad·ow |shăd′ ō| *n., pl.* **shadows** **1.** A shaded area made when light is blocked. **2.** Partial darkness.

sharp |shärp| *adj.* **sharper, sharpest** Not rounded or blunt; pointed.

shel·ter |shĕl′ tər| *v.* **sheltered, sheltering** To provide protection or cover for: *We sheltered the injured animal until it got well.*

Shen·an·do·ah Na·tion·al Park |shĕn′ ən dō′ ə| A scenic area of north Virginia on the crest of the Blue Ridge Mountains.

ship |shĭp| *n., pl.* **ships** A large vessel that can travel in deep water. A ship can be powered by a motor or sails. *v.* **shipped, shipping** **1.** To transport or send: *We ship our fresh vegetables to market by truck.* **2.** To put on board a ship.

ship·yard |shĭp′ yärd′| *n., pl.* **shipyards** A place where ships are built, repaired, and equipped.

shoot |shōōt| *v.* **shot, shooting** To hit, wound, or kill with a bullet, an arrow, or another projectile fired from a weapon.

short·age |shôr′ tĭj| *n., pl.* **shortages** An amount of something that is not enough; lack; scarcity.

short·stop |shôrt′ stŏp′| *n., pl.* **shortstops** The position between second and third bases in baseball.

shoul·der |shōl′ dər| *n., pl.* **shoulders** The part of the human body between the neck and the upper arm.

shov·el |shŭv′ əl| *n., pl.* **shovels** A tool with a long handle and a flattened scoop: *I dug out the ditch with a shovel. v.* **shoveled, shoveling** To pick up or move with a shovel: *Shovel the snow.*

shown |shōn| *v.* A past participle of **show**: *The librarian has shown us where to find books about birds.*

shred |shrĕd| *v.* **shredded** *or* **shred, shred-ding** To cut or tear into small strips.

sigh |sī| *v.* **sighed, sighing** To let out a long, deep breath because of fatigue, sorrow, or relief.

sight·see·ing |sīt′ sē′ ĭng| *n.* The act or pastime of touring places of interest. *n.* **sightseer** *Anne lead a tour through the museum for the sightseers.*

sign |sīn| *n., pl.* **signs** Something, such as a poster, that conveys information. *v.* **signed, signing** To write one's name on, as a form.

sig·nal |sĭg′ nəl| *n., pl.* **signals** A sign, gesture, or device that gives a command, a warning, or other information.

si·lent |sī′ lənt| *adj.* Making or having no sound; quiet.

sim·i·lar |sĭm′ ə lər| *adj.* Alike but not exactly the same.

sim·ple |sĭm′ pəl| *adj.* **simpler, simplest** Not complicated; easy: *The directions are simple.*

sim·plic·i·ty |sĭm plĭs′ ĭ tē| *n.* The condition or quality of being uncomplicated or easy.

sim·pli·fy |sĭm′ plə fī′| *v.* **simplified, simplifying** To make or become less complicated or easier.

sim·ply |sĭm′ plē| *adv.* **1.** In an uncomplicated or easy way; plainly. **2.** Merely; just: *I was simply standing there.*

sin·cere |sĭn sîr′| *adj.* **sincerer, sincerest** Not lying or pretending; honest; genuine: *a sincere apology.*

sin·gle |sĭng′ gəl| *adj.* **1.** Not with another or others; one: *There is a single biscuit*

ă	pat	ŏ	pot	û	fur
ā	pay	ō	go	*th*	the
â	care	ô	paw, for	th	thin
ä	father	oi	oil	hw	which
ĕ	pet	ōō	book	zh	usual
ē	be	ōō	boot	ə	ago, item
ĭ	pit	yōō	cute		pencil, atom
ī	ice	ou	out		circus
î	near	ŭ	cut	ər	butter

left on the plate. **2.** Not married. **3.** A hit in baseball that allows the batter to reach first base.

site |sīt| *n., pl.* **sites** A position or location.

skill |skĭl| *n., pl.* **skills** The ability to do something well.

skim |skĭm| *v.* **skimmed, skimming 1.** To remove (floating matter) from a liquid: *Skim cream off the top of the milk.* **2.** To read quickly, skipping over parts.

slam |slăm| *v.* **slammed, slamming** To shut forcefully and noisily.

slept |slĕpt| *v.* Past tense and past participle of **sleep**: *The baby slept late today.*

slide |slīd| *n., pl.* **slides** A small glass plate on which objects are placed for examination by microscope: *Look at the slide with the flower pollen on it.*

slight |slīt| *adj.* **slighter, slightest 1.** Small in amount or degree. **2.** Small in size; slender.

slip·per·y |slĭp′ ə rē| *adj.* **slipperier, slipperiest** Tending to slip; tending to cause one to lose one's balance or grasp; slick.

slope |slōp| *v.* **sloped, sloping** To slant upward or downward.

smear |smîr| *v.* **smeared, smearing** To cover or spread with a sticky or greasy substance. *n., pl.* **smears 1.** A stain or blotch. **2.** A substance or preparation placed on a slide for microscopic study.

smog |smôg| *n.* Fog mixed with smoke.

snap |snăp| *v.* **snapped, snapping 1.** To make or cause to make a sharp cracking sound. **2.** To break or cause to break suddenly with a sharp sound.

snare |snâr| *n., pl.* **snares** A device, such as a noose, that is used for trapping birds and small animals; a trap.

snow·ball |snō′ bôl′| *n.*, *pl.* **snowballs** A ball of pressed snow.

soar |sôr| *v.* **soared, soaring** To rise, fly, or glide high in the air.
♦ *These sound alike* **soar, sore.**

soft |sôft| *adj.* **softer, softest** **1.** Not hard or firm: *She squeezed the soft melon.* **2.** Smooth, fine, or pleasing to the touch: *She petted a soft, gray kitten.* *n.* **softness** *Lamb's wool is known for its softness.*

sole¹ |sōl| *n.*, *pl.* **soles** The bottom of a shoe, boot, or slipper.
♦ *These sound alike* **sole, soul.**

sole² |sōl| *adj.* Being the only one; single.
♦ *These sound alike* **sole, soul.**

sol·id |sŏl′ ĭd| *adj.* **1.** Not hollow: *The chef carved a swan out of a solid block of ice.* **2.** Strong and firm: *The house has a solid foundation.*

sol·i·tar·y |sŏl′ ĭ tĕr′ ē| *adj.* Being or living alone: *I saw a solitary runner at the side of the road.*

solve |sŏlv| *v.* **solved, solving** To find an answer or solution to: *She finally solved the mystery.*

som·ber |sŏm′ bər| *adj.* **1.** Dark and dull; gloomy: *The somber sky was the first sign of the approaching storm.* **2.** Serious: *The bad news put us in a somber mood.*

som·er·sault |sŭm′ ər sôlt′| *n.*, *pl.* **somersaults** The act of rolling the body in a complete circle, heels over head.

sore |sôr| *adj.* **sorer, sorest** Suffering pain, hurting: *I am sore from running.*
♦ *These sound alike* **sore, soar.**
◇ *Idiom* **stick out like a sore thumb** To be obvious or visible: *That purple car sticks out like a sore thumb.*

sor·row |sŏr′ ō| *n.*, *pl.* **sorrows** Grief or sadness caused by loss or injury.

soul |sōl| *n.*, *pl.* **souls** The part of a person considered to include the capabilities to think, feel, and act.
♦ *These sound alike* **soul, sole.**

sound·track |sound′ trăk′| *n.*, *pl.* **soundtracks** A narrow strip at the edge of a motion-picture film that carries a recording of the sound.

south |south| *n.* The direction to the left side of a person who faces the sunset.

space |spās| *n.*, *pl.* **spaces** The distance or open area between or within objects or between points.

spar·kle |spär′ kəl| *v.* **sparkled, sparkling** To give off sparks of light; glitter: *Diamonds sparkle.* *n.*, *pl.* **sparkles** A spark of light.

spe·cial |spĕsh′ əl| *adj.* Different from what is common or usual: *Birthdays are special occasions.* *n.*, *pl.* **specials** Something arranged for a particular occasion: *lunch special.*

spec·ta·cle |spĕk′ tə kəl| *n.*, *pl.* **spectacles** An unusual or impressive public show, as of fireworks.

spec·trum |spĕk′ trəm| *n.*, *pl.* **spectrums** The bands of color that are seen when light, especially light from the sun, is broken up, as by a prism. You can see the colors of the spectrum in a rainbow.

spec·ta·tor |spĕk′ tā′ tər| *n.*, *pl.* **spectators** A person who watches an event but does not take part in it; viewer.

speech |spēch| *n.*, *pl.* **speeches** A public talk or address: *The President's speech was broadcast at nine o'clock P.M.*

speech·less |spēch′ lĭs| *adj.* Not able to speak for a short time because of shock, fear, or joy.

speed·om·e·ter |spĭ dŏm′ ĭ tər| *n.*, *pl.* **speedometers** A device that measures and indicates speed, as of an automobile or bicycle.

spic·y |spī′ sē| *adj.* **spicier, spiciest** Seasoned with or containing spice, a plant substance such as nutmeg or pepper that has a pleasant or strong smell.

spin·ach |spĭn′ ĭch| *n.* A plant grown for its dark green leaves. Spinach is eaten as a vegetable.

split |splĭt| *v.* **split, splitting** **1.** To divide or become divided into parts, especially lengthwise: *We split logs for the campfire.* **2.** To break, burst, or rip apart with force: *Pressure caused the container to split.*

spon·sor |spŏn′ sər| *n.*, *pl.* **sponsors** A person or organization that pays the costs of a radio or television program in order to advertise a product or service.

spot |spŏt| *v.* **spotted, spotting 1.** To mark or cause to be marked with spots. **2.** To find or locate: *It was hard to spot you in the crowd.*

spy |spī| *v.* **spied, spying** To watch secretly and for unfriendly reasons: *Soldiers were spying on the enemy camp.*

squad |skwŏd| *n., pl.* **squads** An organized team or group, as of police officers.

square |skwâr| *n., pl.* **squares** A rectangle having four equal sides.

squeeze |skwēz| *v.* **squeezed, squeezing** To press together with force: *The baby squeezed the rubber toy.*

squirm |skwûrm| *v.* **squirmed, squirming** To twist about; wiggle.

squirt |skwûrt| *v.* **squirted, squirting** To send out or be sent out in a thin, fast stream.

sta·di·um |stā′ dē əm| *n., pl.* **stadiums** A large structure in which athletic events are held; arena.

ă	pat	ŏ	pot	û	fur
ā	pay	ō	go	*th*	the
â	care	ô	paw, for	th	thin
ä	father	oi	oil	hw	which
ĕ	pet	ōō	book	zh	usual
ē	be	ōō	boot	ə	ago, item
ĭ	pit	yōō	cute		pencil, atom
ī	ice	ou	out		circus
î	near	ŭ	cut	ər	butter

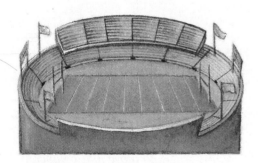

staff |stăf| *n., pl.* **staffs** *or* **staves 1.** A long stick carried to help in walking. **2.** An organized group of employees: *the staff of camp counselors.*

stain |stān| *n., pl.* **stains** A discolored mark or spot.

stair |stâr| *n., pl.* **stairs 1. stairs** A series or flight of steps; staircase. **2.** One of a flight of steps.

stalk¹ |stôk| *n., pl.* **stalks 1.** The stem of a plant. **2.** A part that is attached to or supports a leaf or flower.

stalk² |stôk| *v.* **stalked, stalking** To move in a sly way as if tracking prey: *The tiger stalked through the jungle.*

stan·za |stăn′ zə| *n., pl.* **stanzas** A group of lines that makes up a division of a poem.

star·ry-eyed |stär′ ē īd′| *adj.* Full of youthful hope and enthusiasm.

sta·tion·ar·y |stā′ shə něr′ ē| *adj.* **1.** Not changing: *The price remained stationary.* **2.** Not capable of being moved; fixed in place: *The towers of a suspension bridge are stationary.*
   ♦ *These sound alike* **stationary, stationery.**

sta·tion·er·y |stā′ shə něr′ ē| *n.* Materials, such as paper, notebooks, pens, and envelopes, that are used in writing.
   ♦ *These sound alike* **stationery, stationary.**

stat·ute |stăch′ ōōt| *n., pl.* **statutes** A law.

steal |stēl| *v.* **stole, stolen, stealing 1.** To take without right or permission. **2.** In baseball, to gain (another base) without the ball being batted, by running to the base during the delivery of the pitch.

steer |stîr| *v.* **steered, steering** To direct the course of or guide: *The pilot steered the ship to the dock.*

stern |stûrn| *n., pl.* **sterns** The rear part of a ship or boat.

stim·u·late |stĭm′ yə lāt′| *v.* **stimulated, stimulating** To make active or more active; excite; arouse: *The book stimulates my imagination.*

stir |stûr| *v.* **stirred, stirring** To mix by using repeated circular motions: *I stirred the vegetables into the soup.*

stole |stōl| *v.* Past tense of **steal**: *When the pitcher threw the ball, Luis stole second base.*

strat·e·gy |străt′ ə jē| *n., pl.* **strategies** A clever system or plan of action: *Our strategy is to give a surprise party for them.*

stray |strā| *n., pl.* **strays** A person or animal that has wandered away from home. *adj.* Wandering or having wandered away from home; lost.

stride |strīd| *v.* **strode, stridden, striding** To walk with long steps. *n., pl.* **strides** A long step.

strike |strīk| *v.* **struck, striking** To hit with or as if with the hand: *I struck the ball with the bat.*

strip |strĭp| *v.* **stripped, stripping** To remove the covering from: *I stripped the peel from the banana.*

stroke |strōk| *n., pl.* **strokes** The time indicated by the striking of a bell or a gong: *She had to be home at the stroke of eight o'clock.*

stroll |strōl| *v.* **strolled, strolling** To walk or wander around in a slow, relaxed way. *n., pl.* **strolls** A slow, relaxed walk.

stub·born |stŭb′ ərn| *adj.* Not willing to change a purpose or opinion in spite of urging or requests from others: *The stubborn child refused to wear boots.*

stuck |stŭk| *v.* Past tense and past participle of **stick**: *The car got stuck in the mud.*

stu·dent |stōōd′ nt| or |styōōd′ nt| *n., pl.* **students** A person who studies, as in a school; pupil.

stud·y |stŭd′ ē| *n., pl.* **studies** The act or process of learning; an effort to learn: *Much study went into the new program. v.* **studied, studying** To examine closely and carefully: *Study the questions before you try to answer them.*

stun |stŭn| *v.* **stunned, stunning 1.** To daze or make senseless by or as if by a blow. **2.** To shock or confuse.

stunt |stŭnt| *n., pl.* **stunts** An act showing unusual skill or daring: *The action-packed movie was full of dangerous stunts performed by specially trained actors.*

sub·due |səb dōō′| or |səb dyōō′| *v.* **subdued, subduing** To quiet or bring under control: *I managed to subdue my fear and speak up.*

sub·ject |sŭb′ jĭkt| *n., pl.* **subjects 1.** Something thought about or discussed; topic. **2.** The word or group of words in a sentence that tells what the sentence is about.

|səb jĕkt′| *v.* **subjected, subjecting** To cause to undergo: *My doctor subjected me to some tests.*

sub·mit |səb mĭt′| *v.* **submitted, submitting** To yield to someone else's commands; give in.

suc·ceed |sək sēd′| *v.* **succeeded, succeeding** To carry out something desired or attempted: *We succeeded in our repairs.*

suf·fer |sŭf′ ər| *v.* **suffered, suffering** To feel pain, hurt, or distress: *suffering from illness.*

suit·a·ble |sōō′ tə bəl| *adj.* Right for a purpose or occasion; appropriate; proper.

sum·mit |sŭm′ ĭt| *n., pl.* **summits** The highest point or part; peak; not the base: *the summit of the mountain.*

su·per·hu·man |sōō′ pər hyōō′ mən| *adj.* Being or seeming to be beyond ordinary or normal human ability: *It would take superhuman strength to move that boulder.*

su·per·la·tive |sōō pûr′ lə tĭv| *adj.* Being the very best: *The singer gave a superlative performance.*

su·per·mar·ket |sōō′ pər mär′ kĭt| *n., pl.* **supermarkets** A large store that sells food and household goods.

sup·port |sə pôrt′| *v.* **supported, supporting 1.** To keep from falling; hold in position: *Two steel towers supported the bridge.* **2.** To act in a lesser role to a leading actor: *John supported Lara, who had the starring role.*

sur·geon |sûr′ jən| *n., pl.* **surgeons** A doctor who specializes in treating injury and disease by cutting into and removing or repairing parts of the body.

sur•vey |sûr′ vā| *n., pl.* **surveys** A big investigation, as a sampling of opinions: *A survey of the voters showed that people want honest government.*

sur•vi•vor |sər vī′ vər| *n., pl.* **survivors** Someone or something that has stayed alive: *There were many survivors of the plane crash.*

sus•pect |sŭs′ pĕkt′| *n., pl.* **suspects** A person who is thought to be guilty of something without proof.

sus•pense |sə spĕns′| *n.* **1.** The condition or quality of being undecided. **2.** Anxious uncertainty about what will happen. *adj.* **suspenseful** *This mystery novel is very suspenseful and quite entertaining.*

sus•pi•cious |sə spĭsh′ əs| *adj.* Distrustful; doubtful. *adv.* **suspiciously** *The police officer looked at me suspiciously.*

sway |swā| *v.* **swayed, swaying** To swing or cause to swing back and forth or from side to side: *The willow trees were swaying in the wind.*

sweep |swēp| *v.* **swept, sweeping 1.** To clean with a broom or brush. **2.** To move or flow with steady force: *A strong wind sweeps across the lake all winter.*

sweet |swēt| *adj.* Having a pleasing taste like that of sugar.

sweet•heart |swēt′ härt′| *n., pl.* **sweethearts 1.** A person whom one loves. **2.** A lovable person.

swept |swĕpt| *v.* Past tense and past participle of **sweep**: *He swept the floor with a broom.*

swift |swĭft| *adj.* **swifter, swiftest** Moving or able to move very fast; quick; speedy.

swim |swĭm| *v.* **swam, swum, swimming** To move through water by moving the arms, legs, or fins.

T

tai•lor |tā′ lər| *n., pl.* **tailors** A person who makes, repairs, or alters clothing.

tax•a•tion |tăk sā′ shən| *n.* The act of imposing taxes, or requiring that people or businesses pay money in order to support a government.

ă	pat	ŏ	pot	û	fur
ā	pay	ō	go	*th*	the
â	care	ô	paw, for	th	thin
ä	father	oi	oil	hw	which
ĕ	pet	o͞o	book	zh	usual
ē	be	o͞o	boot	ə	ago, item
ĭ	pit	yo͞o	cute		pencil, atom
ī	ice	ou	out		circus
î	near	ŭ	cut	ər	butter

tel•e•cast |tĕl′ ĭ kăst′| *v.* **telecasted, telecasting** To broadcast by television. *n., pl.* **telecasts** A television broadcast.

tel•e•gram |tĕl′ ĭ grăm′| *n., pl.* **telegrams** A message sent by wire or radio to a receiving station.

tel•e•phone |tĕl′ ə fōn′| *n., pl.* **telephones** An instrument that reproduces and receives sound, especially speech.

tel•e•scope |tĕl′ ĭ skōp′| *n., pl.* **telescopes** A device that uses an arrangement of lenses or mirrors in a long tube to make distant objects appear closer.

tel•e•vise |tĕl′ ə vīz′| *v.* **televised, televising** To broadcast by television.

tel•e•vi•sion |tĕl′ ə vĭzh′ ən| *n., pl.* **televisions 1.** A system for sending and receiving visual images of objects and actions with the sounds that go with them. **2.** A device that receives and reproduces the images and sounds sent by a television broadcast system.

tense |tĕns| *adj.* **tenser, tensest** Anxious or nervous.

ten•sion |tĕn′ shən| *n., pl.* **tensions 1.** The act of stretching or the condition of being stretched. **2.** Stress that affects nerves, emotions, or relationships with other people; strain: *Meeting the deadline caused tension in the office.*

term |tûrm| *n., pl.* **terms 1.** A word that has a certain meaning, usually in a special vocabulary: *"Shutout" is a sports term.* **2.** A period of time, especially one with definite limits: *a term of office.*

ter•ri•ble |tĕr′ ə bəl| *adj.* **1.** Causing great fear; dreadful. **2.** Very great or extreme; severe: *a terrible storm.* **3.** Very bad: *That was a terrible movie.*

test tube |tĕst′ to͞ob′| or |tĕst′ tyo͞ob′| *n.,* *pl.* **test tubes** A tube of glass that is usually open at one end and rounded at the other, used in the laboratory for experiments.

tex•ture |tĕks′ chər| *n., pl.* **textures** The look or feel of a surface: *Velvet has a soft, smooth texture.*

Thanks•giv•ing Day |thăngks gĭv′ ĭng| *n.* A holiday for giving thanks. Thanksgiving Day is the fourth Thursday of November in the United States. It is the second Monday of October in Canada.

the•a•ter |thē′ ə tər| *n., pl.* **theaters** **1.** A building where plays or movies are presented. **2.** The work of writing, producing, or acting in plays.

thief |thēf| *n., pl.* **thieves** A person who steals; a robber.

thigh |thī| *n., pl.* **thighs** The part of the human leg that extends from the hip to the knee.

thirst |thûrst| *n., pl.* **thirsts** **1.** A dry feeling in the mouth related to the need to drink. **2.** A desire to drink liquids.

thou•sand |thou′ zənd| *n., pl.* **thousands** The number, written 1000, that is equal to the product of 10 X 100.

through•out |thro͞o out′| *prep.* In, to, through, or during every part of: *Elections were held throughout the country. adv.* In or through every part: *I found this book interesting throughout.*

throw |thrō| *v.* **threw, thrown, throwing** To send through the air with a fast motion of the arm; fling: *We threw the ball back and forth.*

thrown |thrōn| *v.* Past participle of **throw**: *Jeff has thrown the ball over the fence.*

thun•der |thŭn′ dər| *n.* The deep, rumbling noise that goes with or comes after a flash of lightning.

ti•ny |tī′ nē| *adj.* **tinier, tiniest** Extremely small.

ti•tle |tīt′ l| *n., pl.* **titles** An identifying name given to a book, painting, song, or other work.

to•geth•er |tə gĕth′ ər| *adv.* In or into a single group or place; with each other: *Many people were crowded together. We went to school together.*

to•mor•row |tə môr′ ō| *n.* **1.** The day after today. **2.** The near future. *adv.* On or for the day after today: *I will return your book tomorrow.*

to•paz |tō′ păz′| *n., pl.* **topazes** A mineral, usually yellow, that is used as a gem.

torch |tôrch| *n., pl.* **torches** A device that shoots out a hot flame, as for welding or cutting metals.

tore |tôr| *v.* Past tense of **tear**: *He tore his shirt on a nail.*
   ◇ *Idiom* **tore his [her] hair out** suffered greatly; became very anxious.

to•tal |tōt′ l| *n., pl.* **totals** **1.** A number gotten by adding; sum. **2.** An entire amount. *adj.* Absolute; complete: *Our play was a total success.*

touch•down |tŭch′ doun′| *n., pl.* **touchdowns** A score of six points in football, usually made by running with the ball, or catching a teammate's pass, across the opposing team's goal line.

tough |tŭf| *adj.* **tougher, toughest** Strong and not likely to break or tear with use or wear.

tow•er |tou′ ər| *n., pl.* **towers** A very tall building or a tall structure that is part of a larger building.

tox•ic |tŏk′ sĭk| *adj.* Of, relating to, or caused by a poison: *The child was allergic to bee stings and had a toxic reaction.*

trace |trās| *v.* **traced, tracing** **1.** To follow the track, course, or trail of: *The post office tried to trace the lost letter.* **2.** To copy, as a drawing, by following lines seen through a sheet of transparent paper.

track |trăk| *n., pl.* **tracks** **1.** A path, course, or trail made for racing, running, or hiking. **2.** A rail or set of rails for vehicles such as trains to run on.

trac•tor |trăk′ tər| *n., pl.* **tractors** A vehicle that is driven by an engine and is equipped with large tires that have deep treads. A tractor is used especially for pulling farm machinery, such as a plow or thresher.

traf•fic |trăf′ ĭk| *n.* The movement of vehicles and people along roads and streets, of ships on the seas, or of aircraft in the sky.

trans·mit |trăns mĭt′| *v.* **transmitted, transmitting 1.** To send from one person, place, or thing to another. **2.** To send out an electric or electronic signal by wire or radio.

trans·port |trăns pôrt′| *v.* **transported, transporting** To carry from one place to another.

trans·pose |trăns pōz′| *v.* **transposed, transposing** To put in a new order.

treas·ure |trĕzh′ ər| *n., pl.* **treasures 1.** Wealth, such as jewels or money, that has been collected or hidden. **2.** A very precious or valuable person or thing.

trea·ty |trē′ tē| *n., pl.* **treaties** An official agreement between two or more countries, national governments, or rulers: *The war ended and a peace treaty was signed.*

trek |trĕk| *n., pl.* **treks** A long and difficult journey.

trem·or |trĕm′ ər| *n., pl.* **tremors** A shaking or vibrating movement, especially of the earth.

tres·pass |trĕs′ pəs| *v.* **trespassed, trespassing** To go onto someone's property without permission; intrude.

tri·al |trī′ əl| *n., pl.* **trials** The studying and deciding of a case in a court of law.

trip·le |trĭp′ əl| *n., pl.* **triples** In baseball, a hit that allows a batter to reach third base safely.

troop |tro͞op| *n., pl.* **troops 1.** A group of persons, animals, or things: *police troop.* **2.** A group of soldiers mounted on horses or riding in motor vehicles.

tro·phy |trō′ fē| *n., pl.* **trophies** A prize given or received as a symbol of victory or achievement: *The basketball team won the play-off game and received a trophy.*

ă	pat	ŏ	pot	û	fur
ā	pay	ō	go	*th*	the
â	care	ô	paw, for	th	thin
ä	father	oi	oil	hw	which
ĕ	pet	o͞o	book	zh	usual
ē	be	o͞o	boot	ə	ago, item
ĭ	pit	yo͞o	cute		pencil, atom
ī	ice	ou	out		circus
î	near	ŭ	cut	ər	butter

true |tro͞o| *adj.* **truer, truest** Being in agreement with fact or reality; accurate: *Is it true that you are moving this summer?*

trunk |trŭngk| *n., pl.* **trunks 1.** A sturdy box in which clothes or belongings can be packed for travel or storage. **2.** The covered compartment of an automobile, used for storage.

tu·lip |to͞o′ lĭp| or |tyo͞o′ lĭp| *n., pl.* **tulips** A garden plant that grows from a bulb and has colored cup-shaped flowers. Tulips are planted in the fall and bloom in the spring and early summer.

tun·nel |tŭn′ əl| *n., pl.* **tunnels** An underground or underwater passage.

turn·pike |tûrn′ pīk′| *n., pl.* **turnpikes** A wide highway that drivers pay a toll to use.

twice |twīs| *adv.* Two times: *He saw the movie twice.*

typ·i·cal |tĭp′ ĭ kəl| *adj.* Showing the special traits or characteristics of a group, kind, or class; usual; ordinary: *A typical summer day in Arizona is hot and dry.*

U

um·pire |ŭm′ pīr′| *n., pl.* **umpires** A person who rules on plays in sports, such as baseball: *The umpire called a strike, and the batter was out.*

un- A prefix that means: **1.** Not: *unable, unhappy.* **2.** Lack of: *unemployment.*

un·a·ble |ŭn ā′ bəl| *adj.* Not able; lacking the power to do something: *I was unable to catch the school bus.*

un·a·ware |ŭn′ ə wâr′| *adj.* Not aware or conscious: *My brother and sister were unaware of my presence.*

un·e·ven |ŭn ē′ vən| *adj.* **unevener, unevenest 1.** Not level, smooth, or straight: *The surface of the bumpy road is uneven.* **2.** Not balanced; unequal.

un·for·tu·nate |ŭn fôr′ chə nĭt| *adj.* Not fortunate; not lucky.

uni- A prefix that means "one, single": *unicycle.*

u·ni·corn |yoo′ nĭ kôrn′| *n., pl.* **unicorns** An imaginary animal similar to a horse but with a single long horn in the middle of the forehead.

u·ni·form |yoo′ nə fôrm′| *n., pl.* **uniforms** Clothing that identifies those who wear it as members of a certain group, such as a police force.

u·ni·fy |yoo′ nə fī′| *v.* **unified, unifying** To make or form into a whole; unite; join: *Patriotism unified the community.*

un·known |ŭn nōn′| *adj.* **1.** Not known or familiar; strange: *We bought a drawing by an unknown artist.* **2.** Not identified: *The cause of the fire was unknown.*

un·nec·es·sar·y |ŭn nĕs′ ĭ sĕr′ ē| *adj.* Not necessary or required; needless.

un·sink·a·ble |ŭn sĭngk′ ə bəl| *adj.* Not able to go under the surface or to be sunk.

un·skilled |ŭn skĭld′| *adj.* Lacking skill or special training.

un·sure |ŭn shoor′| *adj.* Not sure; uncertain: *I am unsure about this homework assignment.*

up-to-date |ŭp′ tə dāt′| *adj.* Showing or using the latest improvements, facts, or style: *We bought a new, up-to-date home computer.*

use |yooz| *v.* **used, using** To bring or put into service for a purpose: *Use the soap when you wash.*

u·su·al |yoo′ zhoo əl| *adj.* Happening at regular intervals or all the time; customary; common.

V

va·can·cy |vā′ kən sē| *n., pl.* **vacancies 1.** The condition of being vacant. **2.** An unoccupied job, position, or place, such as a motel room.

va·cant |vā′ kənt| *adj.* Not occupied or rented.

va·cate |vā′ kāt′| *v.* **vacated, vacating** To go away from and no longer occupy: *We vacated our apartment when we bought a house.*

va·ca·tion |vā kā′ shən| *n., pl.* **vacations** A time of rest from work, school, or other regular activities: *This summer my family is going on a camping vacation.*

vac·u·um |văk′ yoo əm| or |văk′ yoom| *n., pl.* **vacuums 1.** A space that does not have any air in it. A perfect vacuum probably does not exist. **2.** A vacuum cleaner.

Val·en·tine's Day |văl′ ən tīnz| *n.* February 14, a day when people send valentines to their friends, relatives, and sweethearts.

val·u·a·ble |văl′ yoo ə bəl| *adj.* Worth a lot of money; precious: *This is a valuable necklace. n., pl.* **valuables** Often **valuables** A valuable personal possession, as jewelry: *We have a safe to put our valuables in.*

val·ue |văl′ yoo| *n., pl.* **values 1.** What something is worth in exchange for something else: *These shoes will give you good value for your money.* **2.** The quality that makes something worth having; importance: *You should recognize the value of a good education.*

van·ish |văn′ ĭsh| *v.* **vanished, vanishing** To disappear or become invisible: *My smile vanished when Martha told me the bad news.*

va·ri·e·ty |və rī′ ĭ tē| *n., pl.* **varieties 1.** Difference or change; lack of sameness: *We enjoy variety in our meals.* **2.** A number of different kinds within the same group or category: *Our library has a wide variety of books.*

vault |vôlt| *v.* **vaulted, vaulting** To jump or leap over, especially with the help of one's hands or a pole.

ve·hi·cle |vē′ ĭ kəl| *n., pl.* **vehicles** Something used for carrying people or goods from one place to another, especially one that moves on wheels or runners. Cars, bicycles, and airplanes are vehicles.

vel·vet |vĕl′ vĭt| *n., pl.* **velvets** A soft fabric with a short, thick pile. Velvet is made of silk, cotton, rayon, or other materials.

ve·ran·da |və răn′ də| *n., pl.* **verandas** A long porch or balcony, usually with a roof, that runs along one or more sides of a building.

ă	pat	ŏ	pot	û	fur
ā	pay	ō	go	*th*	the
â	care	ô	paw, for	th	thin
ä	father	oi	oil	hw	which
ĕ	pet	o͝o	book	zh	usual
ē	be	o͞o	boot	ə	ago, item
ĭ	pit	yo͞o	cute		pencil, atom
ī	ice	ou	out		circus
î	near	ŭ	cut	ər	butter

Vet·er·ans Day |vĕt′ ər ənz| *n.* November 11, a holiday now officially celebrated on the fourth Monday in October in memory of the peace treaty ending World War I in 1918 and in honor of veterans of the armed services.

ve·to |vē′ tō| *n., pl.* **vetoes** The right or power of a president, governor, or mayor to reject a bill that has been passed by a legislature and to keep it from becoming a law. *v.* **vetoed, vetoing** To prevent from becoming law by using the power of veto: *The President vetoed the tax bill.*

vic·to·ry |vĭk′ tə rē| *n., pl.* **victories** The defeat of an opponent or enemy; success.

vid·e·o |vĭd′ ē ō′| *n., pl.* **videos** A recording on special tape of a television program or movie for later playback and viewing.

view |vyo͞o| *n., pl.* **views** Range or field of sight: *The airplane disappeared from view. v.* **viewed, viewing** To look at: *We viewed the stars through a telescope.*

vil·lage |vĭl′ ĭj| *n., pl.* **villages** 1. A group of houses that make up a community smaller than a town. 2. The people who live in a village.

vil·lain |vĭl′ ən| *n., pl.* **villains** 1. A wicked person; not a hero. 2. A main character who harms or threatens the good or heroic characters in a story or play.

vin·e·gar |vĭn′ ĭ gər| *n., pl.* **vinegars** A sour liquid that is made by fermenting wine, cider, or other liquids. Vinegar is used in flavoring and preserving food and in salad dressing.

vi·o·let |vī′ ə lĭt| *n., pl.* **violets** 1. A low-growing plant having small flowers that are usually bluish purple but can be yellow or white. 2. A reddish blue color.

vis·it |vĭz′ ĭt| *v.* **visited, visiting** 1. To go or come to see: *Visit your doctor once a year.* 2. To stay with as a guest: *I am visiting an old friend in California.*

vi·tal |vīt′ l| *adj.* 1. Necessary to life: *The heart and lungs are vital organs.* 2. Very important; essential; necessary: *A good education is vital to a successful career.*

vot·er |vō′ tər| *n., pl.* **voters** A person who casts a ballot or otherwise votes in an election.

voy·age |voi′ ĭj| *n., pl.* **voyages** A long journey to a distant place, made on a ship, aircraft, or spacecraft.

W

waist |wāst| *n., pl.* **waists** The part of the human body between the ribs and the hips.
 ♦ *These sound alike* **waist, waste.**

wait |wāt| *v.* **waited, waiting** To do nothing or stay in a place until something expected happens: *Wait for me here.*
 ♦ *These sound alike* **wait, weight.**

wan·der |wŏn′ dər| *v.* **wandered, wandering** To move from place to place without a special purpose or destination; roam: *We wandered around town.*

ware·house |wâr′ hous′| *n., pl.* **warehouses** A large building where goods are stored.

warn |wôrn| *v.* **warned, warning** To make aware of danger; alert: *The news report warned us that the roads were icy.*
♦ *These sound alike* **warn, worn.**

war·rant |wôr′ ənt| *n., pl.* **warrants** An official paper that gives the police authority, as for making a search or an arrest.

waste |wāst| *n., pl.* **wastes** Worthless or useless material, such as garbage. *adj.* Worthless or useless: *Throw out that waste paper.*
♦ *These sound alike* **waste, waist.**

waste·bas·ket |wāst′ băs′ kĭt| *n.,* *pl.* **wastebaskets** An open container that is used to hold things to be thrown away.

watch·ful |wŏch′ fəl| *adj.* On the lookout; alert.

wa·ter·mel·on |wô′ tər mĕl′ ən| *n.,* *pl.* **watermelons** A very large melon with a hard, thick, green rind and sweet, watery pink or reddish flesh.

weap·on |wĕp′ ən| *n., pl.* **weapons** Something, such as a gun or claw, that is used in defense or attack.

week·end |wēk′ ĕnd′| *n.,* *pl.* **weekends** The period of time from Friday evening through Sunday evening.

weight |wāt| *n., pl.* **weights** The measure of how heavy something is: *The weight of the box is 100 pounds.*
♦ *These sound alike* **weight, wait.**

wel·fare |wĕl′ fâr′| *n.* Health, happiness, or prosperity; well-being.

wheel·chair |hwēl′ châr′| *n., pl.* **wheelchairs** A chair on wheels in which a sick or disabled person can move about.

where·a·bouts |hwâr′ ə bouts′| *n. (used with a singular or plural verb)* The place where someone or something is: *My friend's whereabouts is (or are) unknown.*

wheth·er |hwĕ*th*′ ər| *conj.* **1.** Used to show a choice between things: *Whether we win or lose, we will be glad we tried.* **2.** If.

whip |hwĭp| *v.* **whipped, whipping** To beat something, such as cream, into a foam.

whir |hwûr| *v.* **whirred, whirring** To move quickly with a buzzing or humming sound.

whis·tle |hwĭs′ əl| *n., pl.* **whistles 1.** A device that makes a high, clear sound when air is blown through it. **2.** A sound made by or as if by whistling.

who·ev·er |hoo ĕv′ ər| *pron.* Anyone that: *Whoever wants my sandwich can have it.*

wild |wīld| *adj.* **wilder, wildest** Not grown, cared for, or controlled by people: *The polar bear is a wild animal.*

wil·der·ness |wĭl′ dər nĭs| *n., pl.* **wildernesses** A region in a wild, natural state in which there are few or no people.

wild·life |wīld′ līf′| *n.* Wild plants and animals, especially wild animals living in their natural surroundings.

win |wĭn| *v.* **won, winning 1.** To gain victory in a game, contest, or battle: *Which team won?* **2.** To achieve success in an effort or venture.

win·ner |wĭn′ ər| *n., pl.* **winners** A person or group that wins.

wis·dom |wĭz′ dəm| *n.* Intelligence and good judgment in knowing what to do and being able to tell the difference between good and bad and right and wrong; not foolishness or ignorance.

wise |wīz| *adj.* **wiser, wisest** Having or showing intelligence and good judgment: *A wise student studies for tests.*

wit·ness |wĭt′ nĭs| *n.,* *pl.* **witnesses 1.** Someone who has seen or heard something; observer: *I was a witness to the traffic accident.* **2.** A person who is called to testify before a court of law and promises to tell the truth.

world |wûrld| *n., pl.* **worlds** The earth: *The world is round.*

worse |wûrs| *adj.* Comparative of **bad.** Less well.

wor·ship |wûr′ shĭp| *n.* Religious ceremonies and prayers. *v.* **worshiped, worshiping** *or* **worshipped, worshipping** To honor and love.

worth |wûrth| *n.* The quality that makes someone or something expensive, valuable, useful, or important: *Your education will prove its worth. adj.* Equal in value to: *This rare baseball card is worth $27.50.*

worth·less |wûrth′ lĭs| *adj.* Without worth; useless.

worth·while |wûrth′ hwīl′| *adj.* Worth the time, effort, or cost involved; valuable; important.

wor·thy |wûr′ thē| *adj.* **worthier, worthiest** Having worth, merit, or value; useful or valuable: *Raising money for the homeless is a worthy cause. n.* **worthiness** *Sasha was confident of her worthiness as a pitcher.*

wrote |rōt| *v.* Past tense of **write**: *She wrote an excellent book report.*

Y

year |yîr| *n., pl.* **years** **1.** A period of twelve months. **2.** A period of time, usually less than 12 months, devoted to a special activity: *The school year begins in September and ends in June.*

yearn |yûrn| *v.* **yearned, yearning** To have a deep desire; long; want very much: *I yearn to see my old friends again.*

ă	pat	ŏ	pot	û	fur
ā	pay	ō	go	*th*	the
â	care	ô	paw, for	th	thin
ä	father	oi	oil	hw	which
ĕ	pet	ōō	book	zh	usual
ē	be	ōō	boot	ə	ago, item
ĭ	pit	yōō	cute		pencil, atom
ī	ice	ou	out		circus
î	near	ŭ	cut	ər	butter

Yel·low·stone Na·tion·al Park |yĕl′ ō stōn′| Oldest and largest of United States national parks, mostly in northwest Wyoming, where the geyser Old Faithful is located.

yes·ter·day |yĕs′ tər dē| *or* |yĕs′ tər dā| *n.* The day before today: *Yesterday was windy. adv.* On the day before today.

yield |yēld| *v.* **yielded, yielding** To allow to another: *At a stop sign, yield to the car on your right.*

Yo·sem·i·te Na·tion·al Park |yō sĕm′ ĭ tē| An area of east central California that has high waterfalls and mountain scenery.

youth |yōōth| *n., pl.* **youths** **1.** The time of life between being a child and being an adult: *They had worked hard since their youth.* **2.** A young person, especially a boy or young man.

Content Index

Credits

Series design and cover design by Ligature, Inc.
Front cover and title page photograph:
S. Chenn/West Light.

Illustrations

Meg Kelleher Aubrey: 14, 32, 74, 87, 89, 101, 110, 125, 134, 159, 167, 201, 215, 218.
Mary Azarian: 89, 113, 167.
Holly Berry: 17, 29, 35, 41, 53, 59, 65, 71, 77, 84, 87, 90, 93, 96, 99, 102, 105, 108, 111, 120, 123, 126, 129, 132, 135, 138, 141, 144, 147.
Higgins Bond: 46, 47.
Ray-Mel Cornelius: 17, 95, 101, 125, 149, 173, 203, 221.
John Ellis: 12, 17, 18, 29.
Ruth Flanigan: 287, 300, 306, 314.
Harriet Fishman: 292, 298, 325.
Stephen Gardner: 154, 155.
Josette Gourley: 226, 227.
Nick Harris: 118, 119.
Carol Inouye: 279, 282, 308, 313, 321.
Laurie Jordan: 107, 131, 137, 161, 197.
Margaret Kasahara: 35, 41, 53, 59, 65, 77, 89, 113, 143, 159, 162, 165, 168, 171, 173, 174, 177, 180, 183, 185, 192, 195, 198, 201, 204, 207, 210, 213, 216, 219.
Tom Leonard: 15, 21, 77, 179, 185, 209.
Fred Lynch: 203, 209.
Wallace Marosek: 161, 215, 221.
Martucci Studios: 13, (42), 19, (42), 25, (43), 31, (43), 37, (44), 45, 49, (78),55, (78), 61, (79), 67, (79), 73, (80), 81, 85, (114), 91, (114), 97, (115), 103, (115), 109, (116), 117, 121, (150), 127, (150), 133, (151), 139, (151), 145, (152), 153, 157, (186), 163, (186), 169, (187), 175, (187), 181, (188), 189, 193, (222), 199, (222), 205, (223), 211, (223), 217, (224), 225.
Cheryl Kirk Noll: 297, 310, 322, 327.
Steve Pietzsch: 23, 24, 27, 30, 33, 35, 36, 39, 48, 51, 53, 54, 57, 60, 62, 63, 65, 66, 69, 71, 72, 75, 95, 107, 113, 156, 161, 173, 185, 209.
Bernadette Pons: 149.
John Shipperbottom: 190, 191.

Emanuel Schongut: 23, 131, 143.
Robin Spowart: 137.
George Ulrich: 261, 265, 267.
Charles Waller: 101, 107, 125, 149, 167.
Ashley Wolff: 52, 143.

Photographs

3 Charlie Hogg.
4 Nancy Sheehan.
16 David Carriere/After Image.
22 Bettman Archive.
28 Bettman Newsphotos.
29 The TOPPS CO., Inc./National Baseball Hall of Fame.
34 Comstock.
40 "Purple Gallinule", (Detail), by John James Audubon, by permission of Houghton Library/Harvard University.
58 Alfred Pasieka/Bruce Coleman, Inc.
64 Kirk Schlea/Berg and Associates.
70 B & J McGrath.
76 Gerry Goodstein.
82 Dan Morrill/Reese-Gibson.
83 Ken O'Donoghue/Reese-Gibson.
88 Brian Parker/Tom Stack and Associates.
94 Nancy McFarland/FPG.
100 Peter L. Chapman.
106 Mark Reinstein/TSW-Click/Chicago.
112 Culver Pictures.
124 Tom Pantages.
130 FPG.
131 (left) Bettman Archive.
131 (right) Brown Brothers.
136 John Lund/After Image.
142 Culver Pictures.
148 Courtesy of Elizabeth Fagg Olds.
160 TSW-Click/Chicago.
166 "The Landing of the Pilgrims", (Detail), by Henry Bacon, courtesy of the Pilgrim Society, Plymouth, MA.
172 James Holland/Black Star.
178 Patrick Henry National Memorial.
179 "Washington Crossing the Delaware", (Detail), by Emanuel Gottlieb Leutze. The Metropolitan Museum of Art. Gift of John Stewart Kennedy, 1897.
184 A. C. Nielsen Co.